Twayne's Filmmakers Series

Warren French
EDITOR

Alfred Hitchcock

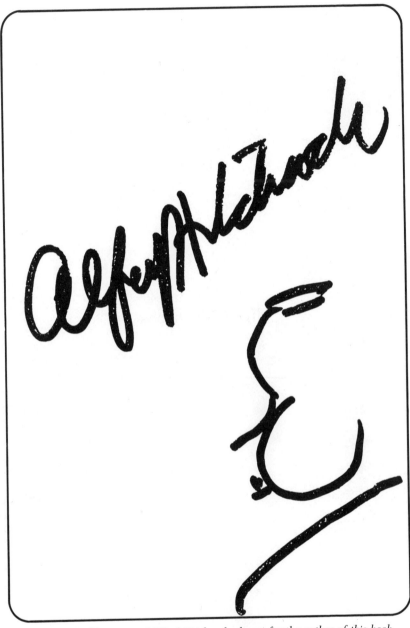

The celebrated self-portrait of Alfred Hitchcock, drawn for the author of this book. (Courtesy of Alfred Hitchcock)

Alfred Hitchcock

GENE D. PHILLIPS

Loyola University of Chicago

BOSTON

Twayne Publishers

1984

Alfred Hitchcock

is first published in 1984 by Twayne Publishers,
A Division of G. K. Hall & Company
All Rights Reserved

Copyright © 1984 by G. K. Hall & Company

Book Production by John Amburg

Printed on permanent/durable acid-free paper and bound
in the United States of America

First Printing, May, 1984

Library of Congress Cataloging in Publication Data

Phillips, Gene D.
Alfred Hitchcock

(Twayne's filmmakers series)
Bibliography: p. 187
Filmography: p. 189
Includes index.
1. Hitchcock, Alfred, 1899–   . I. Title.
II. Series.
PN1998.A3H5496   1984   791.43′0233′0924   83-22786
ISBN 0-8057-9293-7
ISBN 0-8057-9301-1 (Pbk.)

Contents

To Hitchcock's close friend and only peer:
GEORGE CUKOR

"I spent three years studying with the Jesuits. They used to terrify me to death, and now I'm getting my own back by terrifying other people."

—*Sir Alfred Hitchcock*

About the Author

GENE D. PHILLIPS, S.J., has been actively interested in Alfred Hitchcock and his work since watching the director shoot a scene for *Frenzy* in downtown London in the summer of 1971. After that first experience, the author met and talked with Hitchcock and several people associated with the director's work, with a view to one day writing the present volume.

The author is an elected member of the Society for Cinema Studies and teaches fiction and film at Loyola University of Chicago. He received his doctorate in English from Fordham University in New York City and has been chosen to serve on special juries at the Cannes, Berlin, Chicago, and Midwest Film Festivals. He has published more than ninety articles on literature and the film, and is a contributing editor for *Literature/Film Quarterly*, as well as an advisory editor for *American Classic Screen*.

His books include *The Movie Makers: Artists in an Industry; Evelyn Waugh's Officers, Gentlemen, and Rogues: The Fact Behind His Fiction; Stanley Kubrick: A Film Odyssey; The Films of Tennessee Williams; Hemingway and Film;* and three other volumes for this series: *Ken Russell, John Schlesinger,* and *George Cukor.*

Editor's Foreword

NEITHER ALFRED HITCHCOCK nor Gene Phillips needs any introduction to followers of this series. A book about Hitchcock has been planned since the inception of this project. He is not only the genius who literally envisioned a new kind of thriller that no later-comer has been able to duplicate, but the director who made many filmgoers conscious of the significance of those who merited their "name above the title." With his six perfected British thrillers from the original *The Man Who Knew too Much* (1934) to *The Lady Vanishes* (1938), he was responsible for launching in the United States the practice of auteurism while Francois Truffaut was still an infant and two decades before Hitchcock's French admirer gave controversial currency to the term in a famous article in *Cahiers du Cinéma* in January 1954. Any auteurist-oriented series of books like this one is implicitly dedicated to Alfred Hitchcock, whose classic British thrillers crystallized my own dedication to the art of the cinema. The appearance of this tribute to his lifetime's work is the climax of this program.

Father Phillips, Chicago's Jesuit cinephile, has already contributed to this series three books about Ken Russell, John Schlesinger, and George Cukor, about whom he was written from long friendships based on mutual respect. The long-needed appreciation of Cukor is already winning recognition as a model for the study of the careers of those talented figures of Hollywood's studio years who could not so steadfastly devote themselves to the perfection of a single genre as Hitchcock could, but who yet left the imprint of a distinctive sensibility on all the projects assigned them.

Although Phillips did not know Hitchcock as well as he did his former subjects, he had the pleasure of watching the director work on his next-to-last film, *Frenzy*, and of talking over with the subject plans for this book. He has thus been able to set straight the record on many comments and practices attributed to Hitchcock, and to benefit from the director's mellowed recollections of a lifetime's experience.

The most important distinctions of this book, however, as Phillips points out are, first, that in preparing for it, he viewed immediately before writing about it every one of the films Hitchcock directed except for the only one of his many that is apparently permanently lost, *The Mountain Eagle* (1926); and second, that he also viewed consecutively every one of the twenty teleplays that Hitchcock directed personally. Thus the author has been able to correct many small errors about Hitchcock's works that have appeared elsewhere and have gradually crept into the public record.

As Phillips points out, he has also devoted "equal time" to the director's British period, which some earlier writers have "condescendingly dismissed . . . as mere warm-ups for his sophisticated American movies." The freshness and spontaneity of these low-budget films unquestionably contributed greatly to the development of his own unique style and the maturing of film as an art form.

While a more detailed biography of Hitchcock is available, this book will remain permanently valuable as the most complete and accurate record of the experience of *seeing* Hitchcock's films, since some of these materials may not be accessible again. Hitchcock fans and filmlovers generally will also treasure its affectionate effort to explain just what Hitchcock was up to in his work and the unique contribution it made to the continuing pleasure of filmgoers everywhere. Some of Hitchcock's most celebrated films still draw large audiences when they are frequently rescreened in many places throughout the world; this book may introduce the admirers of those films to others equally fascinating.

W.F.

Preface

Alfred Hitchcock: Prankster of Paradox

—Andrew Sarris

DURING HIS LAST YEARS Alfred Hitchcock was granted an honorary degree from Columbia University, an honorary Oscar from the Motion Picture Academy, and an honorary evening with the Film Society of Lincoln Center. The irrepressible spoilsports among us may argue that such honors are ill-advised for a "mere" entertainer, however masterly. . . .

Certainly, Hitchcock's reputation has suffered from the fact that he has given audiences more pleasure than is permissible for serious cinema. No one who is so entertaining could possibly seem profound to the intellectual puritans. Furthermore, did not Santayana once observe that complete understanding extinguishes pleasure? Hitchcock himself seems to have absorbed Santayana's sentiment by focusing attention on the stylistic surfaces of his films rather than on their spiritual depths. He tells us the how, but we must determine the why. By contrast, most modern filmmakers bend our ear with the why before they have figured out the how. The result: An Art Oozing with Obfuscation.

No wonder then that, for Truffaut, the greatest Hitchcockian virtue is clarity. Teresa Wright once told me that the difference between Hitchcock and other directors was that when Hitchcock sat down to tell you the story of the movie he was about to make, it was the same story you later saw on the screen. With other directors, it was one story before the shooting, and another after. The picture story that Master Alfred had told to Teresa Wright was, of course, *Shadow of a Doubt*—itself the quintessentially Hitchcockian title, reflecting, as it does, both the expressionism of his style and the ambiguity of his attitude.

Curiously, Hitchcock's formal elegance seems to pertain to a realm far removed from the precincts of pop art. One can like Hitchcock without liking much else of popular culture, and one can dislike Hitchcock without disliking Hollywood movies on principle. Thus Hitchcock need not necessarily be taken as a prime example of the popular entertainer, and certainly not in the sense of Raggedy-Ann aesthetics. Consequently, the category that Manny Farber once designated as "termite art" applies less to Hitchcock than it does to such burrowing directors as Walsh and Hawks and Wellman and Hathaway. Indeed, Hitchcock is as much his own genre as Kafka was his. That is why Raymond Durgnat's anti-Hitchcock writings are beside the point when they seek to enshroud Hitch within the *film noir*. Only on the most superficial level of narrative development is there any genre affinity between, say, Hitchcock's *Psycho* and Clouzot's *Diabolique*. For most viewers, however, Clouzot's climax is scarier than Hitchcock's the first time around, what with Vera Clouzot's stereophonic gasps of terror virtually inducing coronaries. But once is enough. Repeated viewings of *Diabolique* only verify the efficiency of the director's fright techniques. Quite the contrary with *Psycho:* each successive viewing only deepens our appreciation of the spectacle. The first time I saw the shower scene in *Psycho* I screamed with authentically Freudian fright. (Mother invading my shower with a knife?) I have witnessed this scene many times since, and have even "taught" the scene in a classroom, and now regard it as one of the most profoundly affecting religious expressions of this century. Similarly, *Vertigo* and *Rear Window* and *Notorious* and *North by Northwest* and *Strangers on a Train* and *Stage Fright* and *The Thirty-nine Steps* and *Secret Agent* and the two versions of *The Man Who Knew too Much* and a few dozen more suspense classics sustain repeated viewings without becoming stale or withered.

How then can Hitchcock be designated (and dismissed) as the Master of Suspense? If suspense were all that mattered in Hitch's universe, how could we look at his movies again and again and again without becoming bored by the unvarying mechanisms of the plot? There's a hitch there somewhere, and I'm sure that it isn't Hitch. . . .

On the first few viewings of a film like *Notorious* the screen is saturated with the trappings of melodrama: Good Guys and Bad Guys, Them and Us, Fear and Loathing, Formulas and Poisons. Then, gradually, massive archetypes appear on the screen: Mothers and Sons, Husbands and Lovers, Deceivers and the Deceived. Circles are redrawn as triangles, and sympathies shift back and forth between the bright stars and their dim satellites. Nothing is what it seemed at first glance. Thus Hitchcock is not merely an entertainer for the moment, but a fitting subject for eternal retrospectives. . . .

*

Preface: "Alfred Hitchcock: Prankster of Paradox"

Hitchcock has had his share of failures, but not nearly as many as there seemed to be at first viewing. Some films age, and some films date. Hitchcock's films, good and bad alike, belong to the first category.

Acknowledgments

FIRST OF ALL, I am most grateful to the late Sir Alfred Hitchcock, who encouraged me in this endeavor by personally approving the precís from which it was developed. In addition to him and the artists associated with his work who are mentioned in the text, I would also like to single out the following among those who have given me their assistance:

Novelist and screenwriter Graham Greene for sharing his thoughts about Hitchcock and his work with me. Actor William Devane (*Family Plot*) and screenwriter Ernest Lehman (*North by Northwest* and *Family Plot*), as well as Hitchcock's long-time friend Fr. Thomas Sullivan, S.J., for discussing their recollections of the director with me. John Russell Taylor, Hitchcock's authorized biographer, for comparing notes with me on the director's early films, which we viewed together at the British Film Institute in London. Carl Russell and John Krutzler of MCA-TV, the distributors of Hitchcock's television series, for allowing me to screen all of the telefilms Hitchcock personally directed; Mary Ellen Hayes of Loyola University of Chicago, for collating the filmography and spying out the many discrepancies that have been perpetuated in earlier Hitchcock filmographies; Stuart Kaminsky of Northwestern University and Adam Reilly of the Denver Center for the Performing Arts for invaluable research aids.

I would also like to thank Loyola University of Chicago for granting me an academic leave during which I could finish this book, as well as the Research Committee of Loyola for giving me a summer grant for the same purpose.

Some material in this book appeared in a totally different form in *America*, © 1974 by American Press. The Andrew Sarris essay is © 1974 by Film Comment Publishing Corporation, and is reprinted by permission of the Film Society of Lincoln Center and the author.

Chronology

1899	Alfred Joseph Hitchcock born in the East London suburb of Leytonstone, August 13, to William and Emma Whelan Hitchcock.
1912– 1920	Educated at St. Ignatius College, a Jesuit preparatory school, then at the School of Engineering and Navigation, where he majors in engineering and draftsmanship before switching to fine arts.
1920	After graduation, he enters the film industry by designing inter-titles for silent films at the studios of Famous Players-Lasky (later Paramount Pictures), located in the Islington section of London.
1922– 1925	Continues his apprenticeship in motion pictures by acting as art director, script writer, production manager, and assistant director on various films, and by directing a two-reeler, *Number Thirteen* (1922), which is never completed.
1925	Works in Germany at UFA's Neubabelsberg studio.
1926	Moves on to directing features on his own with *The Pleasure Garden* (filmed partly in Italy), and *The Mountain Eagle* (USA: *Fear O'God*), and *The Lodger*, his first bona fide thriller. Marries Alma Reville, his assistant on these films, on December 2.
1927	*Downhill* (USA: *When Boys Leave Home*), *Easy Virtue*, and *The Ring*.
1928	*The Farmer's Wife; Champagne.*
1929	*The Manxman; Blackmail*, the first major British talking picture.
1930	*Juno and the Paycock; Murder!.*
1931	*The Skin Game.*

1932   *Rich and Strange* (USA: *East of Shanghai*); *Number Seventeen.*

1933   *Waltzes from Vienna*, his only musical (USA: *Strauss's Great Waltz*).

1934   *The Man Who Knew too Much* (first version).

1935   *The Thirty-nine Steps.*

1936   *Secret Agent; Sabotage* (USA: *A Woman Alone*).

1937   *Young and Innocent* (USA: *The Girl Was Young*).

1938   *The Lady Vanishes*, which wins him the New York Film Critics Award for best director.

1939   *Jamaica Inn*; takes up permanent residence in the United States.

1940   *Rebecca*, his first American film, receives the Oscar for best picture of the year; *Foreign Correspondent.*

1941   *Mr. and Mrs. Smith*, his only American comedy; *Suspicion.*

1942   *Saboteur.*

1943   *Shadow of a Doubt.*

1944   *Lifeboat; Bon Voyage* and *Aventure Malgache* (*Madagascar Adventure*), two French-language semidocumentaries made for the British Information Service.

1945   *Spellbound.*

1946   *Notorious.*

1947   *The Paradine Case.*

1948   *Rope* (his first film in color).

1949   *Under Capricorn.*

1950   *Stage Fright.*

1951   *Strangers on a Train.*

1953   *I Confess.*

1954   *Dial M for Murder*, shot in 3-D, but generally shown in the conventional format; *Rear Window.*

1955   *To Catch a Thief; The Trouble with Harry.* Inauguration on October 2 of a weekly TV series called "Alfred Hitchcock Presents," which he supervises and hosts, and occasionally directs, over a period of ten seasons. Becomes an American citizen, April 20.

Chronology

1956   *The Man Who Knew too Much* (second version with James Stewart).

1957   *The Wrong Man.*

1958   *Vertigo.*

1959   *North by Northwest.*

1960   *Psycho.*

1963   *The Birds.*

1964   *Marnie.*

1966   *Torn Curtain.*

1967   Receives the Irving Thalberg Award at the Academy Award ceremonies in April.

1969   *Topaz.* Named an officer in the French Order of Arts and Letters (raised to the rank of Commander in 1976).

1972   *Frenzy.*

1974   Gala tribute by the Film Society of Lincoln Center of New York, April 29.

1976   *Family Plot*, his last film.

1979   Receives the American Film Institute Life Achievement Award, televised March 12.

1980   Knighted by Queen Elizabeth II three months before his death on April 29.

1982   Alma Hitchcock dies, July 6.

1983   Successful theatrical re-release of *Rear Window*, *Vertigo*, the second *Man Who Knew Too Much*, *The Trouble with Harry*, and *Rope*, which for various reasons had not been generally available for two decades.

1

Prologue: The Hitchcock Touch

AT PRECISELY 9:20 PM on the evening of April 29, 1974, Alfred Hitchcock took his place in a special box overlooking the auditorium of Avery Fisher Hall in New York City's Lincoln Center for the Performing Arts. The occasion was a gala tribute sponsored by the Film Society of Lincoln Center honoring Hitchcock's lifetime achievement as a filmmaker. Several cinema artists associated with his career were on hand to pay tribute, and their remarks on this and other occasions such as the American Film Institute's celebration of his career televised on March 12, 1979, will be found throughout this book. But Hitch himself, as always, was the main attraction.

One of the reasons that Hitchcock's career is so fascinating is that he was, of course, one of the very few directors in the history of motion pictures whose name has always been as important on a movie marquee as that of any actor appearing in one of his films. People who usually stay home to watch television will go out to see a Hitchcock movie at a revival house, and people who usually skip the "Late Show" will stay up to watch a Hitchcock picture. As Andrew Sarris suggests in the Preface, Hitchcock's perennial popularity with the mass audience means in effect that he was discovered by his public as a first-rate entertainer long before film critics and scholars got around to realizing that he was also a genuine artist. That is because Hitchcock firmly believed that his first obligation as a filmmaker was to entertain his audience. "I don't try to put on the screen what is called a 'slice of life,'" he once wrote, "because people can get all the slices of life they want on the pavement in front of the cinemas." For him film was, after all, "life with the dull bits removed."

The very popularity of his movies, however, is reason enough for some critics to write him off as a mere crowd pleaser rather than recognize him as an authentic artist of the cinema. That a director can be both is suggested by the fact that his finest films, for example *The Thirty-nine Steps* and *Psycho*, are also among his most popular. Never-

19

*itchcock making his cameo appearance in the Oscar-winning
ebecca (1940), with George Sanders in the phone booth.
Credit: Larry Edmonds's Cinema Bookshop)*

theless, he was not unduly bothered by the fact that his artistry was frequently overlooked by reviewers since, for him, "the mark of good technique is that it is unnoticed."[1]

There are several reasons for Hitchcock's abiding acceptance by the public; these elements taken together are what for me comprise the Hitchcock touch—a term often used but rarely explained.

For one thing, because his heroes are usually not people whose professions are by nature dangerous, such as spies or detectives, moviegoers easily identify with them. Instead, the protagonists are ordinary people who are drawn by circumstances into extraordinary situations. "My hero," he has said, "is the average man to whom bizarre things happen, rather than vice versa." Often the hero cannot confide in the police because they wrongly suspect him of having committed a crime (Hitchcock's own mistrust of the guardians of the law dates back to his childhood, as I will point out later). As a result, he is thrown back on his own resources, and we sympathize with his plight in a way that we cannot with the superhuman heroes bottled in the James Bond image.

Not only his central characters but the settings of Hitchcock's films are quite ordinary on the surface, thereby suggesting that evil can lurk in places that at first glance seem normal and unthreatening. His villains commit their mayhem in amusement parks and respectable restaurants, places where the viewers might often find themselves—not in locations that we tend to avoid in order to escape potential harm, such as dark alleys and dives—and often in the cold light of day rather than under cover of darkness. Nor are Hitchcock's villains obviously menacing, criminal types. "The really frightening thing about villains," Hitchcock has pointed out, "is their surface likeableness." How else, he asks, could they win the confidence of their victims?[2]

All of the ingredients of a Hitchcock thriller enumerated so far combine to make spectators feel that what is happening to the hero up there on the screen could conceivably happen to them, for Hitchcock aims to make us aware that catastrophe surrounds us all and can strike when we least expect it. People have to be made to feel, he once said, that "there but for the grace of God go I." It is just this unsettling reflection that holds one's interest while watching a Hitchcock picture, even after repeated viewings.

It is therefore quite misleading to call Hitchcock the master of suspense, as for example the late Princess Grace did in her brief preface to Spoto's book on the director. For, as Sarris notes, suspense is really only operative the first time one sees a Hitchcock thriller. Yet the picture continues to be gripping on subsequent screenings because Hitchcock has enabled the viewer to identify so closely with the central character.

As Sarris puts it, some films age, some films date. Hitchcock's belong to the former category.

Another reason these movies continue to involve moviegoers even on repeated viewings is that Hitchcock customarily takes the audience into his confidence early in the story by sharing with them information that other directors might withhold for the sake of a surprise ending. "I believe in giving the audience all the facts as early as possible," Hitchcock has explained, because that way a director can "build up an almost unbearable tension."[3] When the viewer knows about a danger of which the characters themselves are unaware, for example, that there is a time bomb hidden beneath the table at which they are chatting, he almost wants to blurt out a warning. Surprise lasts only a moment, Hitchcock concludes, but tipping off the audience to what is really going to happen allows the director to nurture excitement that lasts throughout the movie.

Still another factor often found as part of Hitchcock's recipe, and one that is similarly calculated to keep the film moving, is what he called the MacGuffin, a term he defined as a device that sets the plot in motion and keeps it going. The MacGuffin is simply the thing that preoccupies the hero and heroine and because of which they are thrown into danger, such as a vital secret formula. "The characters on the screen worry about what they're after," he explained; the audience, however, does not care about the MacGuffin directly at all, because "they only care about the safety of the hero and heroine."

The term MacGuffin, incidentally, comes from the old English music hall routine about two men on a British train. One passenger asks the other, "What is that on the luggage rack over your head?" The other replies that it is a MacGuffin, a device used for trapping lions in the Scottish Highlands. When the first man points out that there are no lions in the Scottish Highlands, the second responds, "Well, then, that's no MacGuffin." The point of this droll anecdote for Hitchcock is that, because the sole function of the MacGuffin is to keep the story going, its exact nature is, for all practical purposes, irrelevant to one's enjoyment of the film in question. (René Clement paid homage to Hitchcock in his 1969 French thriller *Rider on the Rain* by naming the fugitive whom the hero must track down Mr. MacGuffin.)

Taken together, then, all of the elements I have elaborated, along with the sardonic bits of black comedy that Hitchcock regularly injected into his movies, serve to define the Hitchcock touch; they are what indelibly and indisputably mark a movie as peculiarly his own, even though most of his pictures are derived from preexisting novels or plays. The sum total of his motion pictures reflects the provocative personal vision and directorial style of the man who made them, regardless of their literary antecedents, because he immersed himself in the entire film-making process, from the inception of the screenplay right up to the last snap of the editor's shears.

In fact, Hitchcock often said that his films were really made on paper, indicating the meticulous planning that went into his preparation for shooting a motion picture. Whenever he heard of a director shooting a film in a slapdash, off-the-cuff fashion, without the benefit of such advance planning, he would comment that it made him think of "a composer composing a symphony before a full orchestra."[4] He preferred instead to do his improvising in the privacy of an office, not on a sound stage in front of a host of highly paid actors and technicians who were being kept waiting while the director tried to figure out what he was going to have them do next.

Although he stopped taking screen credit for working on the scripts of his films after 1932 (except for *Dial M for Murder* in 1954), Hitchcock took a hand in the composition of every screenplay he ever filmed, as I have pointed out. After reading a story that he was going to film, he once explained, he would grab a note pad and sketch out the plot in filmic terms. Only then would he call in a screenwriter to work out the scenario with him. By the time that the final shooting script was ready, "I have virtually the whole film in my head," he continued, "and change and improvise very little on the set."[5] At that point, in fact, he would just as soon not have to shoot the picture, since as far as he was concerned, the creative stage was over.

Few directors have possessed Hitchcock's personal knowledge of every facet of film production, as his co-workers were the first to acknowledge. For example, Edith Head, costume designer for several Hitchcock films from 1954 to 1976, remarked that "every costume is indicated when he sends me the script. . . . There is always a story reason behind his thinking, an effort to characterize. He's absolutely definite in his visual approach, and gives you an exciting concept of the importance of color."[6] Louis Levy, who scored five Hitchcock thrillers in the mid-1930s, has observed that even though Hitchcock did not understand all the technicalities of the composer's craft, his directions were so precise that "I always left our musical conferences with a tune written clearly in my mind, almost as though Hitchcock himself had written it."[7] So much for Elizabeth Weis's assertion in *The Silent Scream* that Hitchcock exercised little control over his composers.

As a result of such careful preparations, Hitchcock rarely needed to look through the camera before shooting a scene. While making *Torn Curtain*, for example, Paul Newman asked the director before a take if he was wearing the right pair of shoes for the sequence. "We are cutting at the second button of your coat," Hitchcock replied without leaving his canvas chair to look through the lens; "so don't worry about your shoes."[8]

In attempting to cover all aspects of Hitchcock's work, this study is designed to give equal time to the director's British period, which makes up the first two decades of his career including his many little-known silent films, as well as to cover his later American period. The majority of the earlier thrillers have often been condescendingly dismissed by commentators on Hitchcock's films as simple exercises in melodrama. Robin Wood, for example, sees the British films as mere warm-ups for Hitchcock's more sophisticated American movies. If the films of the British period are apprenticeship works, as Wood has termed them, they represent the apprenticeship of the entire British motion picture industry, since Hitchcock began working in films when both he and the medium were very young indeed (it was he who made the first successful British talkie). Thus it was as a pioneer that he helped the medium to mature as an art form while he himself was growing to become one of the world's leading filmmakers.

Similarly, previous studies of Hitchcock have largely ignored not only his two wartime semidocumentaries, but the twenty teleplays that he personally directed, mostly for his TV series "Alfred Hitchcock Presents," which he supervised from 1955 through 1965. Since the series remains in permanent syndication (it still airs weekly in Chicago), these telefilms certainly merit treatment in a book that purports to cover all of his work.

The present volume, then, represents an attempt to demonstrate by analyzing all of his work in every medium that Sir Alfred Hitchcock was a genuine cinematic artist and continues to be a popular entertainer. I am not daunted by the fact that Hitchcock personally never really considered himself such an artist at all. "There are a certain number of imperatives that a filmmaker has to respect, and with reason," he once pointed out when this subject was raised. "A production involves much money, other people's money," and a director's conscience told him that it was necessary for these individuals to regain their collective investment. "A movie theater is like a screen facing a pile of seats that have to be filled," and if they were not filled it was the director's fault.[9] Indeed, whenever Hitchcock saw lines of workmen all carrying their lunch pails as they punched a time clock at the studio just like any factory employees, he would say to himself that motion pictures were not so much an art form as an industry. As a matter of fact, he proved that movies could be both.

Now let us turn to Hitchcock's early life to see how his background and education influenced his growth as a film artist. For, as Richard Schickel has noted, beneath the "jolly-macabre" public persona Hitchcock devised, there was a man who remained very much in touch with the anxious, middle-class child he once had been.[10]

2

The Twenties: The Silent Years

ALFRED HITCHCOCK ALWAYS considered himself by nature an American film director because he was so strongly influenced by the American movies he saw in his youth. Also, his first jobs in the film industry were in an American-owned British studio, and he emigrated to Hollywood in 1939 and spent the rest of his life there. But the fact remains that his first forty years were spent in Britain.

He was born Alfred Joseph Hitchcock on August 13, 1899, the youngest of three children. His parents, William and Emma Whelan Hitchcock, were both staunch Roman Catholics in a country where Catholicism represented a scant ten percent of the population. (Hence Hitchcock's remark that being a Roman Catholic in England was something of an eccentricity.) The Hitchcocks lived on the outskirts of London in Leytonstone, and ever after Alfred Hitchcock retained in his speech traces of the quasi-Cockney, East London accent of his origins.

William Hitchcock was a poultry dealer (like the title character in Hitchcock's teleplay "Arthur") and fruit importer (like one of the leading characters in *Frenzy*). His father's business stirred in young Alfred an interest in the world beyond his home in the Soho district of greater London. He would study the labels on the packing cases his father received and, with the aid of his own large collection of maps, chart the journey of the ships that had brought the produce to their door.

William Hitchcock saw to it that his son had a strict Catholic upbringing, as Alfred himself attested in his oft-repeated story about his boyhood encounter with the London constabulary at age six. As a young boy, Alfred made a hobby of riding buses all over London, and one evening he ran out of money at the end of the line. "I made my way back on foot and reached home after 9 PM," he remembered. "My father opened the door and didn't utter a word of reproof."[1] He simply sent little Alfred off to the station house with a note addressed to a policeman friend of his named Watson. Constable Watson read the note and accordingly locked the lad in a cell for five minutes in order to teach him

Hitchcock again—with John Longden and Anny Ondra in Great Britain's first successful talkie, Blackmail *(1929).*
Credit: Museum of Modern Art/Film Stills Archive)

where naughty little boys who come home after 9 o'clock would eventually end up.

This incident triggered in Alfred Hitchcock a lifelong fear of policemen and jails, even causing him in later life to refrain from driving a car lest he should be punished for some traffic violation by one of the dreaded minions of the law, despite the fact that his own maternal grandfather was himself a policeman. In point of fact, the sound of the slamming of the cell door that temporarily incarcerated him would echo ominously down the years in the prison sequences of films as different as *Blackmail, The Paradine Case, The Wrong Man,* and *Frenzy.*

For three years, until he was fourteen, Hitchcock attended St. Ignatius College, a preparatory school conducted by the Jesuits in Stamford Hill, London. In those days corporal punishment was common in European schools, as James Joyce testifies in *A Portrait of the Artist as a Young Man.* "I was terrified of physical punishment," Hitchcock remembered. He dreaded having to face the prefect of discipline at the end of the school day to receive three stinging slaps with a hard rubber cane on each hand (the benumbed hands would not have felt a fourth) to pay the penalty for some misdemeanor committed earlier in the day.[2] Discipline under the Jesuits, whom he thus saw as "religious policemen," created a consciousness of what fear really felt like, on which he later capitalized in his movies; it is just this anxiety that he experienced as a youth at school that he sought to call up and then exorcise in his audience in the course of an entertaining thriller. The Jesuits "used to terrify me to death," he concluded, "and now I'm getting my own back by terrifying other people."[3] Invoking the same principles of Freudian psychology that underlie *Spellbound* and *Marnie,* one can say with considerable justification, I think, that both the Jesuits and the policeman who intimidated Hitchcock as a lad were but extensions of the archetypal authoritarian figure of his stern father, who had frightened him into being a good boy when he was young.

Be that as it may, while as Hitchcock himself admitted, that a person's religious and moral training influences his life and guides the development of his instincts, he rightly denied that he was a Catholic artist in any narrowly parochial sense. We will study this question when dealing with his films that treat overtly of religious issues, for example, *I Confess.*

In addition to the moral discipline inculcated in him by the Jesuits, Hitchcock felt that their training gave him what he termed clarity of mind, self-control, and organization. In fact, he later realized that the very methodical way in which he approached the preparations for making a film, outlined in the previous chapter, had been inspired by his

Jesuit education. That tendency toward order and precision was further nurtured by his subsequent training. It also took on thematic implications in his films that depict a chaotic world in which disorder frequently lurks where one least expects it. Indeed, the progress of the plot of a Hitchcock film often turns on how order is restored to the characters' lives.

From St. Ignatius College Hitchcock went on to attend night school at the London School of Engineering and Navigation to study engineering and draftsmanship. He supported himself during this period with a job at the Henley Telegraph and Cable Company, where he became interested in graphic design. This led him to take a course in fine arts at London University, after which he was transferred to Henley's advertising department. This more artistic line of work, plus his reading of professional film journals, prompted him, upon graduation from technical school in 1920, to seek employment in the budding film industry.

He read in one of the trade papers that Famous Players-Lasky (later Paramount Pictures) was opening a studio in a former power plant on Poole Street in Islington, a North London slum. Their first production was to be a movie called *The Great Day*. On his own initiative Hitchcock quickly designed the decorative illustrations for the movie's opening credits and for several of the narrative and dialogue cards that were to be inserted throughout the silent film. For example, if a narrative inter-title said that the hero was leading a dissolute life, Hitchcock drew a candle burning at both ends. When he turned up at the studio with the portfolio of sketches he had devised for the projected film, he was immediately given a job as a title designer. He was twenty.

The aspiring movie maker quickly rose to the top position in the title department, revising and supervising the work of his subordinates. The Americans who staffed the Islington studio at the time were professional craftsmen whose work and equipment were far superior to any found in other studios in Britain. Hitchcock was always the first to admit how much he learned about the picture business by working under the tutelage of these American technicians, as he continued to gain experience in all the various phases of film production, including script writing and scenic design.

His first real break came in 1922, when he was asked to direct a two-reeler about London low life entitled *Number Thirteen* (called *Mrs. Peabody* in the studio records), starring Clare Greet and Ernest Thesiger. The production money, which had been raised independently, ran out, however, and *Number Thirteen*, true to its name, proved an unlucky project after all. It was ultimately abandoned when Famous Players-Lasky pulled out of Islington to return to Hollywood after the ultimate failure of their entire operation in Britain, and the studio was virtually shut down. Never one to be deterred by such reversals, Hitchcock jumped at the chance of finishing an independent British production being shot at Islington, a one-reeler called *Always Tell Your Wife* (1923) when its director, Hugh Croise, left because of artistic differences with the film's producer-writer-star, Sir Seymour Hicks.

Famous Players-Lasky was in due course succeeded at Islington by a troika of British producers, Michael Balcon, Victor Saville, and John Freedman. They understandably asked Hitchcock to stay on as head of the title department and as an assistant director, a well-earned professional step up. He volunteered to try his hand at writing the screenplay of a picture called *Woman to Woman* (1923), about an English officer having an affair with a French girl during World War I. The front office not only liked his script but appointed him both art director on the picture and assistant to the film's director, Graham Cutts. In those pre-union days a single individual often fulfilled more than one function during the production of a film. In fact, the tasks of script girl and of editor of *Woman to Woman* were both handled by a young lady named Alma Reville, who soon became Mrs. Alfred Hitchcock. Happily, *Woman to Woman* turned out to be a great commercial success.

In 1924 Balcon solidified operations at Islington by founding Gainsborough Pictures. Of course he kept Hitchcock on to continue working in various capacities, starting with the company's first production, *The Passionate Adventure* (1924). Balcon soon made an agreement with the German Erich Pommer to coproduce a film entitled *The Blackguard* (1925) in Germany, where it was easier to obtain financing. The movie was to be shot in the gigantic Neubabelsberg studio of the UFA production company in Berlin; and Hitchcock went along as a member of the production team of Graham ("Jack") Cutts, who had become Gainsborough's top director of the period.

Hitchcock arrived in Berlin not knowing a single word of German, but eventually he picked up a working knowledge of the language and profited a great deal from observing the first-rate German filmmakers who were then working at the studio. One of these was F. W. Murnau, who was shooting one of his greatest silent films, *The Last Laugh* (1924), at Neubabelsberg. Like other German directors of the time, Murnau placed a great deal of importance on telling a story visually, with as few inter-titles as possible. Such emphasis profoundly influenced Hitchcock at this early point in his career to think primarily in visual terms when mapping out a film, a practice he continued for the rest of his creative life.

Hitchcock's growing expertise did not go unnoticed by Balcon, who allowed the young man to shoot whole scenes by himself for this movie. This responsibility extended to the four other films back in England on which Hitchcock acted as Jack Cutts's assistant when the increasingly undependable director did not report for work. Finally in 1925 Hitchcock was promoted to the rank of full-fledged director, and Balcon arranged for him to make two movies in Munich at the Emelka Studios, with which the producer had made another Anglo-German deal.

The Pleasure Garden

Hitchcock's first solo directorial assignment was *The Pleasure Garden* (1926), shot in part on location in Italy (that country was a stand-in for the Far Eastern locations called for in the script) where he devoted much of his time and energy to trying to stretch his meager budget to meet expenses. "Most of my evenings were spent in translating German marks into Italian lira by way of English pounds," he said afterward. The parsimonious German producers to whom Hitchcock was directly responsible had even surreptitiously ordered him to spirit secretly into Italy the raw film stock needed to shoot the location sequences there, in order to avoid paying customs duty. With true Hitchcockian irony, the inexperienced smuggler was caught by the authorities at the Italian border and forced to pay the customs tariff.

The neophyte director had other problems as well while shooting in Italy. The American actress playing the role of a native girl (she was eventually replaced by Nita Naldi) refused to do a scene at the sea shore (in which she was to drown at the hands of her lover) because her monthly period had begun. "I was twenty-six years old and I had never heard of menstruation," said Hitchcock, adding wryly, "I had had a Jesuit education, and such matters weren't part of it."[4] He began to feel more sure of himself when the unit returned to Munich to shoot interiors in the controlled conditions at Emelka Studios, where the balance of filming was completed without incident.

The picture opens with a group of chorus girls trouping down the backstage spiral staircase of a night spot called the Pleasure Garden, on their way to perform a raucous number on stage. As Maurice Yacowar notes in his book on Hitchcock's English films, the director masks the sides of the screen during this opening shot, as if the whole world had shrunk to the dimensions of that staircase. As a matter of fact, for the leering men out front, brandishing binoculars to take a closer look at the girls' legs, "the world *is* that narrow."[5]

One of the chorines is Patsy Brand (Virginia Valli), who naïvely marries a libertine named Levet (Miles Mander) and follows him to a British colony in the Far East where she hopes to get a fresh start in life. Instead, however, Levet attempts to convert the sweltering, sultry jungle atmosphere of their new home into an exotic, tropical pleasure garden of his own by taking a native girl as his mistress and further deteriorating into a drunken, dissolute lecher.

After sinking into total depravity and even insanity, Levet drowns his mistress, then deliriously imagines he sees an apparition of her jealously beckoning him to dispatch Patsy with a scimitar that happens to be handy. But the resident doctor of the jungle outpost intervenes and shoots Levet, who briefly returns to sanity just before he expires. His wife then finds lasting love with an old friend (John Stuart).

Although Hitchcock was not to become associated in the public's mind with thrillers for some time to come, significantly, his first directorial effort dwelled on madness and murder in a way that presaged the films of his later career. For the record, when Hitchcock showed the finished film to its coproducers, one of the Germans complained that its climactic scene was unnecessarily sordid and brutal. For his part, Balcon commented that *The Pleasure Garden* looked more like an American movie than a British-German coproduction. He was undoubtedly referring to the technical polish of the film, which demonstrated just how much Hitchcock had profited by his training with the American technicians of Famous Players-Lasky.

The Mountain Eagle

When his first film was shown to the press, British reviewers hailed Hitchcock as a promising new director, and he went to the Emelka Studios in Munich a second time to make *The Mountain Eagle* (1926). The location work this time was to be done in the Tyrol Mountains— which had to serve for the hills of Kentucky! The plot, which was even more implausible than the choice of the location site, was the creation of Eliot Stannard, who was to collaborate on the screenplays of all the rest of Hitchcock's silent films.

Beatrice (Nita Naldi), a village school teacher, is accused by Judge Pettigrew (Bernard Goetzke) of seducing his cripppled son Edward, in retaliation for her rejection of his own amorous overtures to her. She is rescued from the wrath of her gossipy neighbors by a religious recluse known as Fear O'God (Malcolm Keen), whom she marries. The malevolent judge then jealously tries to railroad Beatrice's husband into prison on trumped-up charges, making Fear O'God the first of many Hitchcock heroes unjustly accused of crimes by unworthy representatives of the law.

Nita Naldi, the popular Hollywood actress who had played Levet's mistress in *The Pleasure Garden*, was asked to stay on to star in the present film. This followed the already common practice, which would continue in the years ahead, of casting at least one American star in a British film whenever possible to assure that the movie would be distributed in the United States, a larger, more lucrative market than Britain itself. (For example, Robert Young would be imported for *Secret Agent*.) Ms. Naldi, who specialized in playing vamps and temptresses of the Theda Bara variety, was manifestly unsuited to enact the role of the demure, put-upon school teacher in *The Mountain Eagle*, but she did her best. Given the combination of a miscast star, a soap opera story line, and an improbable location site, it is not surprising that Hitchcock did not regret in the least that no copies of the film are known to survive, although this is the only one that is lost. It is also not surprising that *The Mountain Eagle* met with little enthusiasm when Hitchcock screened it for its producers, who decided to shelve the film. They eventually released it only after the successful launching of the director's next film, *The Lodger*. Fortuitously, this was set in London rather than alien locales, and was made, in fact, on his home turf at Islington.

The Lodger: A Story of the London Fog

When Hitchcock began shooting *The Lodger* in May 1926, he could not have known in advance that he was making the film that would for the first time demonstrate incontestably his talent for telling a taut suspense tale, a genre with which his name became so closely linked in the years to come. The film was based on a novel by Marie Belloc-Lowndes about Jack the Ripper, a subject to which he returned four decades later in *Frenzy*. The cast was headed by Ivor Novello, Gainsborough's biggest star, as the hero Jonathan Drew (the character's name in the novel; he is nameless in the film). His costar was June Tripp, a popular musical hall performer known professionally simply as June. She took the role of Daisy Bunting, whose family name was inexplicably changed to Jackson in American prints of the film. Arthur Chesney (brother of Edmund Gwenn, who himself appeared in several Hitchcock films) played Daisy's father, and Malcolm Keen of *The Mountain Eagle* was her suitor Joe Betts.

The movie gets off to a strong start with a close-up of a young woman screaming, followed by a shot that Hitchcock would repeat near the beginning of *Frenzy* of the victim's body being washed up on the banks of the Thames. He then depicts the escalation of hysteria throughout

London, as the news spreads around the city that yet another beautiful blonde has been murdered by a madman who styles himself as the Avenger.

Because Hitchcock wanted to highlight the victim's blonde hair in the opening shot, he placed the actress's head on a sheet of glass and spread her hair out until it filled the frame. "We lit the glass from behind, so that one would be struck by her light hair," he explained. "Then we cut to show an electric sign advertising a musical play, 'Tonight: *Golden Curls*,' with the reflection flickering in the water," to suggest that the murderer disposed of the girl's body by throwing it in the river even before her corpse is shown on the shore."[6]

It is appropriate that since *The Lodger* was Hitchcock's first truly characteristic movie, it also marked the first time he appeared as an extra, a phenomenon that became a trademark of his work. His reason for placing himself in the newspaper office scene at the beginning of *The Lodger*, however, was strictly practical. He needed another person in the foreground so as to give the impression of a crowded office, and there were no additional extras available. (Some authors claim to recognize Hitchcock as part of the mob toward the end of the film as well, but I agree with John Russell Taylor, his authorized biographer, that a close examination of the sequence on a Moviola does not bear out this conjecture.)

But what really marks the movie as Hitchcock's very own is his effort to tell the story as much as possible in purely visual terms, with a minimum of printed inter-titles. In this respect *The Lodger* very much reflects the influence of his apprenticeship in Germany (as do the misty photography and shadowy sets, which evoke the somber, nightmare world that characterized so many films of the Golden Age of German silent cinema).

More than one scene in *The Lodger* is played entirely without the need for inter-titles. An example is the one in which Joe Betts, the detective assigned to the murder case, is courting Daisy, who does not reciprocate his feelings. As a gesture of his affection, Joe cuts two hearts out of some cookie batter on the kitchen table. When she pretends not to notice, he dejectedly tears one of the hearts in two.

It is just at this point that the new lodger, Jonathan Drew, arrives, his appearance presaged by his shadow falling menacingly across the front door. (The house number is thirteen, possibly a private reference by Hitchcock to his first, unfinished film.) As Mrs. Bunting opens the door, Drew gradually materializes out of the fog, his face muffled in a scarf, like some unearthly apparition. Daisy takes an immediate liking to the lonely, vulnerable-seeming man; her parents, however, gradually come to suspect that he is the Avenger. Later, as the family sits downstairs

(Top) Virginia Valli and John Stuart in Hitchcock's first feature, The Pleasure Garden *(1926); (bottom) Ivor Novello in the title role of* The Lodger *(1926), the first charac teristic Hitchcock thriller. (Credit: Museum of Modern Art/Film Stills Archive)*

listening to him pacing overhead in his room, Hitchcock inserts a shot of a transparent, plate-glass ceiling, through which the soles of Jonathan's shoes are visible as he treads back and forth. In this way the director depicts the source of the sound that the family is listening to, plus their simultaneous anxious reaction to what they hear. Some critics found this shot extremely artificial, but Hitchcock initially defended it as an inventive substitute for an inter-title, which would otherwise have been needed to explain the source of the family's consternation. Upon reflection, however, he eventually conceded that a shot of the family watching the chandelier swaying because of the movement overhead would have been just as effective and less pretentious.

Circumstantial evidence that Jonathan is the Avenger mounts to the point where Joe, jealous of Daisy's feeling for the lodger, vows to put a rope around Jonathan's neck and a ring around Daisy's finger; hence Joe all too hastily arrests Jonathan for murder. The lodger escapes into the night, still wearing handcuffs. He keeps a secret rendezvous with Daisy on a deserted street corner, where a hysterical mob descends on him. He tries to escape by climbing over a railed fence, only to have his manacled wrists catch on one of the fence spikes and leave him dangling perilously between heaven and earth. Joe, who by this time has learned of the capture of the real culprit, pushes his way through the milling crowd to release the innocent Jonathan.

As Jonathan, bleeding and unconscious, is slowly lowered into Daisy's lap, Hitchcock evokes Michelangelo's *Pietà Della Febbre*, in which the innocent Christ, martyred for the sins of others, lies in the lap of the Virgin after He has been taken down from His cross of anguish. This religious symbolism, by the way, anticipates the crucifixion imagery that Hitchcock associated with the priest unjustly accused of murder in *I Confess* a quarter of a century later.

In the long run, Hitchcock would have preferred to have the lodger disappear into the night, never allowing the audience to know for sure whether or not he really was the Jack the Ripper figure. Since Ivor Novello was the studio's leading matinee idol, however, the front office insisted that the script make it quite clear that he was not playing a sexual psychopath. From *The Mountain Eagle* onward, however, Hitchcock often portrayed his hero as an innocent man mistakenly pursued by wrongheaded emissaries of the law because, for one reason, the director felt an audience could more easily identify with an innocent man on the run than a guilty one. Therefore this studio-imposed alteration of the script would seem, to some extent at least, to have been congenial to him.

Besides, even as the film stands, Jonathan in one sense really is an avenger, given the fact that, as he admits to Daisy earlier in the film, he has for months been carrying a gun with which to demand atonement for his sister's death at the hands of this murderous lunatic, should he happen to find him before the police do. Jonathan's outlook is hardly more edifying than that of the lynch mob that plans to take the law into its own hands and execute him. Thus Jonathan Drew is the first of many Hitchcock heroes who is to some degree impelled by the same dark drives as the villains they seek to vanquish.

The distributors of *The Lodger* thought some of the plot turns hard to follow and found the shadowy atmosphere of one or two of the night exteriors too murky. They therefore asked for some alterations to be made in the film before they would release it. Balcon accordingly asked twenty-two-year-old Ivor Montagu, who was then comanaging another film company, to make some revisions in consultation with Hitchcock. As a result, Hitchcock reedited a couple of scenes to clarify plot details and partially reshot the sequence in which Jonathan runs for his life because the photography was deemed too dark at times for an audience to make out all of the action. Moreover, Montagu managed to pare down the inter-titles still more, reducing them to a scant eighty in number. This was a real feat when one considers that the average silent feature contained close to two hundred inter-titles. Little wonder that Montagu was subsequently hired as supervising editor at Gainsborough, where he served as editor on Hitchcock's next two films. Montagu was linked with Hitchcock still later as a producer of the topnotch thrillers the director made at Gaumont-British in the mid-1930s.

When *The Lodger* was finally released in September, 1926, it opened to both critical and public acclaim and established Hitchcock, who had just turned twenty-seven, in the front rank of British directors. To top off his good fortune, on December 2, 1926, Hitchcock was married to Alma Reville, newly converted to Roman Catholicism, by Rev. J. J. Bevan at Brompton Oratory. She had been working with him in various capacities from script girl to assistant director from his earliest days in pictures, and would be credited with contributing in varying degrees to the screenplays of no fewer than sixteen of his films between 1927 and 1950.

Another version of *The Lodger* was made early in the sound period as *The Phantom Fiend* (1932), again with Novello in the lead, but directed by Maurice Elvey. Almost invariably when a Hitchcock movie has been remade by other hands, the remake, while perhaps all right when considered in itself, suffers by comparison with the original, in much the same manner that the road-company version of a Broadway play is so often judged to be inferior to the original. Elvey's pedestrian version, which reduced the plot to the kind of stolid detective yarn that might be termed little more than "private eye-wash," is surely no exception to this rule. Nor are the two remakes of Hitchcock's 1935 film, *The Thirty-nine*

Steps, done in 1960 and 1978, to cite other examples; and the same can be said of the equally gratuitous 1982 television version of his 1954 motion picture *Dial M for Murder* and the dull 1978 TV version of his magnificent *Rebecca.* All of these lack the panache and flair that in each case he had invested in the original film. Whenever he was asked what he thought of a remake of one of his movies, Hitchcock would always respond laconically, "What remake? I only know one." To a large extent, there *is* only one true version of any film he made. His.

Downhill

His next film was, unfortunately, all too appropriately titled *Downhill* (1927). It was something of a disappointment, despite the fact that the studio, in an effort to capitalize on the popularity of *The Lodger,* had teamed the same star and director again. This time the project turned out to be a routine vehicle for Novello, who was coauthor of the original play with actress Constance Collier (one of the cast of Hitchcock's *Rope* two decades later) under the single pseudonym of David LeStrange. Novello, who had starred in the stage production, was set to repeat the lead role in the film version, in spite of the fact that it was all too obvious that at thirty-five he was well beyond the age of the youthful hero, Roddy Berwick.

Roddy is first expelled from school and then from home because he has taken the blame for the scandalous behavior of his friend Tim (Robin Irvine). Tim has deserted Mabel, a pastry shop clerk whom he has got in a family way. Hitchcock tries hard to dress up the film's predictable plot by employing all sorts of tricks of the cinematic trade, and thus relies on visual devices to tell the story whenever possible. In one such instance he cuts from a shot of Roddy's cap with the school motto "Honor" stitched on it, to Tim's cap, which bears the same emblem, lying on a discarded box from the bakery where Mabel works. A note from Mabel is tucked in Tim's cap reminding him that "Ye Olde Bunne Shoppe" closes early on Wednesdays, a sly suggestion that Tim is welcome to visit her after hours any Wednesday. It is as a result of these clandestine get-togethers in the back room of the bakery that Mabel winds up with "a bun in the oven," as the saying goes. Roddy's cap appears once more, in the scene in which he disconsolately tosses it aside as he packs up to leave school. He has lived up to the school motto embroidered on his cap; Tim has not.

Now an outcast, Roddy sets out for the continent on his way to see the world, but his travels merely send him into a downward spiral toward degradation. As Roddy's fortunes decline, Hitchcock employs a series of visual symbols to mark the character's downhill path, such as showing

Roddy pushing the down button on an elevator or descending an escalator in a subway station. These images of descent are climaxed by a shot of Roddy, who has wound up a drunken wharf rat on the Marseilles waterfront, finally landing in the lower depths of a freighter bound for home.

Visually inventive to the end, Hitchcock employs subjective camera work in the scene in which Roddy, sick with fever, arrives back in England. The camera assumes the delirious Roddy's unsteady point of view while he lurches down a street toward home. Buildings and traffic alike are photographed from Roddy's distorted perspective with the camera, going in and out of focus, recording in double and triple exposure what he sees. The sequence is suitably brought to a close with the inter-title, "Blind instinct led him home." This illustrates how Hitchcock, who began his career in the film industry composing inter-titles, had learned by experience not only to limit the number of narrative and dialogue titles in a film, but to make each one of them really count by packing as much meaning into it as he could. In sum, in a mediocre film like *Downhill*, there is much Hitchcockian wizardry to be admired, even though the whole unfortunately does not equal the sum of the parts.

Easy Virtue

Easy Virtue (1927), based on the Noel Coward play, is an unjustly neglected Hitchcock silent. (Durgnat's ponderous, heavy-handed, four-hundred-page tome on the director devotes a single sentence to the film.) Yet that movie indicates as much as any of the preceding films Hitchcock directed that he was gaining an increasingly firm grasp on the tools of his trade.

William K. Everson is one of the very few film historians to give the picture its due. He points out in his unpublished program notes for the movie that one can measure how basically fine a work *Easy Virtue* is by contrasting it with another film adaptation of a Noel Coward stage work, *The Vortex*, made later the same year by the same studio and scriptwriter, but by an inferior director named Adrian Brunel. "While *The Vortex* has much more dramatic red meat on its bones" than *Easy Virtue*, Everson has written, "it is a dull, far too literal translation of the stage play, drawing most of its excitement from the lifting of Coward's witty one-liners." Hitchcock's screen adaptation does not depend on Coward's dialogue to the same degree that the Brunel film does, but instead characteristically transforms the original material into more than a mere photographed stage play by consistently stressing the visual over the verbal wherever feasible.

The first half of *Easy Virtue* is a visual expansion of a few lines of expository dialogue from the play. As various witnesses testify at a divorce trial, we learn through flashbacks how Larita Filton (Isabel Jeans, who appeared in *Downhill*) has come to be accused by her estranged husband of committing adultery with Claude Robson, a neurotic painter who in fact took his own life after failing to win Larita's affections. In the wake of the scandalous divorce proceedings, Larita takes the name of Gray (supposedly because her reputation, although it may have been sullied by her recent past, has not been altogether blackened by it). She then flees England for the Riviera, where she meets John Whittaker (Robin Irvine, also of *Downhill*), a young man in whose love for her she sees a second chance for happiness.

As Everson points out, Hitchcock constantly uses visual touches to get away from the film's theatrical antecedents. The entire courtship of Larita and John is sketched by simply cutting from a shot of John politely kissing Larita on the hand to one in which he passionately kisses her on the mouth.

When John proposes to Larita over the phone, the camera focuses, not on the lovers, but on the eavesdropping switchboard operator (Benita Hume). As her expression changes from one of anxiety to relief and then glee, the viewer easily surmises, without the need of a single dialogue title, that Larita, after some hesitation, has agreed to marry John. We later learn that the newlyweds have left France and returned to England after their honeymoon when a shot of a French poodle sitting on a trunk at the outset of their trip is immediately followed by one of a British bulldog atop another trunk at journey's end. It is remarkable how Hitchcock tells the viewer so much by showing so little. Larita realizes that the honeymoon is definitely over when John's possessive mother inevitably discovers the truth about Larita's past and forces her weak-willed son to divorce his bride. As Larita walks out of the courtroom after a second sensational divorce trial, she once more is forced to face the glare of exploding flashbulbs, so representative of the scandal-mongering press that has pursued her throughout the film. Looking straight at the camera, Larita delivers what Hitchcock believed to be the worst line of dialogue that he ever came up with: "Shoot! There is nothing left to kill."

But the melodramatic posturing of the film's finale does not in any way dilute the overall accomplishments of what surely is one of Hitchcock's most polished and sophisticated nonthrillers up to this point in his career. In fact, Lindsay Anderson, who later became an important English director himself, was quite right when he wrote in his ground-breaking 1949 essay on Hitchcock that *Easy Virtue* was "almost as prodigious an accomplishment" as the great Ernst Lubistch's elegant

film adaptation of Oscar Wilde's similarly plotted play *Lady Winde-mere's Fan* (1925).[7]
By now Hitchcock was unquestionably one of England's highest-paid and most sought-after filmmakers. In mid-1927 he was accordingly wooed by producer John Maxwell to switch his services to British International Pictures (BIP) at Elstree Studios, where he was promised a freer hand in developing projects than he had enjoyed of late at Gainsborough. For BIP, Hitchcock made the last four of his silent films and his first six talking pictures, all of which were photographed, incidentally, by ace cinematographer Jack Cox (who later shot *The Lady Vanishes*, as well). Hitchcock started off at BIP, however, by filming an original screenplay of his own, composed with the aid of his wife as well as of Eliot Stannard, who had also moved over to BIP.

The Ring

Many Hitchcock commentators place *The Ring* (1927) near the top of the list of his silent films. The creative devices with which the film is studded are still there to be savored today, although Hitchcock maintained that critics and public alike overlooked many of them when the movie first came out.

Hitchcock depicts "One-Round" Jack (Carl Brisson) losing a boxing match for the first time in his career to challenger Bob Corby (Ian Hunter, in his third Hitchcock film in a row) by the same indirect means he had used to portray John's proposal to Larita in *Easy Virtue*. The fight itself is not shown at all, and the viewer must therefore infer the progress of the bout and its outcome by watching the reaction of Jack's second at ringside, just as he had to observe the switchboard operator to learn Larita's response to John. The faith of One-Round Jack's second in Jack's ability to floor the opponent is first shaken when he is obliged to replace the battered card announcing round one with the brand-new card indicating round two, which has evidently never been used before. As the match continues, the second's face registers dismay, disbelief, and finally stunned amazement when Jack lies flattened on the canvas.

By means of the same kind of visual shorthand, Hitchcock telescopes Jack's rise in the boxing world by a series of shots of outdoor billboards, each with Jack's name a notch higher in the line-up than on the poster preceeding it. In addition, the passage of time is implied in the same succession of shots by the gradual change of seasons from one shot to the next, with snow giving way to budding flowers, and so on.

Sad to say, Jack's private life does not keep pace with his successful boxing career, as betokened by a close-up of a glass of champagne that has lost its fizz and gone flat, a metaphor for the way in which the sparkle has disappeared from Jack's marriage to Nelly (Lilian Hall Davis—not Lillian Hall-Davies, as her name is misspelled in Truffaut's filmography and in all of the filmographies copied from it, which have repeated the error). Nelly has been seeing Corby, so Jack smashes the champagne bottle against a framed photograph of his rival, recalling the way in which he hits his punching bag with added vigor during a workout when Corby's visage symbolically appears on it in double exposure.

Another visual symbol of the precarious state of Jack's marriage centers around a snake bracelet given to Nelly by Corby. In addition to recalling Eve's temptation by the Serpent in the Garden of Eden, the bracelet implies that Nelly cannot decide which man she really wants, since she continues to wear both the bracelet and her wedding band. The title of the movie suggests that Jack is grappling for victory over Corby in both the boxing ring and in the domestic arena associated with the wedding ring; for Nelly intimates that Jack's besting Corby in their impending return match will have no little bearing on whether or not he will win back his title to her as well.

The plot, once again living up to the film's title, comes full circle when Jack kayoes his rival, thereby winning both his professional and private battles with Corby at one and the same time. For her part, Nelly, who secretly hoped all along that Jack would be the victor, has at last extricated herself from the coils of the serpentine bangle Corby had given her, and she consequently doffs it once and for all.

During the silent era, British distributors depended so heavily on importing pictures from abroad, especially from the United States, that in December 1927 the British government passed the Cinematograph Films Act. This established a quota system whereby British studios had to produce a specified number of domestic pictures if they were to be permitted to continue importing motion pictures for distribution in England from America and elsewhere. This led to the production each year of several "quota quickies," movies that were mere bargain-basement imitations of Hollywood movies, slipshod affairs turned out on the studio conveyer belt just to meet this need.

As a result, quality movies became something of a rarity among British productions, and were of course the work of directors like Hitchcock. Though still modestly produced by Hollywood standards, these films nonetheless demonstrated the artistry of which filmmakers of his caliber were capable. Although the quota system was to endure in one form or another well beyond his departure in 1939 for the United States, Hitchcock was forced to flirt only briefly with the production of quota quickies when his contract with BIP was running out some four years hence, as we will see. Meanwhile he continued to make films of a relatively high artistic order and managed to keep his distance from any producer who tried to finagle him into turning out these low-grade movies.

The Farmer's Wife

Lilian Hall Davis, who played Nelly in *The Ring*, also starred in *The Farmer's Wife* (1928), which was based on a long-running play. Her touching performance in this domestic comedy makes all the more tragic her suicide in 1933, by which time she had failed to make a satisfactory transition to sound pictures. Here she plays Araminta Dench, the charming, self-effacing housekeeper of Samuel Sweetland (Jameson Thomas), a widower who roams far afield searching for a second wife among the eligible spinsters of the rural region where he lives. He finally realizes, to no one's surprise but his own, the virtues of the lovely lady in his own kitchen, and chooses her.

Hitchcock quite unfairly wrote off the movie in interviews as a too literal transcription of its source, marred as a result, by an excessive number of dialogue titles. Although the movie does have more inter-titles than was customary in a Hitchcock silent, he managed to tighten the film's scenario by excising several minor incidents and characters from the text of the play to accelerate the tempo of the action. Moreover, the exterior shots of rustic landscape of Devon and Surrey that punctuate the scenes in which Sam travels around the countryside in his quest for a bride carry the action well beyond the limits of the play's confined stage setting.

The film's interiors were also handsomely photographed—by Hitch-cock himself during the extended period when cameraman Jack Cox was ill. Sometimes when Hitchcock in the role of substitute cinematog-rapher would finish lighting the set for a scene and announce that he was ready for a take, the assistant director would have to remind him tactfully that Hitchcock the director had forgotten to rehearse the actors and could not shoot the scene until he had done so. "I was able to do the lighting," he remembered, "but I did take the precaution of grinding off a few feet of every scene and sending it across to the lab, which was on the lot," to have them test it just to be sure that the set was properly lit. "But even so it worked out quite well."[8]

Indeed it did, for in the program notes for a London screening of the movie, Anthony Slide calls *The Farmer's Wife* one of Hitchcock's most pictorially beautiful films, pointing to images like the one in which the housekeeper sits wistfully in the chair by the fireside that had once been occupied by the farmer's deceased wife, not daring to hope that it will ever belong to her.

The design of the film's principal interior setting was quite innovative for its time, in that Hitchcock had a composite set built comprising virtually the whole of Sam Sweetland's farmhouse. Director Ronald Neame recalled recently in a talk at the Midwest Film Festival how impressed he was as a lad doing odd jobs at Elstree when he saw this complex set construction. It was designed, like the large penthouse set in *Rope* two decades later, to allow the camera maximum fluidity of movement throughout the various rooms and thus keep the interior scenes from taking on a static quality. Hence the film's adroit camera work, both in the studio and on location, testifies that *The Farmer's Wife* is much more than the filmic record of a theatrical talk piece its director mistakenly labeled it to be.

Champagne

Hitchcock was closer to the truth when he said that his next film, *Champagne* (1928) marked the lowest ebb of his career artistically speaking. Still, like *The Farmer's Wife* immediately before it, the movie is in many ways redeemed by the director's expert use of the camera. In the opening scene he photographs through the bottom of a glass of champagne a girl tangoing in the ritzy ballroom of the SS *Aquitania*. The glass is tilted toward the camera to suggest that the dancer is being gradually revealed to the view of the person as he drains the glass. (Hitchcock uses a similar effect in *Spellbound* when Gregory Peck drinks a glass of drugged milk and the glass empties toward the camera.) The mustachioed gentleman eyeing the ballroom through his champagne glass next turns his gaze upon Betty, a giddy young flapper (Betty Balfour). Although he stares at her with what appears to be lecherous intent, he makes no effort to meet her while they are at sea.

Hitchcock pokes a bit of fun at life on a luxury liner during this sequence, as when he has a drunk staggering down a passageway while the steamer is on an even keel, and then shows the same tipsy gentleman walking perfectly straight when the ship is rolling and no one else can keep his balance.

Once arrived in France, Betty takes a job selling corsages in a Paris bistro where, sure enough, her not-so-secret admirer becomes a regular customer. Hitchcock inserts a visual joke in the cabaret scene whose intent is akin to the one with the drunk in the shipboard sequence. This time he photographs from overhead a dance floor jammed with couples, then cuts to a shot of a flock of sheep crowded into a pen.

In the denouement, the enigmatic figure who has been shadowing Betty throughout the picture is disclosed to be a longtime friend of Betty's well-to-do father, engaged by him to see to it that the immature girl does not get into any real trouble while living in Europe on her own. Although the revelation that this individual is in actuality Betty's secret protector and not a licentious old rake seems after all to be something of a cop out, it illustrates a theme that emerges over and over again in Hitchcock's films: people are not always what they seem—neither as virtuous nor, in this case, as corrupt as we might at first take them to be. Otherwise this superficial, silly little farce is not of any particular significance in the Hitchcock canon. Like the stale champagne described in the scene in *The Ring*, this *Champagne* possesses little effervescence because the director was ultimately defeated by a poor script. Donald Spoto records in his biography of Hitchcock *The Dark Side of Genius* that the director once recalled that he found the screenplay so tedious that he took it home at night and put it between the pages of an almanac, just to see if it would have absorbed anything interesting by morning. It never did.

The Manxman

For what was to be his last silent picture, Hitchcock again took on inferior material that he thought he could turn into something, this time *The Manxman* (1929). Based on a novel by popular writer Sir Hall Caine set on the Isle of Man, inhabitants of which are called Manxmen, the well-known tale concerns two boyhood chums, Pete Quilliam (Carl Brisson of *The Ring*) and Philip Christian (Malcolm Keen in his third Hitchcock film), who grow up to fall in love with the same girl. When Pete, a fisherman, is presumably lost at sea, the girl Kate, a barmaid (Anny Ondra), has an affair with Philip, a lawyer. Hitchcock distills the growth of the love between Kate and the lawyer into a series of brief notations in her diary. "Mr. Christian called," gives way to "Philip came today," and "Phil is meeting me." This last entry dissolves to a shot of them keeping a secret rendezvous in a shimmering meadow.

But Pete unexpectedly returns, and Kate, although she is by now carrying Philip's child, insists that she should make good her promise to marry Pete. Philip, who has become a local magistrate called a deemster, eventually lives up to his last name by doing the Christian thing and admitting his involvement with Kate. He then accepts the responsibility of their child by wedding her himself. Faced with his own transgressions, Philip feels that he can no longer sit in judgment on his fellow citizens. Accordingly, he publicly lays aside the emblems of his office, doffing his judicial wig as if it were part of a disguise.

That leaves Pete with no alternative but to return to the sea, now that his own relationship with Kate has gone on the rocks. Philip's sacrifice of his prestigious position in the town brings into relief the film's printed prologue, a quotation from the New Testament, which is also the epigraph of the book: "What does it profit a man to gain the whole world and lose his own soul?"

The movie's location scenes, which most critics assume were done on the Isle of Man, were actually shot on the craggy coast of Cornwall, with

Hitchcock once more effectively collaborating with Jack Cox, his favorite cameraman. Besides Brisson and Keen, who had appeared in two of Hitchcock's best silent films, *The Ring* and *The Lodger* respectively, the cast included Anny Ondra, who was to appear in Hitchcock's next film, *Blackmail* as well. She, more than any actress in a Hitchcock film before her, is the prototype of the gallery of no fewer than forty-five assorted blondes to grace the Hitchcock pictures to come, including Madeleine Carroll and Grace Kelly.

Hitchcock explained to a BBC interviewer his acknowledged propensity for casting blonde actresses in his films by saying that for him the ideal leading lady was a blonde with an icy facade concealing fiery passions underneath that surface only gradually, rather like a volcano covered with snow that simmers for a long time before it eventually erupts. Such females exude sex appeal in a subtle, sophisticated manner, he concluded, that makes them all the more attractive. This was certainly true of Anny Ondra.

Despite good performances by the principals and outstanding location photography, however, the mawkish plot of *The Manxman* precluded the film being much more than soap opera, and it was largely dismissed as such, even by the director himself, though it was popular with the mass audience which was familiar with the novel.

Blackmail

Blackmail (1929) went into production as a silent picture, but during the shooting period it became increasingly clear that talking pictures were here to stay. A quota quickie with sound, called *The Clue of the New Pin*, premiered in March 1929 according to the eminent British film historian Rachel Low. It was poorly made and employed the unsatisfactory method of transcribing the sound track on separate discs, rather than printing it right onto the film stock itself, which was to become the accepted practice. Hence, although *Clue*, the first British talkie, was itself not very successful, it did demonstrate the potential of sound films. Therefore, in April 1929 BIP, among the first studios to be wired for sound, announced that it was installing the RCA sound-on-film process, rather than a sound-on-disc process, and that the last reel of *Blackmail* would have spoken dialogue as a special added attraction. When Hitchcock screened the final reel of the film for the studio brass, they were just as impressed with the use of sound in the film's finale as he knew they would be. He consequently persuaded them to approve the plan he had been secretly nursing throughout production to convert the film into a full-scale sound picture. As he put it, "When producing the film in silent form, I was imagining all the time it was a talkie."[9] He reshot certain scenes with spoken dialogue; but he was able to incorporate into the finished film several action sequences such as the climactic chase through the British Museum, just as he had originally shot them, with only the addition of background music and sound effects. Hitchcock did encounter one serious snag when transforming *Blackmail* into a talking picture. Anny Ondra, again the female lead, unfortunately had a thick Czech accent, which presented no problem while the movie was being shot as a silent, but rendered her lines barely intelligible when her voice was recorded. Her screen test for the sound version of *Blackmail* shows the director attempting to put her at ease with such saucy quips as, "Stand still in your place or it won't come out right, as the girl said to the soldier." But the results of the test were unsatisfactory, as Hitchcock had feared they would be. Since sound technicians had not as yet devised a method for postsynchronizing dialogue, the director had to resort to the expedient of having British actress Joan Barry speak the star's lines into a microphone while standing on the sidelines out of camera range as Ms. Ondra mouthed the words on camera.

On the other hand, Cyril Ritchard, who played Crewe, the artist who was the heroine's would-be seducer, had relatively little trouble adapting to the making of a sound picture. At the Lincoln Center tribute to Hitchcock he recalled that while the seduction scene was being shot, "mikes were hidden all over the set, and I had to talk into first one and then another as I walked about, sometimes having to pause in midsentence while I walked out of the range of one microphone and into the range of a second. I thought that Anny and I were getting a little glazed from shooting the scene so many times. It turned out that Hitch had substituted real gin in our glasses to give the scene a bit more vitality!"

Hitchcock introduced dialogue into *Blackmail* very gradually at the beginning of the film. The whole first sequence, dealing with the apprehension of a criminal by Detective Frank Webber (John Longden, who would appear in several early Hitchcock talkies), is played entirely without dialogue, just as it was originally shot for the silent version, augmented only by incidental music and sound effects. This introductory sequence, in which Webber arrests a fugitive in the latter's dingy flat, represents the visual style of silent cinema at its best. Frank and a companion quietly open the man's door, revealing him lying on his bed reading a newspaper. The criminal peeks over his paper and sees the two detectives reflected in the cracked mirror over his washstand. Then he glances furtively at his gun, which is on his bedside table. Without the need for one word of dialogue, the director has established that the man knows that he is cornered and that he intends to shoot his way out.

But Frank nabs him before he has a chance to grab his revolver; and the criminal is quickly transported to the police station, where Hitchcock gives us a documentary-like depiction of the routine procedures of fingerprinting, photographing, and finally, incarcerating a prisoner. The sequence, of course, reminds one of the director's personal phobia for prison cells and policemen. Furthermore, this self-contained episode, which would probably be presented as a precredit sequence in a film today, not only looks back to the young Hitchcock's own brief but traumatic "imprisonment," but looks forward to similar sequences in *The Paradine Case, The Wrong Man,* and *Frenzy.*

After booking the culprit at the station house, Frank and his partner are shown walking down the corridor chatting. As they do so, their voices gradually become audible on the sound track; and before the viewer realizes it, the movie has glided into its first dialogue sequence. In prefacing with a wordless prologue the first scene in which the actors are actually heard speaking lines, it almost seems as if Hitchcock wanted to show the silent era giving way to the advent of sound pictures right before the filmgoer's eyes in this, his first British talking picture.

From the very dawn of the sound era Hitchcock realized that sound could and should complement image in an imaginative way. His smooth integration of the techniques of silent and sound pictures, a hallmark of his films from then on, is demonstrated by the fact that some scenes in *Blackmail* are essentially visual, while others depend on the creative use of sound. Besides the prologue, already discussed, another scene that emphasizes sight over sound takes place after Alice, Frank's girl (Anny Ondra), kills Crewe with a breadknife for attempting to rape her. When the dazed girl leaves Crewe's flat and wanders home, she notices a neon sign recommending Gordon's gin, which is white for purity. In her imagination the cocktail shaker on the sign suddenly turns into a phallic knife stabbing at the first syllable of the word *cocktail,* leaving no doubt about the link between the lethal weapon that Alice employed to defend her "purity" and the sexual "weapon" Crewe had intended to use on Alice.

In contrast to Hitchcock's emphasis on the visual elements of certain scenes, other sequences in the film reflect an equally shrewd manipulation of the sound track. In the justly famous breakfast-table scene that takes place the morning after the stabbing, Alice tries to behave naturally while eating with her parents in their living quarters in the back of the tobacco shop that they operate. A gossipy neighbor joins them to discuss the murder that is all over the morning papers. As Alice prepares to slice a piece of bread for her father, the chatterbox's voice fades into an incomprehensible babble on the sound track, with only the word *knife* clearly audible. The word is repeated a little louder on the sound track each time it recurs, until it reaches a crescendo that causes Alice to scream hysterically and throw down the knife she is holding as if it were the one she had wielded the night before against Crewe. No one present, however, guesses the true import of her behavior.

Frank, on the other hand, knows of Alice's implication in the artist's death, as does Tracy (Donald Calthrop, star of *The Clue of the New Pin*), the seedy blackmailer who threatens to expose her to the police. But Frank shields Alice from Tracy by badgering the wretched little man into believing that he is himself the police's prime suspect. Tracy flees in panic, and Frank organizes the manhunt to track him down. Cornered atop the British Museum, Tracy falls to his death through the glass dome of the Reading Room. Later, Hitchcock staged similar scenes of disorder and violence on the top of other symbols of order and peace, such as London's Westminster Cathedral, the Statue of Liberty, and Mount Rushmore.

One sees in retrospect that the prologue in which the police are shown catching a truly guilty party was a forecast of the grim efficiency with which in the movie's climax they hound the wrong man to his death. Hence the film's first sequence is not irrelevant to the story that follows, as some critics have charged.

Hitchcock had originally wanted Alice to be arraigned for killing Crewe, which is what happens to her in the play from which the movie is derived. In such a version the film would end even more closely to the way it began, with a scene portraying the rituals of imprisonment, thus making the prologue still more integral to the film as a whole. In this highly ironic ending, another detective would inquire casually if Frank was going out with his girl that night and Frank would respond laconically, "No, not tonight." The front office vetoed this ending as too downbeat and uncommercial, however.

Whether he consciously meant to or not, Hitchcock nonetheless managed to devise a morally ambiguous ending that is still fairly downbeat. As the ending stands, Alice compromises herself morally by not owning up to what she has done, even though she would undoubtedly have been exonerated of a murder charge on the grounds of self-defense. In addition, Frank just as surely compromises his position as a guardian of the law by encouraging her not to give herself up, as well as by being at least indirectly responsible for a petty blackmailer's not entirely accidental death. As a result, Frank has resolved his conflict between love and duty by sacrificing the latter to the former, rather than the other way round.

In subverting justice with a web of deception that suits his own private purposes, Frank Webber joins Hitchcock heroes like Jonathan Drew of *The Lodger*, whose encounters with injustice leave them, to some degree at least, contaminated with the very evil they profess to combat. Fittingly, then, the closing image of *Blackmail* is that of Crewe's portrait of a jester being carried past Frank and Alice in a hallway at Scotland Yard, as the jester seems mockingly to be pointing an accusing finger at the pair, who must go on living with their guilty secrets. In some sense it is Crewe, by way of his painting, who has the last laugh.

The midnight premiere of *Blackmail* in June 1929 at the Regal Cinema near Marble Arch in London was of course an unqualified success and formally inaugurated the era of talking pictures in Britain, even though *Blackmail* was not the very first English talkie, as nearly all the studies of Hitchcock, including both of Spoto's hefty books, have mistakenly designated it, but the second. Now that Hitchcock had made another superior thriller in the tradition of *The Lodger*, one would have thought that his career would have been firmly established in that genre for good. Just as after *The Lodger*, however, he was assigned a succession of silent comedies and dramas, so in the early sound period his versatility was once more challenged by work in a variety of film genres before he finally hit his stride with the series of first-rate thrillers that date from 1934.

Looking back on the birth of talking pictures in his article on film production in the *Encyclopedia Britannica*, Hitchcock wrote that the introduction of spoken dialogue constituted the final touch needed to make movies realistic. But that, of course, did not mean that filmmakers should abandon the mobility of the camera and other cinematic techniques that had been perfected in the silent era, in favor of making what he often referred to as films that were mere photographs of talking heads. Yet, he points out, "that is what happened on the appearance of sound," when directors often filmed stage plays straight, forgetting that talking pictures should still be moving pictures. "The consequence was a loss of the art of reproducing life entirely in pictures," he concluded.[10]

With *Blackmail* as his guide, he was determined to make what he liked to call "silent talkies," films in which the images as often as possible were allowed to speak for themselves. In this way he would keep his first sound films from degenerating into photographed copies of stage productions. But since such copies were really all that the studios at this point in the sound era expected movies to be, his aim was not going to be achieved easily.

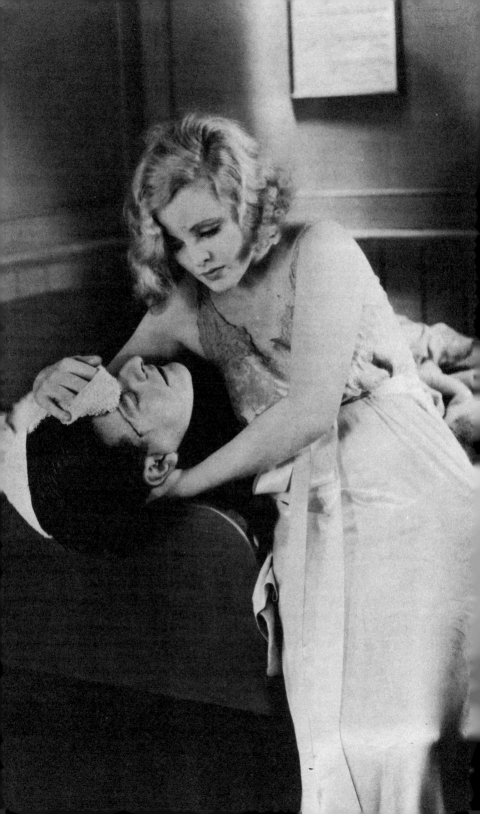

3

The Thirties:
The Early Years of Sound

IMMEDIATELY AFTER INAUGURATING the sound era in British cinema by directing *Blackmail*, Hitchcock participated in making *Elstree Calling* (1930), a star-studded omnibus film directed in part by several different filmmakers that was designed to celebrate—and promote—the arrival of sound pictures. The format of *Elstree Calling* consisted of an assortment of music-hall numbers to which Hitchcock contributed the running gag that was supposed to stitch the disparate segments together. Although the movie was hastily assembled in twelve days, it proved so popular because sound was still a novelty that it was released in no fewer than eleven foreign language versions.

The connecting episode that Hitchcock filmed involved an on-going sketch in which Gordon Harker, a cockney character actor whom Hitchcock had directed in three silents, fails to get his primitive television set to receive the show that is supposedly presenting the potpourri of variety acts that comprise the bulk of *Elstree Calling*. Elstree may be calling, but Harker's recalcitrant television set refuses to heed the call. (Writer Michael Haley gives the false impression that Hitchcock directed the entire film, one of the several real howlers that mar his meager 1981 *Alfred Hitchcock Album.*)

Murder!

Of Hitchcock's next four films, only *Murder!* (1930) comes close to being a thriller after the manner of *Blackmail*, and even *Murder!* is not, strictly speaking, a thriller but a whodunnit. As a rule Hitchcock stayed away from this genre, since, as noted in chapter 1, he preferred to generate suspense by identifying the person who is the major source of menace early on, rather than simply by surprising the audience at the conclusion of the movie, which is the format a mystery calls for. For Hitchcock, a whodunnit was an intellectual exercise like a chess game, presenting a puzzle to be solved, with most of the filmgoer's interest

nry *Kendall and Joan Berry (the voice of the heroine in* ackmail) *in the shipwreck scene of* Rich and Strange *(1932).* redit: *National Film Archive, London)* concentrated on figuring out the ending. A thriller, by contrast, engaged the viewer's emotions in the perils of the central character throughout the film.

Consequently, *Murder!* is not as riveting a picture as *Blackmail*, since as a whodunnit, *Murder!* fundamentally appeals to the mind rather than to the emotions. Still Hitchcock sought to pep up the plot by making the film with maximum reliance on image rather than on dialogue, so that *Murder!* would not betray its theatrical origins in the way that so many stage-bound talking pictures of the period did.

In the opening sequence, for example, the camera pans along a whole row of apartment windows to show the reactions of the dwellers in each flat to a scream in the night that signals the murder of the title. (This image anticipates *Rear Window*, in which Hitchcock would photograph the entire picture from the vantage point of someone looking into apartment windows from outside.) In one apartment a woman is struggling into her bloomers in such a hurry to find out what has happened that she keeps putting both feet into the same leg of the garment. Hitchcock admitted cribbing this image from watching his frightened mother do the very same thing one night, as she said her prayers all the while, during a World War I air raid.

As the film progresses, Hitchcock balances his creative use of the camera with an equally creative use of the sound track, just as he did in *Blackmail*. In the course of the ensuing murder trial, when Sir John (Herbert Marshall), an actor, turns out to be the single dissenter among the jurors to a guilty verdict grounded solely on circumstantial evidence, he is surrounded by the other jurors and browbeaten into acquiescence. The sound of their simultaneous babble merges into an incoherent muddle on the sound track, from which the one world *guilty* emerges in a kind of rhythmic choral chant, similar to the way in which *knife* was the only word clearly discernible in the gossip's chatter in *Blackmail*. When the verdict is finally pronounced, it is heard through the open door of the courtroom while the camera remains outside (a shot Hitchcock would repeat in *Frenzy*) to give the viewer a sense of eavesdropping on the proceedings.

Afterwards, Sir John's misgivings about the guilt of the defendant, actress Diana Baring (Nora Baring), continue to gnaw at his conscience. As he soliloquizes about his scruples for giving into the pressure exerted on him by the other jurors, his voice, prerecorded, is played back; and we hear his inner thoughts. Although technicians at the time apparently could prerecord sound, they had not yet learned to postsynchronize it. Therefore when Sir John switches on the radio in the course of the same scene, Hitchcock had to have a thirty-piece orchestra standing by just off the set at the time the scene was shot to provide the musical background supposedly issuing from the radio. The strains of the prelude to *Tristan and Isolde* swell appropriately to a crescendo just as Sir John, whose words are issuing from a wire recorder out of camera range, decides to track down the real murderer himself.

The culprit is ultimately revealed to be Handell Fane (Esmé Percy), a former member of Diana's repertory company, now a transvestite trapeze artist. He has killed Edna Druce, another member of the troupe and the woman Diana has gone to prison for murdering, who was on the point of divulging to Diana that Fane was a half-breed. This was the reason given in the source story for the murder, and Hitchcock retained the motive in the film. The director also made Fane a homosexual in the screenplay, as he later told interviewer Charles Samuels. Hitchcock modeled Fane's transvestite aerial act on that of a young acrobat who performed his circus act in drag. Hence in the film when Fane finally admits to being a half-caste, the context implies that he is homosexual as well as of mixed blood. That Fane's half-breed status is sexually as well as racially based, of course, represents an even more cogent reason for his wanting to silence Edna for good.

This admission, after all, comes from an affected creature accustomed to appearing in public bedecked in ostrich feathers and sequins, which is surely meant to suggest the homosexual cast to his character, which he nevertheless denies. In addition, earlier in the film Fane is shown wearing woman's attire during the performance of a play ironically entitled *Nothing But the Truth* that is being staged by the repertory company. He quips to the detective waiting backstage to question him, "I assure you, Inspector, I am not the other woman in the case." In point of fact, that is just what he is, since on the night of the murder Handell feigned a high-pitched, feminine voice while arguing with Edna, a ploy that deceived Edna's landlady into testifying that the victim's quarrel was with another woman (Diana), not with a man (Fane).

Hitchcock was forced to telegraph to the audience by visual shorthand rather than by a direct statement in the dialogue that Fane was an invert because homosexuality was at that time a taboo topic for films. It would be another twenty years before Hitchcock could deal with the subject more directly in *Rope* and *Strangers on a Train*. Fane, who anticipates the transvestite killer in *Psycho* by three decades, hands his written confession to Sir John just before going out to do his high wire act for the last time. He ends his performance by grabbing a nearby rope and hanging himself from the top of the circus tent, thereby executing himself in the most flamboyant fashion imaginable.

Juno and the Paycock

The two other film adaptations of plays besides *Murder!* that Hitch-cock undertook to direct in the early days of sound were based on famous works by Sean O'Casey and John Galsworthy. Hitchcock expressed his desire to make a film of O'Casey's *Juno and the Paycock* (1930) when he was introduced to the playwright by Ivor Montagu, Hitchcock's former editor, on the set of *Blackmail*. Asked by the dramatist why he wanted to film "the bloody thing,"[1] the director, three of whose four grandparents were in fact Irish, gave as his motives that *Juno* was set against the colorful background of the civil war that raged in Ireland in the early 1920s. He admired both the play and the performances by Dublin's Abbey Players, whom he hoped would re-create their roles on the screen.

By and large he got his wish, except for the fact that the part of the proud peacock of the title, Captain Boyle, was taken over in the film by British actor Edward Chapman, who also appeared in *Murder!*, because the original player, Arthur Sinclair, was touring with the play at the time the movie was made. Still, Sara Allgood, who was playing Alice's mother in *Blackmail* at the time that O'Casey and Hitchcock met, was on hand to record permanently on film her brilliant performance as Boyle's long-suffering wife Juno, along with numerous other veterans of the original stage production.

As always when he brought a play to the screen, Hitchcock strove to avoid merely photographing the actors reciting the dialogue, despite the handicaps attendant on shooting talkies at the beginning of the sound period. In those primitive days the camera was enclosed in a soundproof case resembling a telephone booth so that its grinding mechanical noises would not be picked up on the sound track. For this reason Hitchcock had to use different stationary cameras for long shots, medium shots, and close-ups, somewhat after the manner of live television shows years later. He would sometimes mount one of the cumbersomely crated cameras on a dolly and move it around the set to capture different bits of action.

Hitchcock makes an interesting blend of both sight and sound in a scene that opens as we hear an Irish tenor apparently singing in the dark. Then the camera slowly pulls back to disclose the horn of the gramophone into which it had been peering. Hitchcock achieved the effect of a phonograph record being played in *Juno* in much the same way that he engineered the radio playing in *Murder!* and for the same reason. Because techniques for the postsynchronization of sound had yet to be developed in the film industry, he accordingly had to place a small orchestra near the set and have the prop man sing the ditty while pinching his nose to approximate the tinny sound of an old-fashioned gramophone.

In a subsequent scene the family is gathered around the phonograph listening to a recording of "If You're Irish Come into the Parlor." The song is interrupted as the funeral procession of Robbie Tancred, a die-hard rebel, passes the house. The marchers are heard chanting a hymn to the Blessed Virgin Mary, which in turn is punctuated by the rattle of scattered sniper machine-gun fire in the street. Since all of these sounds had to be produced on the sound stage while the scene was being shot, Hitchcock squeezed into the cramped quarters that surrounded the set not only the singer and the orchestra for the Irish ballad, but the choir for the Marian hymn, plus the sound-effects men who beat pieces of leather with canes on cue to simulate the gunfire.

But the director achieves his most moving effect in the final scene, in which the heartbroken Juno speaks to her dead son Johnny, who has been liquidated by the rebels for having informed on Robbie. She addresses his empty chair near the fireplace, recalling *The Farmer's Wife*, in which the chair often occupied by Sam Sweetland's wife came to represent the now-deceased person.

When one considers the trouble that Hitchcock took to bring O'Casey's play to life on the screen, his conviction that the ecstatic reviews the film elicited were largely undeserved seems unduly modest.

The Skin Game

Hitchcock sought to keep his film of Galsworthy's *The Skin Game* (1931) from becoming a slavish reproduction of the stage play by liberating his camera even more than he had done in *Juno*. Notably, he opened out the play spatially for the screen with the addition of some rustic location sequences that recall the superb location work in *The Farmer's Wife* and *The Manxman*. The stand-out location photography in *The Skin Game*, which was mostly shot silent to ensure maximum camera mobility, is enough to give the lie to the misleading screen credit that reads "a talking film by John Galsworthy." The film is certainly much more than talk.

The Skin Game is Galsworthy's study of a nouveau riche industrialist who is making inroads on the vast real estate holdings of the landed gentry in rural England. Hitchcock introduces several visual metaphors that establish the conflict between Hornblower (Edmund Gwenn), the enterprising manufacturer who wants to build a factory in a farming area, and Hillcrist (C. V. France), the local squire who resists the encroachment of the industrial revolution on his domain.

At one point Hillcrist looks out his window at a meadow on which Hornblower has designs, and this bucolic image momentarily dissolves into a shot of a factory on the same site, a projection of Hornblower's plans for the property. In another scene Hornblower's son and Hillcrist's daughter, the story's obligatory love interest, are pictured bickering about the feud between their two families while she is astride a horse, a traditional form of transportation in the country, and he sits in a motorcar, which is the harbinger of technological progress. This scene is complemented by another in which one of Hornblower's trucks is stalled at a crossroads by a herd of sheep. The impatient hornblowing of the trucker as he insists upon the right of way is matched by the shepherd's studied intransigeance in letting his sheep take their time crossing the lane. Here is a perfect embodiment of the stalemate that industry and agriculture have reached at this point in social history, and a palpable representation of Hornblower's warning to Hillcrist in another scene that "anyone in my path doesn't stay there long." Equally threatening is Hillcrist's reply to Hornblower, "We'll play your skin game," a reference to the boxing ring and a brutal, bare knuckles bout.

Hitchcock further emphasizes the mutual hostility of the two men in the auction sequence when each is determined to buy a piece of property they both covet. All during the bidding the camera rapidly pans from one to the other with a restlessness that communicates the tension between them, barely hidden beneath the surface of their controlled facial expressions. Although Hornblower ultimately comes off as relatively less ruthless than his rival in double-dealing, the two implacable foes patently deserve each other.

Durgnat is wrong in misidentifying Hornblower and Hillcrist as Hornblow and Hillcrest (careless oversights of this kind undercut the quality of his book all the way through), but he is right in blaming Galsworthy's dated 1920 play as the reason that the film does not hold up as well as *Juno and the Paycock*. The director had to contend with such creaky plot contrivances as a character ducking behind a convenient pair of window curtains just in time to overhear a vital conversation. The movie was nonetheless recognized as a polished piece of cinema, whose flaws in plot construction had to be laid at the playwright's door, not the filmmaker's.

Rich and Strange

Unlike the Hitchcock sound films that preceded it, *Rich and Strange* (1932) was not derived from a stage play, though its title does come from a play, Shakespeare's *The Tempest*, in which Ariel sings of someone lost at sea undergoing "a sea-change into something rich and strange" (1.2.399–401). The title refers to the film's bored and immature couple Fred Hill (Henry Kendall) and his wife Emily (Joan Barry, the voice of Anny Ondra in *Blackmail*), who squander a legacy on an expensive world cruise and wind up figuratively all at sea when their extravagant plans go awry.

Restless from shooting several films that were largely confined to studio sets, Hitchcock was pleased with the prospect of filming an original screenplay (the first since *The Ring*) that called for a maximum number of location exteriors, including some as far away as Ceylon. Most of these far-flung location sequences were shot silent to avoid having to cope with the complex logistics of recording sound properly on various remote location sites.

Hitchcock compensated for the absence of dialogue in these sequences by interspersing them from time to time with a narrative title or two, after the manner of the silent pictures of not so long ago. Moreover, he kept the dialogue to a minimum in the scenes that were shot on the sound stages at Elstree, with the result that when all the footage was assembled, nearly four-fifths of *Rich and Strange* had no spoken dialogue whatever. This made the picture a real rarity in an era when movie ads proclaimed the "100 percent all-talking picture" to be the order of the day.

The opening sequence is case in point. In it Hitchcock satirizes the regimented existence of office workers in a scene that recalls a sequence from King Vidor's *The Crowd* (1928). At 6 PM sharp, Fred and his fellow clerks rise as one from their desks, reach for their bowlers and umbrellas, and head for the crowded subways. As Fred walks toward his house in the rain, he struggles manfully to open his recalcitrant umbrella, which finally collapses, as does the spirit of this harried commuter by the time he finally reaches home.

In the course of their ocean journey to the Far East, Fred and Emily both drift into extramarital affairs; Hitchcock deftly foretells that their estrangement will be short-lived in a shot of them riding along an Oriental street in separate rickshaws in the company of their new lovers. Significantly, the wheels of the two rickshaws become interlocked, and the drivers cannot disengage them.

Withal, *Rich and Strange* remains rather underrated, characteristically by Hitchcock himself, who thought afterwards that among other things, Henry Kendall who, like Ivor Novello, was a homosexual in private life, seemed a trifle effeminate at times to be convincing as a stuffy suburban husband. Contemporary critics like John Grierson thought that Hitchcock had missed the boat by making the film so episodic, since the individual segments were not linked together into a sufficiently cohesive whole.

Nevertheless Grierson added that many of the individual incidents were quite clever in themselves. Pointing to vignettes like the one just described, Grierson wrote approvingly of Hitchcock's "great ability to give a novel twist to his sketch of an episode." Another instance occurs when Fred and Emily are quarreling about their depleted finances in a hotel room. They are constantly interrupted by the entry of an apologetic Chinese janitor who wants to sweep the floor, until finally Fred throws him out for good. No one, the viewer infers, can clean up the mess the Hills have made of their lives but themselves. "The film is full of details of this kind," Grierson concludes.[2]

Their troubles come to a head when the leaky liner on which they are sailing home sinks, and they are rescued by a Chinese pirate's junk. On board they are served some chop suey, in which too late they discover remnants of the ship's cat. The cat, however, provides only one of the unappetizing experiences the Hills are forced to swallow on their increasingly unpleasant pleasure cruise. Ironically, the shipwreck saves their foundering marriage by literally throwing them together for mutual support.

But once they have returned home, the Hills seem to have experienced no "sea-change" as a result of what could have been a voyage toward maturity for them both. Instead of reflecting on their misadventures, they prefer to forget all about them as quickly as possible. So Fred disdainfully sweeps the family cat off the dinner table in order to squelch any recollection of the cat meat served on the Chinese junk.

Settling once more into their routine existence, Fred and Emily begin sniping at each other at the dinner table, so that the storm warning on the radio does not seem to call up salutary memories of the stormy seas they have weathered together as it should, so much as to presage more tempests in a teacup as they continue their old ways. On this discordant note, the film concludes.

Perhaps because it begins as a frivolous farce and then takes some relatively serious turns near the end, both audiences and critics were by and large disconcerted by the movie when it was originally released. Today, however, audiences are more prepared to accept such a disquieting blend of comedy and drama than they were half a century ago. Hence this somewhat strange movie richly deserves reevaluation. The same cannot be said of Hitchcock's last non-melodrama of the period, *Waltzes from Vienna*, made for independent producer Tom Arnold.

Waltzes from Vienna

Waltzes from Vienna (1933) is a musical about Johann Strauss, Senior (Edmund Gwenn) and Johann Strauss, Junior (Esmond Knight), nicknamed Schani. Hitchcock has described the film as a bargain-basement production for which the producer could not afford to stage many musical numbers. But like *Rich and Strange*, it has some clever Hitchcock touches, as when Schani, to please his fiancée (Jessie Matthews), temporarily accepts employment in her family's pastry shop. The aspiring composer registers his distaste for the regimented, stifling lot of the day laborer by marching around the bakery in lockstep fashion, as if he were part of a chain gang, while his face, all whitened by flour, looks ghostly pale.

Since Schani is always preoccupied with his music, even while he is going about his duties in the shop, he is inspired to compose "The Blue Danube Waltz" by listening attentively to the rhythmic sounds of bakers making pastry: the churning of the batter in a mixer, the tossing of freshly baked loaves from one baker to another, the dropping of hard rolls on a wooden table top before they are boxed—all provide the shifting tempos of Strauss's great waltz, which gradually takes melodic shape on the sound track during this sequence.

Both the icy jealousy that the elder Strauss initially harbors for his son's talent and the warm acceptance of it that he ultimately feels are depicted in striking images. Arriving late for a concert he is to conduct, the elder Strauss finds to his chagrin that Schani has replaced him on the podium, and that his very own orchestra is being led by his very own son in the premiere performance of the latter's "Blue Danube." "The late Mr. Strauss," the older man mutters morosely as he surveys his son accepting the adulation of his well-wishers when the waltz ends. As he stands in the foreground, the elder Strauss's imposing figure looms large on the screen, an ironic reminder of his domineering nature at the very moment when he is losing ascendancy over his son.

Schani, surrounded by his fans, moves away from the camera and recedes into the distance, just as his father walks toward the camera and goes off alone in the opposite direction. What Hitchcock was shooting for in the composition of this shot was the effect of wide screen on the conventionally shaped movie screen of the day. He created what was really a wide-screen shot photographed sideways by positioning the two Strausses at different distances from the camera with only empty space between them to emphasize their growing isolation from one another.

The older man's eventual reconciliation to his son's success is reflected in the way he signs his autograph for one of his own young admirers. He first inscribes "Johann Strauss" on the page; then after a moment's hesitation, he adds for the first time "Senior." With that, he strides away while the strains of his son's acclaimed composition surge to a peak on the sound track.

As always, there is more to be said on behalf of even one of Hitchcock's less significant movies than he was prepared to grant. The movie, as I have described it, can be seen to boast a felicitous integration of image and score that is exemplary for a musical of its time, since the numbers do grow out of situations in the story and are not merely tacked on to it, as was usually the case with the Hollywood backstage musicals of the period.

Yet during production Hitchcock himself became so disenchanted with the entire project that Esmond Knight remembers him ruefully confessing to the cast and crew that he simply had no real feeling for this kind of material. "Melodrama is the only thing I can do," he lamented.[3] True to his word, all of the rest of the pictures he made in his pre-Hollywood period were suspense melodramas.

Jamaica Inn

In fact, the only other costume film that Hitchcock made in England before going to America was *Jamaica Inn* (1939), a suspense yarn. He never found directing period pictures like this and *Waltzes from Vienna* much to his taste because the characters, belonging as they did to the past, seemed remote to him, more like figures from a waxworks than live human beings. He once confessed that he personally could never get a sense that such characters, all trussed up in the elaborate costumes of some bygone era, ever went to the bathroom, or to the dentist, for that matter. Since he had no personal experience of the details of their daily lives, therefore, he was at a loss to know how to bring them to life convincingly on the screen. As he put it, he felt he had to know things like how much a loaf of bread would have cost the characters at the time in which they lived if he were really to understand them.

Like the Strauss picture, *Jamaica Inn* was an independent production, made in this instance under the aegis of Mayflower Pictures, a short-lived joint producing venture of Charles Laughton, the star of the film, and Erich Pommer, for whom Hitchcock had worked as an art director and assistant director on the British-German coproduction of *The Blackguard* at Neubabelsberg in 1925. The scenario was developed from a novel by Daphne Du Maurier, niece of Sir Gerald Du Maurier, who starred in the only film Hitchcock ever produced without directing, *Lord Camber's Ladies*, which will be mentioned again shortly.

Jamaica Inn is a turgid tale tale of Cornish pirates that focuses on Sir Humphrey Pengallan (Charles Laughton), who is by day a respected country squire and by night the mastermind of a secret smuggling operation centered around the inn of the title. Sir Humphrey's careful cultivation of a worthy exterior to cloak his inner malice makes him resemble Professor Jordan in *The Thirty-nine Steps* and other high-class Hitchcock villains; otherwise *Jamaica Inn* has little in common with the director's better films of the period.

Hitchcock took one look at the first draft of the stodgy script and asked to be let out of the project; but the coproducers cajoled him into honoring his contract, though the final shooting script was not appreciably better than the preliminary version he had rejected. Hence he approached the direction of the film half-heartedly, with predictably indifferent results.

Graham Greene, whose mainly negative reviews of Hitchcock's British films of the 1930s I will return to later, was the first to point out that the director had ultimately been defeated by working in the genre of the historical saga, one that was manifestly uncongenial to him, a statement with which Hitchcock would have been the first to agree. Moreover, the hackneyed plot, Greene went on, offered the director little opportunity to exercise his talent for devising suspenseful scenes: "We can see everything that will happen half an hour away." The reviewer rounded out his remarks with the observation that "the unsatisfactory picture has been most lavishly produced, though the whole set of the sinister inn creaks like its own signboard."[4]

Nevertheless, there is a sharply defined moment or two in the film that stays with the viewer long after he has seen it. We know that a chance witness of the pirates' skullduggery has been murdered when an off-screen howl of pain is followed by a band member rejoining his cohorts on screen while casually wiping his bloody cutlass on his sleeve. After Pengallan is discovered by the authorities to be trafficking in contraband ship's cargo, he is trapped at the waterfront by a group of soldiers sent to arrest him. Determined to die rather than submit to capture, he climbs the rigging of a vessel anchored at dockside and grandiosely jumps to his death from the top of the mast. Because Hitchcock photographed the squire's suicidal descent from above, the sight of Pengallen's cape billowing around him as he hits the deck far below makes for a stunning shot.

Other compensations in a film that is admittedly one of Hitchcock's lesser efforts include a promising performance by Maureen O'Hara, in one of her first films, as the rambunctious heroine; first-rate cinematography by Bernard Knowles, who photographed most of Hitchcock's top-notch thrillers of the mid-1930s (which we will take up shortly); and a fine incidental score by the well-known British composer Eric Fenby.

Because Fenby was unused to writing movie music, however, he later complained that Hitchcock "cut up my score unmercifully."[5] Fenby's distinguished colleague William Walton (who wrote background music for several British films, but not, as Rothman's Hitchcock book erroneously states, for any of Hitchcock's) tactfully told Fenby that the composer of film music inevitably has to be at the disposal of the director of the picture, and not vice versa.

Jamaica Inn was a thoroughgoing hit at home when it opened in London on May 20, 1939, because the names of Hitchcock and Laughton (despite the latter's rather mannered performance) assured a healthy box office in England. But the film failed to find an audience just about everywhere else, and Hitchcock understandably did not make another historical movie for some years thereafter, when he returned to England to make the equally unsuccessful *Under Capricorn* (1949), his last venture of this kind.

4

The Thirties:
The Peak Years in Britain

Number Seventeen

NUMBER SEVENTEEN (1932) was the unpretentious precursor of the cycle of superior thrillers that Hitchcock would soon launch and that constituted the peak of his British period. Shot on a shoestring because BIP was in acute financial straits at the time, *Number Seventeen* is little seen today because the film's sound recording, which was substandard even for an early talkie, makes the dialogue at times hard to catch. This is particularly true of the Cockney accent of Ben, the dopey hobo (Léon M. Lion) who is on hand to supply the comic relief the throwaway plot sorely needs.

This serious technical flaw coupled with the film's skimpy sets and brief running time of little over an hour mark *Number Seventeen* as looking more like a quota quickie than any other film that Hitchcock directed while the quota system was in force. Nonetheless, in spite of the director's efforts in interviews to sweep the film under the rug, William K. Everson, one of the few long-standing champions of Hitchcock's early films, has wisely written in some unpublished program notes for the picture: "Most of the Hitchcock trademarks are here—the mixing of melodrama with urbane comedy, ultra-civilized villains, and a smattering of piquant sex (the regular searching of the two leading ladies)." The screenplay, which possesses all of the substance of a Saturday matinee serial, frequently tosses logic aside, Everson continues, and never to greater advantage than in the stylish opening sequence: "howling wind, a hat blown away, feet running after it, hat and owner coming together outside a mysterious house, and curiosity drawing him inside. Within a few moments and with no time wasted, the plot is under way visually and excitingly." What matter if five reels later we find that the hero (bent on intercepting the exchange of some stolen gems) was going to the house anyway, and did not need to be lured there as if by chance!

The heroine (Nova Pilbeam) of Young and Innocent *is not aware of potential danger, but the audience is. (Credit: Museum of Modern Art/Film Stills Archive)*

67

The bulk of the film, set in a deserted ramshackle house whose address is number seventeen, demonstrates just how much Hitchcock had learned about visual design during his stint in Germany in the 1920s, Everson notes. Distorted shadows and bizarre lighting transfigure the otherwise fairly commonplace setting into a living nightmare, which is climaxed by the collapse of the creaky bannister to which the jewel thieves have tied together the hero, Detective Barton (John Stuart) and the heroine, Miss Ackroyd (Anne Grey) (another Hitchcockian image of bondage, as in *The Lodger* and other films) and left them temporarily swinging in midair.

Once free, Barton pursues his prey in a chase sequence that accounts for the last third of the picture. In this episode, which is almost totally free of dialogue, Hitchcock has more leeway to tell his story visually. Barton commandeers a motor coach at gunpoint in order to catch up with the freight train on which the crooks are escaping as it steams along the railway track that runs parallel to the highway on which the bus is traveling. The pursuit ends with a spectacular crack-up when the speeding train reaches the end of the line at the waterfront. The engine crashes into another train and plows it directly toward the camera, with the cars of the latter train splashing one by one into the sea and managing to sink a ferry boat near the dock in the bargain.

It is a great tribute to Hitchcock's cinematic sleight-of-hand that the majority of this chase sequence, aside from the shots done with the actors on a sound stage, was a combination of stock footage from the studio vaults and additional material photographed with scale models standing in for trains, bus, and boat. Although money-saving miniatures were very often employed in British films of this period, they were never put to more prolonged and satisfactory use than in the finale of *Number Seventeen*, which is right out of Hitchcock's top drawer, and as such proved a fitting forecast of the group of fascinating chase melodramas soon to follow.

Number Seventeen was not itself a success, however, and like the railway carriages at the film's conclusion, it quickly sank without a trace after its release. The film's failure augured the end of Hitchcock's association with producer John Maxwell and BIP, where he had not really made a strong commercial movie since *Blackmail.* He finished up his contract there by producing but not directing an out-and-out quota quickie with Sir Gerald Du Maurier and Gertrude Lawrence called *Lord Camber's Ladies* (1932). Then he departed BIP for good and soon after accepted the invitation to rejoin Michael Balcon, his old mentor from his Gainsborough days, who was now production chief at Gaumont-British. Since Gaumont-British's Lime Grove Studios, located in the Shepherd Bush section of London, was the most thriving

Anne Grey and John Stuart in suspense in Number Seventeen
(1932); one of many images of bondage in Hitchcock's work.
(Credit: Cinemabilia)

motion picture company in Britain at the moment, and since Hitchcock's career was at its lowest ebb since he made *Champagne* five years before, he gratefully accepted the offer.

At Gaumont-British Hitchcock found himself working once more not only with Balcon, but with Ivor Montagu, the editor of three of Hitchcock's silents including *The Lodger,* and now a producer; and with Charles Bennett, who had coscripted *Blackmail* and had also come over to Gaumont-British from BIP. Together this team collaborated on Hitchcock's next four films, with Bennett staying on for a fifth after Balcon and Montagu left Lime Grove.

In their company Hitchcock embarked on the string of six thrillers that were to make his name forever synonymous with that genre. These relatively low-budget, high-quality movies are straightforward, fast-paced action films with a minimum of plot and character development, and a maximum of excitement. Largely underrated by critics who prefer Hitchcock's American-made movies, they have, as we have seen, been condescendingly characterized by Hitchcock commentators such as Robin Wood as little more than the buds of which the director's longer, more elaborate American suspense dramas are the full flowers. Yet even Wood concedes that the later films, which may be technically more finely wrought and sophisticated, somehow lack the freshness and spontaneity of this earlier group.

This sextet of movies, furthermore, marks an enormous step forward beyond the circumstances in which Hitchcock had directed *Number Seventeen,* their most immediate forerunner among his thrillers. Balcon allowed his former protégé a freer hand and better budgets than the director had enjoyed for some time. Hitchcock's first film for Gaumont-British was from a scenario that he and Bennett had brought along with them from BIP, a kidnapping tale entitled *The Man Who Knew too Much* (1934), which I will discuss in tandem with the second version of the story filmed two decades later in Hollywood. Suffice to say here that the 1934 version turned out to be Hitchcock's most rewarding venture in some time.

The Thirty-nine Steps

With *The Thirty-nine Steps* (1935), one of Hitchcock's finest achievements ever, his critical reputation and popularity reached well beyond Britain to the world at large. The film is loosely based on a novel by John Buchan (later Lord Tweedsmuir, Governor General of Canada). Another of Buchan's works, *The Three Hostages,* had provided some of the details of the kidnapping plot of *The Man Who Knew too Much.* The present film departs substantially from its source, to the extent that, while the script was being written, the concrete explanation of the story's title got lost along the way. In the book, the "thirty-nine steps" refers to a flight of stairs leading down to the remote strip of English seacoast from which a group of foreign operatives plan to make their getaway. But since this element of the novel's story line would no longer fit into the film's plot as Hitchcock had revised it, he simply made the Thirty-nine Steps the code name of an organization of enemy spies and let it go at that. (He managed more than two decades later to incorporate a scene from the Buchan book—that of the hero being pursued from the air as he flees across open country—into the similarly plotted *North by Northwest,* which he rightly dubbed for this and other reasons his "American *Thirty-nine Steps.*")

In overhauling Buchan's story for the screen, the director and his writers transfigured it into the archetypal Hitchcock chase movie, for it is a compendium of every one of the elements that comprise the Hitchcock touch enumerated in the first chapter.

Richard Hannay (Robert Donat) is the typical Hitchcock hero, an ordinary man drawn against his will into an extraordinary situation. He attends a vaudeville show headlined by a memory expert whom Hitchcock in fact modeled, like the acrobat in *Murder!,* on a real-life performer, in this case a music hall artiste named Datas. When he asks Mr. Memory (Wylie Watson) the distance between Winnipeg and Montreal, Hannay unconsciously identifies himself as a foreigner, and attracts the notice of another foreigner in the audience whose alias is Annabella Smith (played very authentically by German-born actress Lucie Mannheim).

Ms. Smith, it develops, is a counterspy from the continent (presumably Nazi Germany, judging by her accent) who is working for Britain against her own country. She assumes that a fellow foreigner will sympathize with her plight and entreats him to let her hide out in his flat temporarily until she can shake off the two enemy agents sent to liquidate her. "It's your funeral," Hannay shrugs as he invites her home, blissfully unaware that his casual remark is prophetic, for she does not survive the night. Hannay's sardonic remark is an excellent example of the dark Hitchcockian humor that is sprinkled throughout the film, and which by contrast is nowhere in evidence in Buchan's straightfaced novel.

Hannay's own status as a transient is underscored by his uninviting apartment, where he has to keep his coat on most of the time because the heat has still to be turned on in the wake of his arrival, and in which almost everything, including the telephone, is covered with dust sheets he has not yet bothered to remove.

While fixing Annabella a late supper, Hannay listens skeptically to her tale about some vital Air Ministry secrets, which she is committed to keeping out of the hands of the espionage agents who are stalking her. These state secrets, of course, constitute the film's MacGuffin in the sense of that term explained in chapter 1.

Too late, Hannay realizes that she was on the level, when he is awakened in the night to see Annabella stagger forward and collapse across his bed, only then revealing the kitchen knife with which he prepared her last meal to be buried in her back. (A knifing is staged with the same visual shock effect in *North by Northwest*.) With her last breath she warns, "Clear out, Hannay! They'll get you next." Ashamed of not having taken the desperate woman's pleas for help more seriously, Hannay personally assumes responsibility for her mission.

One of Hitchcock's most celebrated manipulations of a film's sound track occurs when the scream of the charwoman who discovers Annabella's corpse turns out to be the screeching whistle of a train barreling out of a tunnel, anticipated from the next scene. The train is, in fact, the Flying Scotsman rushing northward, carrying Hannay away from the scene of the crime of which he is wrongly accused, as well as from the clutches of Annabella's rival spies who rightly guess that he is a man who knows too much. Hannay in turn is on the trail of their ringleader, who, he is aware, can be identified by a disfigured finger on his right hand.

In a Hitchcock movie the villain is usually an individual endowed with misleading charm and respectability, and *The Thirty-nine Steps* is no exception. The chief of the enemy espionage agents is revealed to be Professor Jordan, an apparently amiable laird who is ensconced in a baronial manor where Hannay is lured to visit him, mistakenly looking for help. (The role was played by Godfrey Tearle, who looked all the more respectable in the part because of his coincidental resemblance to President Franklin D. Roosevelt, whom he in fact later played in the 1947 film *The Beginning or the End.*)

Jordan literally shows his hand by holding it up, so that Hannay can see that it is missing one fingertip, which is also a symbolic tip-off that the power-mad Jordan is maimed psychologically as well as physically. While the arch spy holds Hannay at gunpoint, his wife enters the drawing room to summon him to luncheon. With an impeccable grace that matches her husband's refinement, she diplomatically chooses not to notice the revolver with which he is holding Hannay at bay. Hitchcock's penchant for demonstrating that danger is everywhere, especially where it is least expected, has never been better exemplified than by the Jordan country house, whose splendid facade conceals a vile lair of foreign agents.

Robert Donat and Madeleine Carroll in The Thirty-Nine Steps
*(1935), Hitchcock's best British film. (Credit: Bennett's Book
Store)*

Later on, Jordan's henchmen handcuff Hannay to a feisty girl named Pamela (Madeleine Carroll), whom they misapprehend to be in cahoots with him. Besides recalling the hero and heroine roped together on the stairway in *Number Seventeen*, the manacles that bind the two serve as an ironic visual comment on the rural couple with whom Hannay had taken temporary sanctuary on the way to Jordan's estate. That hapless pair proved to be fettered by an unhappy domestic alliance more confining than any metal shackles could impose.

Hannay in due course discovers that the classified information that Jordan and his co-conspirators covet is the design of an improved airplane engine. The specifications of the engine have been memorized by none other than Mr. Memory, whom Hannay had watched perform in the music hall at the beginning of the movie. Hannay's mission comes to an end, then, in what is once more a most unlikely place in which to play out a danger-fraught adventure: the London Palladium, where Memory is now appearing.

This time Hannay puts a crucial question to the memory expert by asking him to identify the Thirty-nine Steps. A look of dismay crosses Mr. Memory's face as he hesitates on the one hand between refusing to reveal that the term is the code name of the organization of foreign operatives with which he is covertly associated or, on the other hand, maintaining inviolate his peerless public image as an unlimited reservoir of information and thus giving the game away. He is photographed at the moment of his decision from a tilted camera angle to dramatize how Hannay's seemingly innocuous inquiry has caught him off balance. The professional artist in him finally opts to vindicate his cherished reputation, and he begins to explain the meaning of the phrase when he is struck down by a bullet fired by Jordan from his box overlooking the stage.

As Mr. Memory dies backstage, a bevy of gaudily clad chorines is visible from the wings doing their number, since the show must go on. Against this incongruous background the old trouper spends his last drop of life proudly reciting for Hannay the intricate equations that comprise the scientific formula he has so painstakingly memorized, even though it is, of course, incomprehensible to Hannay's untutored mind. Perhaps Hitchcock took the trouble in *The Thirty-nine Steps* to spell out the specific nature and import of the MacGuffin, in this case the mathematical formula for an aircraft engine, to demonstrate once and for all his conviction, noted above, that the precise character of the MacGuffin is of no consequence whatever to the audience, so long as they understand that it is of sufficient importance to the hero for him to be willing to endanger himself by competing for its possession. It is the hero, after all, that they are interested in, not the MacGuffin.

Young and Innocent

Young and Innocent (1937), is reminiscent of *The Thirty-nine Steps* largely because of the conspicuously blithe spirit in which its fundamentally similar picaresque story line unfolds. Its lighthearted tone is especially evident in the flippant romantic repartee in which the hero and heroine indulge as they gradually fall in love.

Hitchcock also employs a trick with the sound track in this film that is virtually lifted from its predecessor. The scene in question begins with the body of a film actress being washed up on the seashore. The swell of the surf raises one of the corpse's arms into the air as if she is still somehow swimming in death, or perhaps eerily beckoning to the group of girls who happen by. When the frightened young females open their mouths to scream, we hear, not their voices, but the strident shriek of the seagulls overhead, anticipating the next shot. The frantic swooping to and fro of the gulls, furthermore, subtly symbolizes the girls' hysteria. This substitution of the birds' noises for the girls' screams obviously parallels the way in which the shrill blast of the train whistle replaces the cleaning lady's cry in *The Thirty-nine Steps*.

As the story of *Young and Innocent* unfolds, Robert Tisdall (Derrick de Marney), a former lover of the dead woman, is falsely accused of doing away with her. Like Richard Hannay, he must expose the real culprit to clear himself. He is aided in this endeavor by, of all people, the daughter of the local police superintendent, Erica Burgoyne (Nova Pilbeam). She is still young enough to recognize innocence in someone who her cynical elders too readily assume is guilty of murder. Together Robert and Erica survive a comic string of mishaps and reversals, including encounters of a farcical kind with a pair of befuddled cops and with a near-sighted lawyer, topped off by a hilarious free-for-all in a roadside diner. Through all of this the dynamic duo must continuously outdistance the police while they search for the real criminal. Because fast pace is the essence of chase melodramas of this sort, Hitchcock actually timed certain scenes with a stopwatch, de Marney remembers. "Too slow," he would mutter after a take. "I had the scene marked for thirty seconds, and it took you fifty seconds flat. We'll have to retake."[1]

By contrast, Hitchcock took his time with other key sequences. As a matter of fact, *Young and Innocent* contains the most intricate shot in any Hitchcock film except *Notorious*, where he virtually reproduced it. The context of the shot is that Robert and Erica know only that the killer, whom they have trailed to a seaside hotel, can be identified by the nervous twitch of his eyes (cf. Professor Jordan's telltale shortened finger). As she sits with a friend in the crowded hotel ballroom listening to an orchestra performing minstrel style in blackface, the camera slowly glides downward from its vantage point high above the dancers and crosses the floor to the bandstand 145 feet away. There it comes to a halt four inches from the blinking eyes of Guy, the drummer (George Curzon). For reasons already elaborated, Hitchcock has once more chosen suspense over surprise, so that the spectator is gripped by the frustration of knowing what the characters on the screen do not, that the person they are looking for is so near to them and yet, because he remains unrecognized, so far away.

Guy at last unwittingly draws attention to himself, however, by becoming so distraught that his bothersome eyes may possibly give him away to his pursuers that he downs too many tranquilizers. In reaction, he begins erratically beating time out of tempo with the rest of the band and finally goes completely to pieces before the startled, unblinking gaze of everyone in the enormous room. With supreme irony the lyrics of the melody that the orchestra had been playing referred to the drummer as the one player among the boys in the band most often overlooked by music fans. Thus while the song on the sound track was singling out the drummer for praise, the camera in its long sweeping descent toward his twitching eyes was pinpointing him for blame. To accomplish this stunning shot, Hitchcock moved his crew from Lime Grove, where space was limited, to a much larger sound stage at the recently opened Pinewood Studios, where the shot took two days to film.

The technical problems involved in this and some of the other complex shots he filmed while at Pinewood may have inspired Hitchcock's personal appearance in *Young and Innocent*. He cast himself as a flustered photographer whose prize snapshot of Robert outrunning some policemen is spoiled when passersby keep getting in his camera's way. This may just be Hitchcock's joking way of suggesting the trials of a harried movie maker trying to capture action on film. The humor of this brief vignette is characteristic of the comic tone of the delightful incidents that occur throughout the film. On the whole, then, *Young and Innocent* seems to be one movie that Hitchcock made just for fun; and while it is not the rehash of *The Thirty-nine Steps* that at least one film historian has dubbed it, it is by comparison a rather lightweight, not to say slight work.

Between *The Thirty-nine Steps* and *Young and Innocent*, Hitchcock directed two movies that have a decidedly darker, more disturbing tone to them. This may at least partially account for their lack of popularity at the time of their initial release, in contrast to the two films just discussed, which bracketed them. They are *Secret Agent* (usually incorrectly referred to as *The Secret Agent*), based on Somerset Maugham's

Ashenden stories; and *Sabotage*, adapted (with attendant confusion of titles) from Joseph Conrad's *The Secret Agent.*

Secret Agent

Secret Agent (1936) was derived principally from Campbell Dixon's stage adaptation of "The Hairless Mexican," one of the short stories in Maugham's volume of tales about secret agent Richard Ashenden, along with additional details borrowed from other short stories in the collection, particularly "The Traitor." John Gielgud, who played the central character in the film, recalls that Hitchcock, in tandem with his team of screenwriters, overhauled this material considerably in shaping the screen story. Hitchcock started off, says Gielgud, "with various locations that had caught his fancy," and then concentrated on getting his characters from a situation set in one of these scenic locations to another as quickly as possible, "with a minimum concern for probability."[2] Gielgud was quite correct in suggesting that Hitchcock liked to integrate the basic locale with incidents in the plot; since the present movie was set in Switzerland, he saw to it that both a Swiss chocolate factory and the Alps would figure in it.

During World War I, Edgar Brodie, whose code name is Richard Ashenden, is sent to Switzerland to ferret out and exterminate an enemy agent operating there. His collaborators are Elsa Carrington (Madeleine Carroll) and a seedy little man known only as the hairless Mexican general. It is appropriate that, as a master spy experienced in misleading others, this incredible creature turns out to be none of the things his nickname describes him to be. Actually, the hairless Mexican general is a curly-headed, middle-European civilian, whose thick mop of hair and madcap antics when he is off duty are perhaps intended to conjure up Harpo Marx. In any event, he is played by Peter Lorre, who during filming regularly stole away from the set to shoot up with morphine, a habit that surprisingly made no discernible inroads on his superlative performance.

The opening sequence is a worthy sample of Hitchcock's best black comedy. A casket draped with military decorations and topped by Brodie's officer's cap is surrounded by a group of mourners. After the last of them has departed, the one-armed veteran who has solemnly attended the deceased all the while, nonchalantly lights a cigarette from one of the candles that stands near the coffin (a touch appropriated by Tony Richardson in his 1965 film *The Loved One*). Then, while unceremoniously picking up the coffin to stow it away for the night, he carelessly knocks the lid off and reveals that it is empty.

Hitchcock cuts immediately to Brodie, now called Ashenden, whose death has been faked to facilitate his undercover work. He is being given his assignment by his chief. "Do you love your country?" his superior inquires. "I ought to," Ashenden replies, "I just died for it."

In a beautiful bit of silent cinema, Hitchcock implies that the local milk-chocolate factory in the Swiss town where Ashenden is stationed is fronting for enemy espionage agents. The routine goes this way. A respectable-looking, bearded gentleman purchases a candy bar, then slyly discards the chocolate and pockets the wrapper, which contains a coded message alerting him and his co-conspirators to beware of Ashenden. That people and places are not what they seem to be is illustrated even more disconcertingly as the film progresses. When Ashenden and the general go to meet one of their own contacts, a church organist, they find his corpse in the choir loft slumped over the keyboard producing thereby a prolonged chord that reverberates with an unearthly echo throughout the vacant church. In the organist's hand is a coat button belonging to his assailant, the man Ashenden is after.

In what seems for Ashenden an unexpected windfall, Robert Marvin (Robert Young, in an immaculate performance), an apparently agreeable American playboy, points out to Ashenden and his companions that the man they want is Caypor, a German tourist (Percy Marmount, in one of his three Hitchcock films). While playing baccarat in the casino, Ashenden carelessly drops the incriminating button on the gaming table, and Marvin casually identifies it as Caypor's.

After arranging for the general to push the unsuspecting Caypor to his death from an Alpine peak, Ashenden withdraws to a nearby observatory to witness the deed through a telescope. His insistence on viewing the murder from a distance dramatizes his not very firm conviction that his involvement in the man's death is only marginal. Throughout the sequence Hitchcock intersperses shots of Caypor's devoted dachshund back at the hotel whining apprehensively for its master. The animal's woeful whimpering continues on the sound track as Caypor is seen disappearing down the mountain side into the abyss below. This makes the filmgoer suspect Caypor's innocence, which the dog seems to be proclaiming, long before Ashenden does.

Ashenden and the general later learn for a fact that Marvin, who is their real target, deliberately manipulated them into assassinating the wrong man so as to divert their suspicions from himself. Ashenden cannot rid himself of a gnawing sense of guilt for his role in the meaningless death of a harmless traveler. The general, however, cavalierly dismisses their miscalculation as an inevitable part of the hazardous fortunes of the business of espionage, which is small consolation to his partner, who no longer can dissociate himself from Caypor's death.

Here we have a clear example of yet another Hitchcock hero finding out that he has compromised himself, however unintentionally, in his confrontation with the forces of evil. Despite good intentions, Hitchcock implies, we are usually left tarnished by a brush with the powers of darkness; he would no doubt by extension have us see in his flawed heroes a reflection of our own capacity for corruption. We have already seen this theme hinted at in films like *Blackmail*, to go back no further; it will crop up again in such films as *Shadow of a Doubt* and *Strangers on a Train*, and most immediately, in *Sabotage*.

Sabotage

In reviewing *Sabotage*, Hitchcock's other film of 1936, Graham Greene, usually Hitchcock's nemesis among the English critical fraternity, wrote with guarded approval that the film preserved at least some of what Greene termed the ruthlessness of the classic novel by Joseph Conrad from which it was adapted. Hitchcock generally shied away from using the revered works of major writers because critics too often expected film versions to be too rigidly faithful to the originals. In choosing to film Conrad's 1907 book, however, Hitchcock was really not breaking his rule, because Conrad's works in general and certainly this novel in particular had not as yet attained anything like the prestigious critical stature that would come to them later. Hence the present book was not considered to be any more sacrosanct a literary source for a movie than the Buchan novel.

In addition, Conrad's own 1922 stage version had already demonstrated the dramatic possibilities of his suspenseful tale of international intrigue. This was a subject, furthermore, that was naturally tempting to the director; and Conrad's austere Catholic vision of man as God made him, adrift in a hostile, barbaric world, that God never made, most likely appealed to Hitchcock's own Catholic sensibilities as well. What is more, although Conrad was never much taken with the silent pictures of his time, he did speculate at one point on whether this particular novel might make a better movie than a play, since he had found it very difficult to confine the story's action within the limitations imposed by the proscenium arch of the conventional theater.

In Hitchcock's updated movie adaptation, Mr. Verloc (Oscar Homolka), a down-at-the-heels middle-European, operates a grubby flea-ridden cinema in East London (Hitchcock's old stamping grounds as a boy), instead of the combination stationery/pornography shop he owns in the book. In any event, his business is but a front for his subversive activities on behalf of an unnamed foreign power, although actor Homolka's bona fide German accent suggests that the country in question, as in *The Thirty-nine Steps*, is Nazi Germany. Verloc's duties include spreading hysteria throughout London by dynamiting the subway station at Piccadilly Circus and thus distracting the police's attention from some of his terrorist band's more covert operations.

Verloc is supplied with bombs made to order by Professor Chatman (William Dewhurst), the harmless-looking owner of a pet shop. Greene thought Dewhurst was superb as "a soapy old scoundrel who supports his shrewish daughter and her bastard child with a bird business, concocting his explosives in the one living room among the child's dolls and the mother's washing."[3]

Verloc entrusts his wife's younger brother Stevie (Desmond Tester) with the task of delivering an ordinary-looking parcel, which in fact contains a time bomb set to go off at 1:45 PM, to the men's room at Piccadilly Circus station on the way to return a film ominously entitled *Bartholomew the Strangler* to Verloc's distributor. As luck would have it, the well-meaning but inept youngster is delayed by the congestion surrounding the Lord Mayor's Day parade, and decides to take a bus the rest of the distance to make up for lost time. The affable bus conductor at first hesitates to let the boy on board carrying motion-picture film, which in those days contained combustible nitrate, but finally gives in to the lad's pleading.

It is not the cans of celluloid, ironically enough, but Stevie's other package that should have been the conductor's chief concern; it is that which explodes before Stevie can reach his destination, killing himself and the whole busload of innocent people. Hitchcock often said that portraying this lovable, freckle-faced boy perishing in such a dreadful fashion was a cardinal sin, since it elicited a severely negative audience response. In the novel, the young man dies in like manner, but Conrad was careful not to engage the reader's sympathy for Stevie to the same degree Hitchcock does in the film. Conrad's Stevie is not an awkward adolescent, but a mental retardate who remains a remote figure whom the reader never really gets to know.

Besides, the disaster takes place "off stage" in the book, where it is reported after the fact, thus keeping the boy's personal fate from absorbing the reader's attention more than his subsidiary function in the story would warrant. For Conrad, in short, Stevie is more of a plot device than a person, since his death drives Mrs. Verloc (who inexplicably has no first name in the film, though she is called Winnie in the book) to wreak vengeance on her husband at the climax of the story.

On reflection, Hitchcock thought that at the very least he should have followed Conrad's lead by having Stevie's demise occur off screen. His reasoning was that when a director stages a suspenseful incident of this kind, usually the audience implicitly assumes that he does so for no other

Sylvia Sidney, Desmond Tester, and Oscar Homolka during a calm before the storm in Sabotage *(1936). (Credit: Museum of Modern Art/Film Stills Archive)*

purpose than to show the helpless person who is endangered being saved in the nick of time, thus relieving the tension that has built up. The audience consequently feels cheated if the threatened peril actually overtakes the innocent party and they are therefore denied the satisfaction of seeing the individual emerge unharmed. In depicting the gruesome bus calamity as he does, Hitchcock is rather like the director of an old silent serial showing the heroine who is tied to the railroad tracks really being run over by an oncoming train!

After Stevie is dead, Hitchcock prefaces the sequence in which Mrs. Verloc (Sylvia Sidney) murders her husband to avenge her brother's death with a brief scene in which she wanders in a state of distraction through the cinema on her way back to the Verloc quarters behind it. On the screen is a Walt Disney cartoon in which an unidentified bird shoots a robin with an arrow, and a bass voice intones on the sound track the old ditty "Who Killed Cock Robin?" Mrs. Verloc winces, for she knows who killed Stevie, and she wonders exactly what to do about it.

Shortly afterwards, while carving a roast at the dinner table, she finds herself contemplating Stevie's senseless death. His model ship and his bird cage, plus his empty chair at the table, all serve as mute reminders of the absent boy. The two caged parakeets, moreover, suggest Mrs. Verloc's horrible realization that, without being aware of it, both she and Stevie had been imprisoned like captive canaries with a man who, unbeknownst to them, has been engaged in dangerous undercover work that could well have resulted in some catastrophe long before this.

Close-ups of Mrs. Verloc's tormented face, and of her hands grasping the carving knife to slice the meat and scoop vegetables onto her husband's plate, are intercut with shots of his watching apprehensively, sensing that she is unconsciously forming an inner resolve to turn the knife on him. Verloc lunges for the instrument, but struggles with his wife in such an ineffectual way that one can only assume that he is accepting his death as justly imposed by her, as the knife is plunged into his stomach like the arrow that found its mark in Cock Robin.

Sylvia Sidney was initially upset by the director's insistence that this scene be played without recourse to dialogue. But Hitchcock, who never lost his predilection (dating back to the silent era) for stressing the visual elements of cinema over the verbal, assured her that she could convey wordlessly the emotions called for by the tense situaton. She could and did.

This stabbing scene is a clear-cut example of Hitchcock's conviction, expressed in his 1937 essay on direction, that "the screen ought to speak its own language, freshly coined; and it can't do that unless it treats an acted scene as a piece of raw material which . . . can be woven into an expressive visual pattern." Specifically, the filmgoer is much more involved in a scene that is broken up into a series of individual shots taken at close range, than by one recorded from some distance away in a single static take, as if it were "a long piece of stage acting." Using the camera to focus on each significant detail, he contended, enables the director "to draw the audience right inside the situation instead of leaving them to watch it from outside," as if they were at a play rather than a film.[4]

It is in this context that Hitchcock's droll remark that film actors must be as compliant as cattle takes on serious significance: since in Hitchcock's view the movie actor is at the service of the camera and not vice versa, he does not have the same amount of freedom to build his performance that a stage actor has. The most spectacular example of Hitchcock designing a scene in this fragmented fashion is of course the shower stabbing in *Psycho*, made fourteen years later. By then, Hitchcock could dispatch a sympathetic character right before the very eyes of the audience (as he did Stevie in *Sabotage*) without protests, since the public had certainly learned to expect the unexpected from his films.

Although Hitchcock eschews Conrad's conclusion to the story, in which Winnie Verloc drowns herself in despair after killing her husband, the ending he substitutes is still fairly bleak and very much in keeping with Winnie Verloc's oft-repeated observation in the book that things do not stand much looking into; that is, the unspoken motivations that frequently underlie people's behavior generally will not survive close scrutiny. In this instance, Ted (John Loder), the police detective charged with keeping Verloc under surveillance, successfully blocks Mrs. Verloc's attempt to confess to the police that she knifed her husband accidentally-on-purpose during a scuffle at the dinner table. He does so, not particularly because of his conviction that the anarchist got his just deserts, but because of his own ripening love for Verloc's widow. Like his counterpart in *Blackmail*, Ted is aware that by covering up his beloved's implication in a crime, he has compromised his integrity as an officer of the law; and the secret guilt they share will permanently sully their relationship.

Given the less-than-enthusiastic popular reception accorded both *Secret Agent* and *Sabotage*, Hitchcock hurried back to less thought-provoking fare along the lines of *The Thirty-nine Steps* by directing films like *The Lady Vanishes*. Although *Young and Innocent* was shot at the Gaumont-British Lime Grove Studios, it was made for release by Gainsborough, a company long associated with Gaumont-British. It was at Gainsborough's own studios in Poole Street in Islington that Hitchcock began his career in the film industry back in 1920; hence the shooting of *The Lady Vanishes* there was the occasion of Hitchcock's triumphant return to Poole Street, where he made the last of his set of six major English thrillers.

The Lady Vanishes

The Lady Vanishes (1938) takes place principally on a transcontinental express. It is extraordinary that Hitchcock was able to achieve a sense of a train speeding across Europe in a movie that had to be shot on the tiny Gainsborough premises, which boasted only two small sound stages, one on each of its floors. He was able to accomplish this cinemagic, as he had before on films like *Number Seventeen*, by the judicious mingling of stock footage and model shots of trains and other vehicles with the material actually filmed in the studio.

The lighter tone of *The Lady Vanishes* is typified by Hitchcock's pairing of Basil Radford and Naughton Wayne as a couple of British cricket enthusiasts so preoccupied with the test match they are missing back in England as they journey across the continent, that they seem blithely unconcerned that Europe is on the brink of chaos. (Carol Reed employed them in similar roles two years later in *Night Train to Munich*.)

The vanishing lady of the title is amiable old Miss Froy (May Whitty), who is in reality an English spy who must at all costs smuggle to her superiors in London the contents of the key clause of a top-secret international treaty (which is, of course, the MacGuffin). This classified information happens to be couched in the music of a Ruritanian folk song that she must commit to memory.

In keeping with Hitchcock's fairly light treatment of his material, a considerable amount of mayhem is suggested without actually being portrayed on the screen. Thus a troubadour, who is imparting the vital tune to Miss Froy while serenading her beneath her window in a Tyrolian inn, abruptly breaks off his song in mid-melody as two hands reach into the frame and yank him off screen. That he has been silenced for good is implied by the fact that a coin, which had been tossed to him by his grateful listener to signal that his coded message had been received, lies on the ground unclaimed.

Similarly, Hitchcock later telegraphs to the filmgoer that counterspies have kidnapped Miss Froy aboard the train, by fading out one scene on a shot of the elderly lady sitting in her compartment contentedly perusing a needlework magazine, and fading in the next scene on a shot showing her seat now occupied by a grim-looking central-European female attired in Miss Froy's tweedy salt-and-pepper suit and snap-brim hat. This imposter is accompanied by a bogus nun whose stylish high heels, so at odds with the rest of her prim religious regalia, reveal more obviously still that an outrageous hoax is being perpetrated. Miss Froy has been whisked away by the heartless arch agent Dr. Hartz (Paul Lukas, whose genuine-sounding German accent suggests that Hartz is a Nazi), a malevolent brain specialist who plans to get rid of her by allowing her to expire on the operating table in the course of "emergency surgery." But first he must dispose of Iris (Margaret Lockwood) and Gilbert (Michael Redgrave), two of Miss Froy's fellow passengers who suspect that he is up to something. Hartz hopes to do this by offering them drugged liqueurs. To make the doped drinks loom ominously large on the screen, Hitchcock had two outsized glasses made to order that would appear all the more menacing when placed in the foreground of the shot in which the doctor coaxes them to share a drink with him. Hitchcock's colleague Carol Reed subsequently recalled in an interview the director's instructions to the prop man on that occasion. Hitchcock asked to be provided with a couple of glasses six and one-half inches high and four inches wide, which were to be placed three feet from the camera, with the actors five feet beyond that. "Hitchcock is the greatest technician in the business," Reed concluded, since he could "do that sort of thing in his head."[5]

The false nun switches her allegiance just in time to help Iris and Gilbert, along with Miss Froy, to escape Hartz and his cohorts. When

Paul Lukas (right) hopes to drug Michael Redgrave and Margaret Lockwood in The Lady Vanishes *(1938). (Credit: Larry Edmonds's Cinema Bookshop)*

the doctor realizes that he has been bested, Nazi or not, he remarks with a graciousness that is in the best tradition of Hitchcock's gentlemanly villains, "Well, jolly good luck to them."

The Lady Vanishes enjoyed popular and critical acclaim in the United States that was unprecedented for an English film of the period, as demonstrated by the New York Critics' Award to Hitchcock as best director of the year (and not for best picture of the year, as Taylor mistakenly states in *Hitch*).

Hitchcock, Realism, and the Critics

Not even Hitchcock's vintage English thrillers were universally applauded, however. Graham Greene, himself a screenwriter (*The Third Man*), who was also one of England's most imposing cinema critics throughout the 1930s, consistently voiced disapproval of Hitchcock's films of the period, as I have already noted. Greene's basic complaint was that Hitchcock too often contented himself with gimmicky cinematic tricks and ingenious but implausible melodramatic incidents at the expense of solid plot construction and narrative continuity. As a result,

Greene maintained, this talented director managed merely to amuse his audience, when his artistry could have been more effectively employed in genuinely involving them with the characters and their perilous predicaments.

As far as Greene was concerned, Hitchcock's suspense melodramas were strewn with eye-catching, clever little set pieces, which, though engaging for the moment, in the long run contributed little to the overall fabric of the film as a whole. Such would be the housekeeper's scream being supplanted on the sound track by the train whistle in *The Thirty-nine Steps*, and the murderer's coat button bouncing on the baccarat board in *Secret Agent*. "Very perfunctorily he builds up these tricky situations (paying no attention on the way to inconsistencies, loose ends, psychological absurdities), and then drops them," Greene wrote in reviewing the latter film. Consequently, for Greene, Hitchcock's characters were not believable, his plots not true to life.

Admittedly, as John Gielgud had pointed out about *Secret Agent*, Hitchcock was more interested in riveting his audience's attention with a number of visually exciting individual scenes than he was in knitting together the overall continuity of the story to the extent of neatly tieing up every loose strand of the plot. As he once remarked to Andre Bazin, "I am not so much interested in the stories I tell as in the means of telling them."[6] On another occasion, when he was asked by a journalist what happened to the member of Hartz's gang of kidnappers who hid out in the baggage car in *The Lady Vanishes*, Hitchcock retorted that as far as he knew the chap was still there. As a matter of fact, the character in question is a magician who gets away from Gilbert in the course of the film by doing a vanishing act into one of his rigged trunks in the luggage compartment. But Hitchcock did not bother to point this out to his inquirer simply because he did not think that it mattered all that much in the development of the plot as a whole.

Hitchcock believed that the fast-paced plot of an action film of this sort was not meant to be analyzed too closely. The moviegoer should be so caught up in a suspense melodrama that he buys the story completely, warts and all, while he is seeing it, and only detects faulty plot contrivances while reflecting on the film as he raids the icebox before going to bed. So long as the film absorbed the viewer's attention the whole time he was watching it, Hitchcock was not personally concerned about any flaws in the machinery of the picture's plot that might come to light only with the application of what he aptly tagged "icebox logic."

The narrative architecture of Hitchcock's more sophisticated American films would be more foolproof than that of his English thrillers, since in those slower-paced films he would have to worry more than he had previously done about icebox logic. As Pauline Kael has written, however, part of the fun of seeing one of Hitchcock's British thrillers was that it "distracted you from the loopholes, so that, afterwards, you could enjoy thinking over how you'd been tricked and teased."[7]

As for Greene's charge that Hitchcock's approach precluded their being true to life, Lindsay Anderson remarked that in the director's best English suspense films he builds up a realistic atmosphere that endows them with "immense conviction." The characters are presented in common-sense, unglamorous terms, and the actors who play them "dress with credible lack of extravagance, get dirty, and behave like average human beings" rather than like movie stars. This overall sense of realism, Anderson contended, "makes it all the more thrilling when the unexpected occurs, as it inevitably does."[8]

For his part, Graham Greene saw no reason over the years to alter his judgment of Hitchcock as a filmmaker. (In fact, Pauline Kael reports that in the course of dinner in Nice in 1973, Greene argued with Francois Truffaut about Hitchcock. One need not wonder which man was pro and which was con.) Although they were both English and Catholic in background, and both more or less specialized in the thriller genre— Hitchcock's *Secret Agent* might easily be mistaken for Greene's *Confidential Agent*—their artistic views clearly were in many ways fundamentally incompatible. Little wonder, then, that Greene refused to permit Hitchcock to film any of his fiction. In a letter dated October 30, 1981, Greene wrote to me that Hitchcock "announced in the press once that he had bought the film rights of *Our Man in Havana*, and I had to contradict him. . . . I had no confidence in him as a director." (Greene's espionage novel was filmed in 1959 by Carol Reed.)

On the other hand, David O. Selznick, an independent producer in Hollywood, had enough initial confidence in Hitchcock's capabilities as a filmmaker to consider bringing the director over to America. Accordingly, Selznick signed Hitchcock to a multipicture contract. Originally, Selznick suggested that Hitchcock launch his Hollywood career by directing a picture for him about the sinking of the *Titanic*, but countered that proposal subsequently with the offer of a much more promising project, Daphne Du Maurier's best seller, *Rebecca*.

At the time Hitchcock went to America no one would have predicted that his "exile" in Hollywood would last the rest of his life (he returned to England to make only three feature films during the balance of his career); still it is not surprising that he decided to sign a long-term contract with Selznick at this crucial point in his career. For one thing, Hitchcock had all but outgrown the modest resources that the British film industry could offer him. If he could turn out a lovely film like *The Lady Vanishes* in a cramped, two-story studio that had once been a power plant, what wonders could he work if he had at his disposal the more sophisticated studio facilities, not to mention the larger budgets and wider choice of scripts, that Hollywood guaranteed him? What is more, Hitchcock saw working in America as affording him a better chance than he had ever had in Britain of reaching the vast international audience Hollywood films more readily commanded.

In addition, there was little doubt that a foreign director could make authentic movies about life in the United States that would appeal first and foremost to the widely diverse American audience. Foreign filmmakers, precisely because they are not native born, are sometimes able to view the culture and customs of a country with a vigilant, perceptive eye for the kind of telling details that home-grown directors might easily take for granted or simply overlook. In fact, immigrant Hollywood directors such as Fritz Lang had already proved this conclusively with films like *Fury* (1936).

As we will see, Hitchcock indeed caught in his American movies the atmosphere of the United States as genuinely as he had captured the ambience of his native land in any of his British films. In the last analysis, it is easily understandable that Hitchcock—who remained by temperament a dyed-in-the-wool Englishman to the end of his days—should come to feel at home living and working in America. As he said, the United States is, after all, a nation made up of people of foreign extraction just like himself.

So he departed England with his wife and small daughter Patricia to set up shop in Hollywood in the spring of 1939. Many years later he quipped to a TV interviewer that he came to America as part of a cultural exchange. No one knows what Britain got in return, he added ruefully; "They're still afraid to open it."

5

The Forties: The Selznick Years

IT IS TRUE, certain of Hitchcock's American-made movies would represent something of a reprise of what John Russell Taylor has called the swift, corner-cutting style of his great prewar English chase melodramas. But such films would now be the exception rather than the rule; with his arrival in Hollywood Hitchcock began to turn out longer, more costly motion pictures that allowed greater screen time for the kind of probing of the psychology of character that Graham Greene and others had found conspicuously absent in the director's British thrillers.

Naturally it took some time for a director accustomed to working in the relatively intimate surroundings of a small British film studio to adjust to the factory atmosphere of the larger and more complex Hollywood accommodations (although the Selznick studios where he started out were smaller than most). He told a TV interviewer that while visiting another director's set during his first days in Hollywood he was astonished to observe this filmmaker bellowing at everyone through a public address system. When a director indulges in this sort of pretentious posturing, Hitchcock commented, "all the drama is on the set and none of it gets onto the screen."

By contrast, Hitchcock's own formal, businesslike approach to cast and crew, mirrored in the conservative, formal suit and tie he wore on the set, impressed French critic Andre Bazin as radiating bored indifference. "It's been said that no one can tell that I'm directing," Hitchcock countered. "That's because I discuss the scene with the actor in his dressing room beforehand." He likewise conferred with the technicians in advance, all in accordance with the careful plans he had drawn up long before the cameras turned. In this regard he had no intention of changing his ways to coincide with those of other Hollywood directors.

David O. Selznick, for whom he worked off and on throughout the 1940s, was a driven man committed to making motion pictures that were considered "big" even by Hollywood standards, capped by the mammoth *Gone with the Wind* (1939). As a producer who was in reality a frustrated director, Selznick once explained that he ultimately found it easier to criticize another man's direction of a film he was producing than to direct it himself, since he did not have time both to produce and direct. He therefore sought to dominate the individual taste and talent of all of the directors he hired by bombarding them throughout the production period with a staggering succession of memos, a practice that earned him the unflattering nickname of "the great dictater." Selznick became more of a martinet as he grew older, as is clear from the steady stream of communiques he compulsively churned out for Hitchcock while the latter was in his employ, this despite the fact that the director he was treating like a tyro was already a well-established movie veteran.

Rebecca

Selznick, as Hitchcock summed him up, was the kind of old-fashioned Hollywood producer who saw himself as undisputed king of the lot; and Hitchcock encountered his royal displeasure more than once while making a film of Daphne Du Maurier's *Rebecca* (1940). The first occasion was when Selznick rejected out of hand the substantial alterations Hitchcock had proposed making in the novel's story line. To put Hitchcock in his place once and for all, Selznick let it be known around the studio that he had assured Daphne Du Maurier, who had reportedly wept bitter tears over the reception of Hitchcock's film of her *Jamaica Inn*, that he had made clear to the director his intention in the case of *Rebecca* "to do the book," and not some "botched-up" version "such as was done with *Jamaica Inn*."[1]

But Selznick's more fundamental and abiding criticism of Hitchcock, which would continue to surface from time to time in the years ahead, was focused on the director's painstaking shooting methods, already described in detail. Never before had a producer seriously called into question Hitchcock's ways of working on the set, much less referred to them as infantile, as Selznick did in one infamous memo, which in a belated display of good judgment he decided not to send.

Selznick's objections to Hitchcock's procedures on the set were twofold. First, Selznick wrongheadedly complained that Hitchcock did not photograph a scene from a variety of angles so as to provide the editor with a number of alternative shots that would give the latter flexibility in choosing, under the producer's watchful eye, the ones he wanted to include in the finished film. Instead, Hitchcock shot just enough footage to enable the editor to put together a given scene one way—Hitchcock's. For example, if Hitchcock had decided ahead of time that he did not want a close-up in a particular scene, he simply did not film one.

What Selznick failed to comprehend was that, because of Hitchcock's precise preproduction planning, there was no need for him to supply the editor with a surplus of footage to ensure sufficient material to assemble the film in final form. Nonetheless, Selznick condemned this procedure, known as "precutting the film inside the camera," because he contended that it reduced the editing process to what he disdainfully designated as "goddamned jigsaw cutting,"[2] since the individual shots would only fit together, like pieces in a puzzle according to the director's predetermined plan. To this objection Hitchcock could only respond in essence that he wanted to make the movie on the set, and not allow the editor and the producer to remake it in the cutting room.

Selznick's other major grievance was that the director was so meticulous in setting up each shot according to his predesigned scheme that he fell behind schedule. In the case of *Rebecca*, shooting commenced on September 8, 1939, and was supposed to last a total of thirty-six days; principal photography was not completed until November 20, about twenty days beyond schedule. Hitchcock remarked in his own defense to his assistant director Ridgeway Callow that "regardless of the schedule, they'll forget about it if it's a good picture."[3] So it was, for *Rebecca* not only earned its cost back twice over in its first year of release, but went on to be hailed by the Motion Picture Academy as the best picture of the year.

Rebecca concerns the marriage of Maxim de Winter (Laurence Olivier), a wealthy, aloof, widower, to the youthful heroine (Joan Fontaine, in her first major role). Like Mrs. Verloc in *Sabotage*, the heroine of *Rebecca* is not given a first name in the film. In this case she did not have a given name in the literary source either. Presumably, it is only by living through the harrowing experiences that confront her after she takes up residence with Max in the stately but menacing mansion of Manderley that she gains maturity, and hence forges for herself a clearly defined identity that goes beyond being merely "the second Mrs. de Winter."

Because of the importance of Manderley to the plot, Hitchcock had two large-scale models of its exterior built, one of which would be destroyed in the climactic fire sequence. (The other model, which survived the shooting of the picture, showed up a year later in the Charlie Chan film *Castle in the Desert* as the home of a "Mr. Manderley".)

In the picture's prologue, Manderley is first glimpsed at the end of a drive overgrown with underbrush, where its gutted ruins materialize out of the mist in spooky silhouette, as the heroine's voice muses wistfully over the sound track, "Last night I dreamt I went to Manderley; . . . but we can never go back again." The next time we see the house, as the story unfolds in the extended flashback that comprises the bulk of the film, the heroine is arriving there with Max after their honeymoon. The sun shines bright as Max's car enters the imposing gates of the estate; but by the time he and his bride arrive at the manor house, the brooding clouds overhead have unleashed a thunderstorm, foreshadowing the bleakness of the girl's immediate future in the forbidding family castle.

Throughout the film the disconsolate heroine lives in the shadow of Rebecca, Max's deceased first wife with whom, she is assured by his family and friends, he was deliriously happy. Max, however, eventually reveals to his second wife that the faithless Rebecca had sadistically sought to make his life a veritable hell, epitomized by her attempt to goad him into murdering her by cruelly informing him that she was pregnant with the child of another man, possibly her own cousin, playboy Jack Favell (George Sanders). Later the real reason for Rebecca's suicidal death wish is brought to light: she wanted to be spared a prolonged and unglamorous death from cancer by having Max in effect put her out of her misery.

In the novel Max takes the bait and in a fit of anger summarily shoots Rebecca during their final confrontation in the beach house on the grounds of the estate. Since the censor would not allow the film's hero literally to get away with murder, however, Hitchcock had to depict the incident with studied ambiguity. In the film version of *Rebecca,* therefore, Max intimates to his present wife that he would have taken Rebecca's life had she not, as they quarreled, tripped over some ship's tackle on the floor, fallen, and struck her head, thereby dying accidentally. The sole novelty of the indifferent four-part 1978 BBC-TV mini-series based on the novel, by the way, was that Max's murder of Rebecca was allowed to be accurately portrayed for what it was.

Hitchcock wisely refrained from directly depicting Rebecca's demise, the better to gloss over the implausible aspects of the censor-imposed death by accident, as well as to make the event all the more mysterious and to keep any image of Rebecca off the screen. Instead, while Max is recounting the traumatic event for his second wife in the beach house, the camera virtually reenacts Rebecca's death by panning around the room, momentarily pausing as it does so on various key objects as Max mentions them, such as the ship's tackle coiled on the floor like a snake ready to strike. In this manner Hitchcock vividly presents this crucial scene without really portraying it at all.

Conversely, Hitchcock adroitly creates the final destruction of Manderley in all its compelling detail. The mansion is burned to the ground by Mrs. Danvers (Judith Anderson), the dour, demonic housekeeper who had adored Rebecca with a passion bearing a decidedly lesbian tinge. When she learns the whole hideous truth about her deceased mistress, the crazed woman puts a torch to the house and is herself burned up in the blaze, as if consumed in the fires of her own destructive fury. When the flames ravaging Rebecca's sumptuous bedroom reach her ornate bed, they devour her monogrammed pillowcase. The embroidered R finally disappears behind a curtain of fire, as Rebecca's spirit is at last dispelled from the lives of Max and his new wife.

Despite the finely crafted film that Hitchcock delivered to his producer, Selznick remained relatively unimpressed by the director whom he had imported from England with such fanfare. In addition to the Academy Award that cinematographer George Barnes won for the film, Hitchcock was himself nominated by his new colleagues in Hollywood as the best director. Yet, when the film was voted best picture of the year, Selznick made a point of wiring congratulations to Daphne Du Maurier, who had nothing directly to do with the movie at all.

Because Hitchcock found Selznick's incessant interference so galling, he arranged to be loaned out to other studios as often as possible during the seven years he was under contract to Selznick; thus by the time he and the producer finally parted company, Hitchcock had made only three pictures for Selznick. This is understandable, since as soon as Hitchcock was working for someone else, he invariably found that official, not to say officious, supervision of his work was lessened.

Suspicion

Suspicion (1941), which Hitchcock made on loan to RKO, reunited him with Joan Fontaine. She noted at the time of the 1974 Lincoln Center tribute to Hitchcock that he was very effective with actors, "except when the front office interfered" (a reference to Selznick?) or "the actor's ego got in the way." Hitchcock's effectiveness with Ms. Fontaine was made manifest when she won for her work in *Suspicion* the best actress Oscar, which she had deserved even more for her similar role in *Rebecca*.

As Lina in *Suspicion*, Joan Fontaine is once again an immature young lady who marries a husband with a mysterious past. She first encounters Johnny Aysgarth (Cary Grant, in the first of his four Hitchcock films) when they find themselves sharing a railway compartment at the beginning of the film. Significantly, the first shot begins in total darkness, which gradually gives way to daylight as the train on which they are traveling emerges from a tunnel, forecasting how Lina will remain in the dark about Johnny's true character until she finally comes to see him in the clear light of day as he truly is.

Looking aloof and spinsterish in her frumpy outfit and horn-rimmed glasses, Lina is reminiscent of Pamela, the heroine of *The Thirty-nine Steps*, whose spectacles and prim demeanor make her seem equally unappealing to Richard Hannay when he happens upon her in a railway carriage. In both films the heroine's eye glasses are a clue to her faulty perception of others: Hannay in reality is a good deal better than Pamela at first takes him to be; the ne'er-do-well Johnny, who eventually marries Lina for her money, is a good deal worse.

In a very telling shot, Hitchcock suggests that Lina would rather not know the truth about Johnny. It begins with a close-up of a photograph of Johnny in a fashionable magazine, looking more winning than ever; then Lina's hand comes into the frame as she places her glasses directly over Johnny's picture, as if the (by now) lovesick girl is deliberately refraining from taking a good look at him, lest she see through the superficial gloss of his external charm to the flawed character underneath. Hitchcock also tunes in a lush Strauss waltz on the sound track from time to time as another emblem of Lina's romantic infatuation with Johnny, and which, coincidentally, is a subtle reminder of the director's Strauss film.

Things change, however, when she begins to suspect that her husband may be plotting to do away with her so that he can have her fortune all to himself. As Johnny carries a glass of possibly poisoned milk up the dark staircase to his wife's bedroom, the viewer's suspicions of its contents are visually heightened by the liquid's eerie glow, accomplished by Hitchcock's placing a luminous bulb inside the glass. Johnny's figure is interlaced with sinister shadows cast by the framework of an enormous window overlooking the steps, a visual metaphor for the dark web of doubt and distrust his wife is spinning around him.

Hitchcock had initially hoped that he could be more faithful to the novel by Francis Iles on which the film was based than an earlier draft of the screenplay co-authored by Nathaniel West had been, by having Johnny actually murder Lina for her money. To head off objections from the industry's censor, who would certainly not permit Johnny to get away with killing off his wife any more than he would allow Max de Winter to do so in *Rebecca*, the director came up with what he thought to be an ideal solution. He proposed that in the final scene of *Suspicion*, after Johnny has slain Lina, he would unwittingly seal his own doom by mailing an incriminating letter to his dead spouse's mother, in which Lina expresses her conviction that her husband was planning to poison her. But this time it was the front office, not the censor, that persisted in giving Hitchcock trouble. The RKO officials categorically refused to sanction Cary Grant's playing a murderer, just as years before Hitchcock's bosses at Gainsborough spurned the notion of Ivor Novello enacting the role of a killer in *The Lodger*. In any event, it is just possible that Hitchcock's signature appearance in *Suspicion*, which shows him posting a letter in a mail box, may be a playful private reference to his favored ending for the film, which he was never even allowed to shoot. As Hitchcock later wrote, he was pressured into making the wife's misgiv-

*Joan Fontaine (center) with Cary Grant in her Oscar-winning
role in* Suspicion *(1941). Sir Cedric Hardwicke (to her right)
looks on. (Credit: Bennett's Book Store)*

ings about her husband "a figment of her imagination," because the
official consensus at the studio was that "audiences would not want to be
told in the last few frames of a film that so popular a personality as Cary
Grant was a murderer doomed to exposure."[4]

Another ending, in which Johnny, desperately despondent over his
mounting personal debts, tries to kill himself instead of Lina, was
actually shot, but previewed badly. It was replaced by the compromise
ending with which the film was finally released. In it Johnny is totally
exonerated of Lina's doubts about him, and a passing reference to his
contemplating suicide (salvaged from the first of the endings that were
shot) is even tossed in for good measure to explain away the manual of
poison he had been surreptitiously studying. But this studio-engineered
denouement is not the cop-out it might at first appear to be. It does
nudge the reflective viewer to consider how Lina's paranoid fears about
Johnny had come close to poisoning their marriage as surely as the
deadly draught with which Lina suspected Johnny had laced her bed-
time milk.

Hitchcock's own suspicions that the last-minute tinkering with the
film's conclusion might have done the film permanent damage were

quickly dispelled when *Suspicion* quickly became, like *Rebecca*, a big box-office favorite.

Foreign Correspondent

During his first years in America, Hitchcock began to notice in the press suggestions that the critics and the public as well hankered for him to direct a few more chase melodramas like the ones he used to make back in England. Thus he occasionally returned to that genre by making films like *Foreign Correspondent* (1940) and later, *Saboteur*. Bolstered by a nimble, witty screenplay on which Charles Bennett, a close creative associate of Hitchcock's in his peak British period, collaborated, the film belongs to the grand tradition of Hitchcock's English thrillers. It is composed of a series of cunningly devised episodes all built around an innocent bystander who at the start is thrown into jeopardy quite by accident. The droll wit that periodically pops up in the script was largely the work of American humorist Robert Benchley, who also wrote his own part, that of the hero's drunken sidekick Stebbins.

The foreign correspondent of the title is Johnny Jones (Joel McCrea), a gauche American reporting on European trouble spots just before the outbreak of World War II. He writes under the name of Huntley Haverstock, a pompous pseudonymn coined by his editor to impress Johnny's readership back home. Johnny has no desire whatever to become enmeshed in undercover work, yet while he is following up on what he considers a routine assignment in Amsterdam, he happens to witness the feigned assassination of a foreign diplomat. The mock murder is intended to cover up the fact that the real statesman, who is still very much alive, has already been spirited away by a group of spies determined to compel him to disclose the secret clause of a foreign treaty (here is a plot twist that owes more than a little to the kidnapping of Miss Froy in *The Lady Vanishes*).

In the guise of a press photographer, the bogus assassin fires a gun that is concealed by the camera with which he was ostensibly going to shoot a photo of the captive diplomat's double. The progress of the rain-drenched fugitive's escape is pictured by a high-angle shot of a cluster of umbrellas bobbing up and down in succession as he forces his way through the crowd of stunned spectators.

"It gave me a turn," Hitchcock remembered, when a year after *Foreign Correspondent* was finished an assassination occurred in Tehran possibly modeled on the one in the film. Eventually he comforted himself with the thought that "the whole thing was a coincidence."[5] By the same token, two decades later when a journalist informed him that a confessed murderer who had systematically done in three wives announced that he killed the third one after seeing *Psycho*, Hitchcock was no longer perturbed by issues of this kind. Gamely he inquired which of his films had prompted the individual to eliminate the first two.[6]

Since the shaky political situation in Europe precluded extensive location work, several elaborate sets representing various overseas locales had to be built in the studio under the supervision of the film's chief production designer, William Cameron Menzies, responsible for *Gone with the Wind*, among other films. With uncanny accuracy, Menzies and his staff created, for example, the observation deck on the tower of London's Westminster Catholic Cathedral, which serves as the setting of an attempt on Johnny's life by the mob of enemy espionage agents who want him silenced. Their ringleader, Stephen Fisher (Herbert Marshall of *Murder!*) hires a jovial, mild-mannered, middle-aged contract killer named Rowley (Edmund Gwenn of *The Skin Game* and *Waltzes from Vienna*) to push Johnny to his death from the church's hallowed heights. The would-be murderer, however, loses his balance and himself plummets to the pavement, just as, appropriately enough, the strains of the Requiem Mass for the dead, which is being chanted inside the cathedral, can be heard on the sound track.

Hitchcock chose as the site for this scene the Catholic Cathedral of London, rather than any of the better-known non-Catholic edifices in the city such as St. Paul's or Westminster Abbey. This was not just because he happened to be a Catholic himself, but because the Cathedral's Spanish architecture featured a tall, lean tower—the ideal setting for photographing someone falling to his death. (The same can be said for the similarly structured Spanish Catholic missions in California, one of which provided the setting for another fateful fall in *Vertigo* nearly two decades later.)

The most spectacular scene in the film occurs when the commercial seaplane that is carrying Johnny home is forced to crash land in the middle of the Atlantic. Just as the nose of the plane meets the surface of the sea, a torrential deluge smashes through the windshield of the cockpit and rushes right at the camera, making the filmgoer feel that he too is awash. Hitchcock engineered this stunning effect by having a shot of a plane diving toward the sea, which had been photographed from the pilot's point of view, projected on a tissue-paper screen placed in front of the mock-up of the cockpit that had been constructed on a studio sound stage. Behind this screen he placed two tanks filled with 54,000 gallons of water, aimed directly at the plane. The director then photographed the crash over the shoulders of the two pilots, showing the plane coming closer and closer to the ocean as it plunges relentlessly downward. At the moment of impact Hitchcock released the contents of the two water tanks and sent them crashing through the flimsy screen with such intensity that filmgoers do not notice the tissue paper being torn away by the gushing water as it cascades in on the cockpit.

The crash landing, which was done in a single, uninterrupted take, is a prime example of Hitchcock's customarily smooth, unpretentious camera work; filmgoers are usually so mesmerized by this marvelously executed scene that they never even think to wonder how it was done. In principle, Hitchcock always shunned showy camera work so his cinematography did not draw attention to itself. He believed that a director's goal should be apparent simplicity, and declared emphatically that he would never take a shot, for example, from behind the flames in a fireplace with the camera looking into the room. He reasoned that it would be humanly impossible in real life for anyone to observe a scene from such an incredible point of view.

Yet he went against his own principle in the sequence just described, which begins with a shot photographed from outside the plane with the camera evidently gliding across the wing, moving up to one of the portholelike windows, and then going through the window and into the cabin. Obviously, in real life no one could observe a scene from such an impossible vantage point as the wing of an airplane in flight. Aside from this one distractingly artificial shot, however, Hitchcock's camera work is as unobtrusive as ever.

Foreign Correspondent, which was generally well received, was nominated for but did not win the Oscar for best picture of the year— only because *Rebecca* did.

Saboteur

Saboteur (1942), which was made at Universal, is another manhunt melodrama, cut from the same cloth as *Foreign Correspondent*. In it Robert Cummings is cast as Barry Kane, who is unjustly blamed for setting fire to a wartime defense plant, which in fact was burned down by a foreign saboteur fittingly named Fry (Norman Lloyd). Kane thus has a pronounced kinship to the wrongly accused heroes of Hitchcock's British cloak-and-dagger films, especially Hannay in *The Thirty-nine Steps* and the hero of *The Lodger*, because he is for a time handicapped in hunting down his man until he can get free of the handcuffs he was wearing when he escaped police custody.

Kane finally traps Fry on the observation platform attached to the torch of the Statue of Liberty, a setting that calls to mind most immediately Johnny Jones's deadly confrontation with Rowley at the top of another memorial to civilization in *Foreign Correspondent*. As Kane grapples with Fry, the latter slips over the railing and is left suspended in midair. Kane clutches at the helpless man's coat sleeve, which gradually gives way stitch by stitch until Fry plunges to his death. With true

Archetypal Hitchcock villain Otto Kruger (right) menaces Robert Cummings in Saboteur *(1942). (Credit: Cinemabilia)*

poetic justice the enemy arsonist who put defense factories to the torch has met his death at America's shrine to the torch of liberty.

Hitchcock said more than once that the filmgoer's involvement in this scene might have been stronger had it been a sympathetic rather than an unsympathetic character whose life was hanging by a thread. Yet he liked the basic setup of the sequence well enough virtually to repeat it more than a decade later in *To Catch a Thief*, in which the hero tightly clasps the hand of a robber who is dangling from a rooftop in an endeavor to haul the criminal to safety. By contrast, Hitchcock did finally reverse the situation a few years after *To Catch a Thief* in *North by Northwest*, when the hero finds himself hanging onto the edge of a precipice on Mount Rushmore while the villain tries to force him to let go and fall to his death. For my money, all three of these cliff-hanging scenes are equally exciting regardless of whether the individual in danger is sympathetic or unsympathetic, because filmgoers can readily share anyone's fear of falling from a great height.

Fry's iniquitous employer in *Saboteur* is Charles Tobin, a wealthy cryptofascist. As Tobin, Otto Kruger gives what is perhaps one of the best renderings ever of the prototypical Hitchcockian villian, next to Godfrey Tearle's Professor Jordan after whom the character of Tobin was

clearly fashioned, just as Kane was modeled on Hannay. (Perhaps Hitch-
cock should have said of *Saboteur*, as he did of the later *North by
Northwest*, that it was really *The Thirty-nine Steps* transplanted to
American soil.)

Hitchcock temporarily toyed with the idea of casting Harry Carey
against type in the part of Tobin, since Carey usually played good-
natured, wholesome characters, but he stuck with Kruger, who frequently played sleek villains. (The director would later brilliantly cast
winsome, boyish Robert Walker against type as the homosexual
psychopath in *Strangers on a Train* about a decade later.) To my mind
Kruger essays impeccably the role of the urbane, debonair, silver-haired
gentleman rancher who devotes his spare time to presiding over the
clandestine operations of his fellow fifth-columnists. One moment he is
playing at poolside with his baby granddaughter, and the next he is
impassively plotting more arson, while the pipe smoke wreathing his
head suggests both the hellfire and brimstone associated with his satanic
character, and the flames enkindled on his order by the arsonist Fry.

When Kane confronts Tobin for the last time, the latter is photographed in long shot to make him look all the more remote and inacces-
sible, for he is serenely confident that he is beyond the reach of Kane or
anyone else who might try to bring him to justice. In point of fact, he
does ultimately escape capture, and the thought that Tobin and his kind
will continue to carry on their treasonous activities against the United
States lends a disturbing note to the ending of a film that was released
shortly after World War II commenced.

Mr. and Mrs. Smith

There was really nothing very disturbing about the daffy screwball
comedy in which comedienne Carole Lombard asked Hitchcock to
direct her. The mutual admiration of director and star induced him to
agree. Hence Hitchcock found himself filming a full-fledged comedy
laced with considerable helpings of farcical material for the first time
since *Rich and Strange*, his hard-edged comedy of a decade before,
which also dealt with a marriage on the rocks.

Mr. and Mrs. Smith (1941) features Robert Montgomery and Carole
Lombard as David and Ann Smith, a feisty married couple who try to
rejuvenate their sagging relationship by, among other things, making a
sentimental journey to Mamma Lucy's, a small Italian restaurant in
Greenwich Village, which they frequented when they were courting.
Struggling into her wedding outfit for the occasion, Ann muses, "I can't
understand a suit shrinking so much by just hanging in the closet." Try as
she might to laugh it off, this uncomfortable reminder that her figure is

not as slim as it used to be is not lost on Ann, and serves as an apt prelude to the woeful evening ahead, in which the pair is forced again and again to acknowledge that they are neither as young nor as resilient as they used to be.

Nor is Mamma Lucy's any longer the cozy, romantic rendezvous of the couple's nostalgic memories, for it has degenerated into a sleazy dive where the affluent Smiths are resentfully assumed by the seedy clientele to be slumming. When the mangy cat that climbs up on their table insolently turns up its nose at the rancid minestrone the Smiths themselves cannot swallow, one is reminded of the cat-meat chop suey Fred and Emily Hill heroically tried to force feed themselves in *Rich and Strange*. This nifty comic sequence in *Mr. and Mrs. Smith* also makes the serious point that any attempt on the part of David and Ann to take refuge in rosy recollections of the past, in lieu of facing the realities of the present, is doomed to failure.

Throughout the extended sequence that encompasses the Smiths' trip to Greenwich Village and back, the witty dialogue is nicely balanced by Hitchcock's sly visual humor. One visual double entendre that Hitchcock somehow managed to smuggle past the censor, despite the more stringent strictures of that day, is especially worthy of note. It occurs in the scene following the distressing dinner at Mamma Lucy's, when David makes one last gallant endeavor to salvage the situation by a little love making. The disenchanted Ann, still smarting from the bitter disappointments of the evening, is persistently disinclined to respond to his amorous overtures. Hoping to coax her into a more receptive mood by plying her with champagne, David provocatively twirls the bottle by its neck between his palms as it protrudes ever so erectly from the ice bucket. Then he coyly asks Ann if she will take over for him, while he gets into his pajamas. She does so, until she suddenly realizes the phallic connotations of her action, and abruptly lets go of the bottle and allows it to sink back into the bucket.

The Smiths' inevitable reconciliation takes place at a winter resort and is signaled by the film's final image. As Ann pulls David down into a chair, the skis she is wearing rise upward and cross each other in a refreshingly original symbol of conjugal union.

Another plus value in the picture is that Hitchcock had no hesitation in asking his costars to indulge in slapstick, specifically in the scenes of marital mayhem built around some dish-shattering quarrels. Back in 1927 the front office would not allow the director to film Ivor Novello in a scene of knockabout farce because it was thought to be undignified for a star of Novello's stature to engage in such ridiculous roistering on the screen. In those days, Hitchcock commented afterward, a director was prohibited from doing anything that might chip any of the glamor off his leading players. This was no longer the case by 1941.

Although Hitchcock had enjoyed working with the first lady of screen comedy in the film, he had not felt totally at home in the frenetic world of farce. After finishing the picture at RKO he immediately returned to the thriller genre, which by now was clearly his acknowledged stock in trade.

Shadow of a Doubt

Shadow of a Doubt (1943), which Hitchcock made at Universal, was always one of the director's personal favorites, largely because he had as his principal collaborator on the screenplay the distinguished American playwright Thornton Wilder, to whom he gave a special acknowledgment in the picture's screen credits. One of Wilder's most endearing and enduring dramas is *Our Town*, filmed three years before the present picture was made. It is a work steeped in Americana, which portrays the day-to-day trials of ordinary citizens living in a New England whistlestop. Hitchcock had Wilder populate *Shadow of a Doubt* with the same sort of small-town types, thus bestowing on the film a richness of characterization rarely equaled in the director's other films.

Into this wholesome atmosphere Hitchcock injected the corrosive presence of evil in the person of Charles Oakley (Joseph Cotten), a psychotic gigolo who has romanced and murdered a succession of wealthy widows, and whom the press have therefore sardonically dubbed the Merry Widow murderer. Taking his cue from the killer's macabre nickname, Hitchcock uses as background for the film's opening credits a shot of couples dancing to the "Merry Widow Waltz" in a turn-of-the-century ballroom, and repeats the image throughout the picture.

This Gay Nineties ballroom scene, which might have been lifted from his Strauss film, represents the only time that Hitchcock ever employed a visual image primarily for its symbolic value, for it has no direct connection whatever with any dramatic episode. In *Suspicion*, for example, when Lina imagines that Johnny has committed a murder, a shot of her husband pushing his victim off a cliff is superimposed on a close-up of her face to indicate that this is a visual image of her very thoughts. By contrast, the image of the old-time waltzing couples in *Shadow of a Doubt* is never identified precisely with Charles Oakley or anyone else in the film.

Charles does refer in passing to this bygone era, while reminiscing about his parents, as a time when it must have been great to be young; he opposes it to the modern world that he contemptuously characterizes as a foul sty filled with grotesque creatures like the fat wheezing sows whom we know to be his prey. One must infer, therefore, that the fanciful image of the dancers represents an idealized picture of the past that is meant to crystallize for the viewer Charles's nostalgic yearnings for a vanished romantic epoch. But this glamorous and enchanting age can never be recaptured because, in his distorted vision, it has been irrevocably replaced by the corrupt modern world, that richly deserves whatever mayhem he is capable of visiting upon it.

Charles Oakley is just the kind of male menace preying on helpless females whom studio officials prohibited Hitchcock from making the central character of *The Lodger* and *Suspicion*, because they feared such a role would damage the screen image of the star in each picture. Apparently movie moguls no longer viewed this as such a threat, since they had no qualms about Joseph Cotten taking the part of a monstrous lady killer in *Shadow of a Doubt*. Or else they didn't consider Orson Welles's protégé such a valuable investment.

Charles is first seen reposing on the rumpled bed in his seedy room in the Philadelphia rooming house where he is hiding out from the law. Although he looks harmless enough on the surface, the smoke wafting upward from his cigar in this and other scenes makes the same implicit reference to his satanic personality as the pipe smoke that rims the head of another malefactor named Charles, Charles Tobin in *Saboteur*. This shot is paralleled by one in the next sequence of Charlie (Charlotte) Newton, his niece and namesake (Teresa Wright), the daughter of his doting sister (Patricia Collinge), lying on the bed in her room in her home in Santa Rosa, California. Young Charlie is pictured stretched out in the opposite direction in which her uncle was just shown, so that it seems like the pair are equivalently facing each other as in a mirror image, an indication of their close affinity.

The dark, brooding ambience coupled with the sullen, not to say cynical, vision of life reflected in this tale of obsession, despair, and death marks *Shadow of a Doubt* as having more than a superficial resemblance, which is all that Sarris will allow, to the sort of work French critics christened film noir (dark cinema). This trend in American cinema, which also includes other Hitchcock films such as *Spellbound, Notorious,* and *Strangers on a Train*, was already flourishing when he made *Shadow of a Doubt*. The pessimistic view of life exhibited, itself an outgrowth of the disillusionment spawned by World War II and its aftermath, is clearly evident here.

Also in keeping with the conventions of film noir is the movie's air of spare, unvarnished realism typified by the authentic, newsreel-like quality of the location cinematography, especially the grim scenes that take place under cover of darkness. The milieu of film noir was essentially one of shadows, and it is exemplified in the present, appropriately named film, in the scene in which Charles is holed up in his cell-like room, lying on his bed like a prisoner on a cot. As his intrusive landlady solicitously pulls down his window shade to encourage him to take a nap, the shadow that gradually envelops his face suggests the murky, morbid world in which his madness has imprisoned him.

With the police hot on his heels, Charles decides to take sanctuary with the Newtons in sleepy Santa Rosa. When his train steams into the depot, the engine belches black smoke that ominously darkens the station platform, as if to presage the arrival in town of the prince of darkness himself. Hitchcock remembered that while shooting this sequence on location in Santa Rosa, the sun at just the right moment passed conveniently behind a cloud, thereby casting a shadow over the scene and making the atmosphere even more sombre than the smoke from the engine had already managed to do.

Charles remains safe in Santa Rosa until his once-devoted niece little by little ceases to ignore his increasingly ambiguous behavior and begins to nurture the shadow of a doubt that he is in actual fact the Merry Widow murderer for whom the police are combing the country. After her ghastly suspicions are verified, her Uncle Charles devilishly manipulates her into becoming an accomplice to his crimes by convincing her that she should keep his true identity a secret to spare their family the grief and scandal of his exposure.

In their book on Hitchcock, Eric Rohmer and Claude Chabrol (both of whom became film directors themselves) used the phrase "transference of guilt" to describe the situation in Hitchcock's films in which a character becomes, however unwillingly, implicated in the evil of another. In point of fact, whatever guilt an individual contracts by complicity in the corrupt behavior of another in no way lessens, much less eliminates, the original culpability of the other party, as the imprecise word transference seems to suggest in this context. It is rather a question of guilt by association, in that the innocent person becomes infected with the evil of the other individual by implicitly condoning it. Nevertheless, I shall use their phrase to refer to their theory whenever it comes up again.

In the present case, Charlie shares her uncle's guilt to the extent that, by agreeing to shield him, she ipso facto gives him the chance to go free and kill again. Similarly, each of the detectives in *Blackmail* and in *Sabotage* participates in the guilt of the woman he loves by willfully hushing up her involvement in a killing.

In *Shadow* Charlie gets the opportunity to expiate the guilt she has incurred for compromising with the forces of evil represented in the person of her Uncle Charles. When, for the sake of appearances, she goes to the railroad depot to see him off as he leaves town Charles tries to kill her and thus shut her up for sure. As they struggle, he loses his balance and falls backward into the path of an oncoming train, and is himself crushed beneath its wheels. Charles's hideous demise is an example of genuine poetic justice, since the other man suspected by the authorities of being the Merry Widow murderer, we learn, was horribly killed in the course of his capture at an airport by falling into a whirling airplane propeller. Charles Oakley surely deserved no better fate than the innocent man whom the police wrongly hounded to death for his crimes.

As for Charlie, being in some degree responsible for the death of her uncle seems to exorcise his unholy influence on her. It is supremely ironic, therefore, that her family, who know nothing of Charles's true nature, will continue to call her by his name in tribute to his memory.

In contrast to the extensive location shooting (then an unusual practice in Hollywood) that the script of *Shadow of a Doubt* called for, the story of Hitchcock's next film required that he shoot nearly all of it in the Fox studio. This was done in a tank to simulate the stifling sense of enclosure experienced by a group of people cast adrift for several days in a lifeboat on the open sea. This is probably the most constricted playing area to which the director of a commercial Hollywood film has ever limited himself before or since. Hitchcock challenged himself to shoot *Lifeboat*, and also *Rope* a few years later, within the borders of a single principal set and thus give the lie to the assumption on the part of some filmmakers that a movie can hold an audience's attention only if it covers a great deal of territory. On the contrary, Hitchcock contended that a skillful director should be able to make an intriguing movie in a closet with the door shut, provided that he knew how to reveal character and motivation through the dexterous use of his camera. "This presupposes, of course, an interesting story and characters worth revealing,"[7] Therein lies the ultimate failure of *Lifeboat*; unlike *Rope*, neither the plot nor the principal characters are particularly engaging.

Lifeboat

Lifeboat (1944) begins with a freighter being torpedoed in the Atlantic by a Nazi U-boat, a disaster that recalls the midocean plane crash in *Foreign Correspondent*. Given the cross section of survivors, the lifeboat represents a microcosm of a world at war. But when studied in such close quarters, too many of the passengers on this tiny ship of fools seem to be mere stereotypes rather than three-dimensional human beings, even though the original screen story was by John Steinbeck.

The one fully realized character is Constance Porter, a sophisticated journalist splendidly played by Tallulah Bankhead in a rare screen appearance. In fact, Hitchcock chose her for her part, as he did the rest of the cast, because none of them was especially well known to the majority of the filmgoing public. "For the sake of realism," he explained, "I am partial to people whose faces are not familiar to movie audiences," at least for the supporting roles (since the stars of a film will probably be well known), so that most of the actors in a movie will not be closely identified in the viewer's mind with a number of previous parts they have played.[8] That is why he used continental actors such as Lucie Mannheim, Oscar Homolka, and Paul Lukas as featured players in his British thrillers, and later imported several German actors to fill subordinate roles in *Torn Curtain*.

In any case, when she first boards the open boat, Constance is not above callously photographing a baby bottle for its "human interest" value as it drifts among the debris of the wrecked steamer. As one of her fellow travelers chides her caustically, "Why don't you wait till the baby floats by and photograph that too!" Constance is gradually humanized by being thrown together with the others in the narrow confines of their craft. Little by little, Robin Wood has written, Constance loses the earthly possessions that earlier seemed to compose her identity, as first her camera, then her typewriter, her mink coat, and finally her jewelry are all claimed by the sea through one mishap or another. By the time a friendly ship comes into view, Constance feels truly liberated from the external trappings on which she so depended in the past. Still, by hastily primping and applying lipstick to look her best when the rescuers arrive, she demonstrates that old habits die hard, and also indicates how genuinely human she really is.

Despite some stark dramatic passages, such as the revelation that one of their number is really a Nazi U-boat commander in disguise, *Lifeboat* all but sinks under the weight of its loquacious screenplay. It contains some arid stretches of dialogue that not even Hitchcock can enliven by constantly working his camera in and around the boat. In fine, this austere film is surely Hitchcock's most obvious attempt to make sheer cinematic technique triumph over indifferent scripting.

One of his most ingenious touches is the delightful way he chose to intrude his signature appearance into the film. Since he could hardly swim by a lifeboat marooned in the middle of the ocean, he decided to appear in an advertisement for "Reduco," a weight-reducing wonder drug that is printed in an old newspaper that happens to be lying in the bottom of the boat. He was subsequently so deluged with letters requesting further information about the fictitious slimming preparation that he playfully slipped in a further reference to it in *Rope*, which takes place entirely in a penthouse. Outside the livingroom window of the apartment there is a neon sign endorsing the same spurious product.

Rope

The action of *Rope* (1948), which was derived from British playwright Patrick Hamilton's stage melodrama, unfolds not only in a single setting, as did *Lifeboat*, but in a single evening, so that the time span covered by the story corresponds to the running time of the finished film. To emphasize the plot's uncompromising unity of time and place, Hitchcock committed himself to shooting the eighty-minute movie in ten unbroken takes of approximately ten minutes apiece. This is the maximum amount of time a motion picture camera can run before it must be reloaded, whereas the reels on which a movie is projected are twice that length.

During production, which lasted twenty-one days, Hitchcock as often as possible camouflaged the switch from the end of one ten-minute reel to the beginning of the next by tracking his camera forward into an extreme close-up of some object, usually an actor's back, thereby causing the image to go black, and then pulling back from the same object at the start of the next reel. To facilitate the focusing of each twenty-minute projection reel when the movie was shown in theaters, however, he began the shooting of each of those reels that would eventually come at the beginning of a double projection reel with a barely noticeable cut to a new camera setup, rather than with a blackout.

To permit the camera to rove unimpeded around the penthouse set during each reel-long take, moreover, the furniture was mounted on rollers and special sliding walls were constructed. This enabled the crew to whisk every obstacle out of the camera's path as it followed the action from room to room. Because each ten-minute reel was not broken up into a series of several individual shots while it was being photographed, there was ultimately little need to edit the picture once it was shot. The overall effect of all of this cinematic sleight-of-hand is to give the impression that the action moves along fluidly from beginning to end, without any discernible break, in one extended shot that runs the length of the entire movie.

Based on the infamous Leob-Leopold murder case, which was also the subject of the 1959 courtroom drama *Compulsion*, *Rope* opens with two homosexuals, Brandon (John Dall) and Philip (Farley Granger), using a rope to strangle David (Dick Hogan), an acquaintance from their prep school days, just for the thrill of it. (Durgnat, once again ill-advisedly trusting to memory, mistakenly asserts that David never appears in the film at all.) After stowing the lad's corpse in an ornate antique chest, they prepare to serve an elaborate buffet supper to David's relatives and friends right on top of what is now the young man's coffin. The fluttering candles that adorn the chest thus add a funereal note to the proceedings of which the guests are of course totally unaware.

Since the action never strays from Brandon and Philip's suite, Hitchcock saw to it that the movie did not turn into a static photographed stage play by keeping his camera perpetually on the go. It unobtrusively

James Stewart (left) and virtually the entire cast of Rope
*(1948), Hitchcock's first color film. Lobby posters informed
latecomers that "there is a body in the box" (foreground, with
buffet). (Credit: Bennett's Book Store)*

glides from one group of characters to another, closing in at times to
capture a key gesture or remark, then falling back for a medium or long
shot as the action and dialogue continue. By using a total of 150 different
camera movements to achieve the equivalent number of individual
shots, Hitchcock was "cutting the film inside the camera" to achieve the
same effect as if he had actually photographed 150 separate shots and
then spliced them together. (Selznick, to be sure, would have condemned such precutting of virtually the whole movie as "jigsaw cutting"
with a vengeance.) By allowing the camera to draw the filmgoer into the
scene and explore the action at close range, the director was in effect
making the viewer feel as if he were another guest at the dinner party,
and not simply a remote observer watching the action from a distance
like a spectator at a stage play.

Nonetheless the pace of the action sometimes falters during those
long unbroken takes, while the viewer waits for the camera to move from
one significant detail to another. When Rupert Cadell (James Stewart), a
former teacher of the two killers, is about to leave, he is handed the
wrong hat. The camera trundles in to show that it bears the initials of the

mysteriously absent David, then tilts up to record Rupert's disturbed reaction as he notices this fact. All of this could have been accomplished much more briskly by simply cutting from Rupert to the hat and back again, without having to wait for the camera to move from one position to another.

Once his suspicions are aroused, Rupert returns to the boys' flat after all the other guests have gone and asks enough probing questions to give the two amateur murderers enough rope with which to hang themselves. It is during this crucial sequence that the long take is exploited to best advantage. The camera follows Rupert as he paces around the room relentlessly interrogating Philip and Brandon. When the moment of truth is at hand, the camera holds on the trio, with the towering figure of Rupert dominating the foreground, while the culprits whom he has overwhelmed with his imposing personality and penetrating powers of deduction retreat into the background.

At this point occurs the most successful of the masked transitions from one reel to the next. When Rupert throws open the chest to peer down on the corpse that he by now assumes he will find there, the lid comes up right in front of the camera, causing the screen to go black. By the time he closes the lid once more, the switch to the final reel has been made imperceptively during the momentary blackout.

Rupert then opens a window to summon the police with a gunshot. By so doing he dispels the stifling, claustrophobic atmosphere of tension that Hitchcock has steadily built up by filming the entire movie within the confines of one setting and with what was for all practical purposes one prolonged, uninterrupted shot.

Hitchcock matched his innovative experiments with protracted takes in *Rope* with deft use of color in this, his first color feature. To give the movie a somber cast in keeping with the morbid tale, he reduced the color to a minimum, favoring muted pastel shades over the garish, unnaturally bright hues that all too often characterized the technicolor cinematography of the period. He was even willing to reshoot whole reels of footage whenever he felt that the color tints were not sufficiently subdued for his purposes.

Rope was also a pace-setter in its treatment of homosexuality in a way that was relatively forthright for American movies. Thus the manner in which Brandon and Philip clutch at their "straight" victim to restrain him during the strangling subtly suggests symbolic rape as much as murder. Scriptwriter Arthur Laurents remembers that, while the industry film censor allowed the homosexual implications of such images to slip by him undetected, he demanded the deletion of some innocuous phrases in the dialogue that Laurents had in fact brought over from the original English play. Expressions such as "dear boy" are commonly used by teachers and students in British boarding schools, and do not necessarily carry homosexual connotations at all.

Nonetheless, in spite of some censorial interference, Hitchcock depicted the homosexual ambience of the story more satisfactorily in *Rope* than he had in *Murder!* nearly two decades before, in which this element was presented in so indirect a manner that it baffled some moviegoers. As Higham and Greenberg have written about *Rope*, the two young men's "slightly over-decorated apartment, their 'understanding' housekeeper, . . . and their mutually suspicious and resentful relationship with the dead boy's girl friend" all testify to the sexual orientation of the pair. [9] Be that as it may, Jean Renoir, accustomed to the franker portrayal of homosexuality in European films, still thought that Hitchcock had skirted the issue too timidly in *Rope*. "I thought it was supposed to be about homosexuals," he remarked, "and you don't even see the boys kiss each other." [10]

Under Capricorn

Under Capricorn (1949) demonstrates that although the long unbroken take could prove tiresome when employed exclusively throughout an entire movie as it was in *Rope*, a film could profit immeasurably from the insertion of an extended take in one or more key sequences. Adapted from a novel by Helen Simpson, who had worked on the screenplay of *Murder!* and *Sabotage*, the present film derives its title from being set in Australia, the heavily populated parts of which are under the Tropic of Capricorn. Sam Flusky (Joseph Cotten), a well-to-do businessman, is also an ex-convict who has served time for slaying the brother of his aristocratic wife Henrietta (Ingrid Bergman). Actually, Henrietta herself took her brother's life because he had blocked her marriage to Sam, a commoner, and she then permitted Sam to take the rap for her.

She confesses all of this to Charles, a sympathetic relative (Michael Wilding), in a long take of nearly ten minutes à la *Rope*, a virtual monologue that represents a brilliantly sustained piece of acting on Ms. Bergman's part. Yet while the picture was in production, even such a seasoned actress as she looked upon the prospect of filming extended takes of this sort as daunting indeed. Besides the feat of memory required to recite a lengthy, taxing speech word-perfect, there was the additional worry that slips on her part or any member of the cast and crew would mean exhausting and expensive retakes, something about which James Stewart had complained while making *Rope*. In a letter to a confidant written half-way through the production period, Ms. Bergman confessed that one day she had become so exasperated with the complications involved in working out the intricate logistics of his precious long takes that she told Hitchcock in no uncertain terms that they were getting to be more trouble than they were worth. In the particular instance to which she referred, the camera was to follow her around the set for the length of an entire roll of film, "which meant that we had to rehearse a whole day with the walls or furniture falling backwards as the camera went through," she wrote. "So I told Hitch off. How I hate this new technique of his." By the time she had finished her tirade, "little Hitch," as she called him, was long gone. Loathing as he did confrontations of any kind, he simply slipped away while Ms. Bergman's back was turned and left her talking to herself. By the time the picture was nearly finished, however, she grudgingly admitted that "some of those damned" long takes had worked out pretty well.[11]

In one of these the camera circles around the perfidious housekeeper Milly (Margaret Leighton) as she seeks to discredit Henrietta in Sam's eyes with a view to displacing her as mistress of the household. The circular camera movement visually underscores the web of deception Milly is weaving round the as yet unsuspecting Sam. Similarly, as Higham writes in *The Art of the American Film* apropos of *The Paradine Case*, the sinuous spiral of the camera around Mrs. Paradine as she spins out her perjured testimony in court signifies the spidery creature that lies behind her Madonna-like countenance.

Milly in the present film also brings to mind the scheming housekeeper in *Rebecca*, Mrs. Danvers; but all of Milly's malicious machinations cannot sustain the moviegoer's interest in a motion picture that is top-heavy with too many scenes of tedious talk. When one considers Hitchcock's two previous historical films, *Waltzes from Vienna* and *Jamaica Inn*, it is no wonder that *Under Capricorn* proved to be his final foray into what always remained for him the unfamiliar terrain of the costume picture.

Since *Under Capricorn* was shot at Elstree Studios, where Hitchcock had made no fewer than ten films during his British period, it was unfortunate that although it was both a popular and critical failure, it did not mark a more felicitous homecoming for Hitchcock than it did. Happily, Hitchcock had had much better luck with the other two movies he had previously made with Ingrid Bergman, *Notorious* and *Spellbound*.

Notorious

Notorious (1946), was originally set up in 1944 by David Selznick, with Cary Grant and Ingrid Bergman as American spies in Brazil. But Selznick ultimately lost interest in the project and sold the whole production package he had put together, including the director, the stars, and the screenwriter, Ben Hecht, to RKO. While conferring on the script with Ben Hecht, Hitchcock, who Hecht later said gave off plot twists like a Roman candle, came up with an interesting MacGuffin. Having read *The Mighty Atom* by H. G. Wells, the director decided that the MacGuffin in *Notorious* would be a secret substance needed to manufacture an atomic weapon.

When the FBI got wind of the fact that the film involved FBI agents, Selznick received a letter from the Bureau in May, 1945, while he was still officially in charge of the project, advising him that any film script involving American intelligence agents would have to be cleared by the State Department. Selznick therefore cautioned the director not to be too specific about the MacGuffin in *Notorious*. According to Spoto, who researched this matter in both the Selznick and FBI files for his Hitchcock biography, it was this warning letter from the FBI that led Hitchcock to jump to the wholly unwarranted assumption, accepted as Gospel in Taylor's biography, that the FBI had the director under surveillance for three months while he was working on *Notorious*, when in fact there is no record that the FBI did any such thing. This is not the only example of one of Hitchcock's favorite anecdotes being proved to be at least partially apocryphal, but it is a salient one.

In any event, by the time Hitchcock started shooting *Notorious* in October, 1945, the United States had unveiled the atomic bomb by unleashing it on Japan the previous August; and he was able safely to specify in the screenplay that uranium ore was the essential component of atomic explosives which his hero and heroine were after.

Notorious is fundamentally a romantic tale built around Devlin (Cary Grant), an American agent, and Alicia Huberman (Ingrid Bergman), the daughter of a notorious Nazi fifth-columnist. Devlin must assist Alicia in forming an amorous liaison with Alex Sebastian (Claude Rains), a confederate of her father's living in Rio, so as to gain access to the atomic secrets Alex is guarding.

Devlin's own growing feeling for Alicia is manifested in what must be one of the longest kisses ever committed to celluloid. To get around the censorship regulation of the time, which forbade a kiss lasting more than three seconds of screen time, Hitchcock had Grant and Bergman keep moving around her apartment suite from the balcony to the living room while they nuzzled and nibbled at each other, exchanging whispered endearments and even answering the phone at one point, so that every three seconds the kiss was interrupted. But since the pair never once broke their embrace the whole time, the kiss "looked endless," Ms. Bergman has written, and "became sensational in Hollywood" because of its audacity. [12]

After encouraging Alicia to romance and even to marry the middle-aged Alex, Devlin jealously berates her because she has sold herself for the sake of obtaining information from an enemy operative. The hero of *North by Northwest*, also played by Grant, similarly heaps abuse on his girl because she too has become a "patriotic prostitute" in the service of her country. Nevertheless Devlin and Alicia continue to work together. Suspecting that Alex has stashed samples of the special ingredient in his wine cellar, Alicia steals his key to his vintage collection of wines. She plans to pass it on to Devlin so that he can investigate the wine supply during the elegant ball Alex is giving in his bride's honor, and thus unlock the mystery of the atomic formula he is seeking. In a virtual repetition of the astonishing crane shot in *Young and Innocent*, Hitchcock's camera starts from above a shimmering chandelier to swoop down the grand staircase of Alex's mansion into a close-up of the crucial key clenched tightly in Alicia's fist. Moreover, the checkered pattern of the ballroom floor, when photographed from the high angle from which this shot begins, resembles a chessboard, implying Alicia's unenviable position as a pawn in the game of international intrigue.

When Alex finds out how his wife has duped him, he abjectly complies with his steely willed mother's brutal proposal to liquidate Alicia by slowly poisoning her to death so that she will appear to have died of natural causes. At the movie's climax, Devlin arrives to rescue Alicia from dying by installments. As Devlin moves down the grand staircase toward the front door with the dazed Alicia in his protecting arms, their painfully slow descent is intercut with reaction shots of Alex, his mother, and some other Nazis. The couple's open display of physical intimacy, as Gavin Lambert observes, seems justified by Alicia's weakened state. "But they are also playing a love scene at a moment of immediate danger, and Alex becomes humiliatingly aware of it."[13]

Alex follows Devlin and Alicia to their waiting car and begs to be allowed to escape with them. But Devlin's vindictive response to the man who married the woman he loves is to lock Alex out of the car and drive off, leaving the bereft husband to the mercy of his Nazi associates. Devlin's behavior at this moment forcefully illustrates that the motives of Hitchcock's central characters are often a disturbing mixture of good and not-so-good elements. In refusing Alex's plea for asylum, the develishly cunning Devlin is not just eliminating an enemy spy, but conveniently disposing of Alicia's husband.

Claude Rains richly merited but did not win the Oscar for which he was nominated. He gave the performance of his career as Alex Sebastian, a complex man who is both victim and victimizer of the woman whom he very likely loves more deeply than the rival for her affections

Hitchcock, Gregory Peck and Ingrid Bergman rehearsing a scene for Spellbound *(1945). (Credit: Larry Edmonds's Cinema Bookshop)*

who eventually takes her from him. Bergman's and Grant's performances were not far behind Rains's. As a matter of fact, Hitchcock later paid a round-about compliment to Grant in *Rope,* when David's aunt remarks that Grant "was thrilling in that new thing with Bergman."

Spellbound

Ingrid Bergman had already appeared in one other Hitchcock film during this period, *Spellbound* (1945). This was also one of the three films Hitchcock directed under the Selznick banner after making six straight films for other producers. Although Hitchcock himself saw the film as "just another manhunt story, wrapped up in pseudo-psychoanalysis,"[14] *Spellbound* turned out to be the first in a series of popular 1940s films employing pop psychology as their basic premise.

Spellbound is the heavily Freudian tale of John Ballantine (Gregory Peck), who is obsessed with the notion that he murdered his psychiatrist, Dr. Edwardes, while they were skiing together. An amnesiac, Ballantine unconsciously assumes the identity of Edwardes at Green Manors, the private sanatorium of which Edwardes was to have been the new superintendent had his untimely death not intervened. When Ballantine's true identity is inevitably discovered, one of the staff psychiatrists, Dr. Constance Petersen (Ingrid Bergman), who by then has fallen in love with John, flees from the asylum with him in the hope of finding out what really happened during Edwardes's last skiing expedition.

The film is prefaced by a printed prologue that explains that the function of a psychoanalyst is "to open the locked doors of the mind," and Hitchcock visualizes this concept on the screen at the point when John and Constance kiss for the first time. Superimposed on their passionate embrace is a shot of a series of doors, which recede down a seemingly endless corridor, opening one by one. This signifies that the constant Dr. Petersen will give John the courage to open the secret doors beyond which lie the traumatic experiences by which he has been spellbound. The visual imagery that Hitchcock incorporated into this romantic scene bears out Gregory Peck's observation that for Hitchcock, "a love scene is not just two people grabbing at each other. He makes the symbolism count."[15]

With the help of her mentor Dr. Brulov (Michael Chekhov, nephew of the Russian author), Constance is able to uncover the hidden meaning of several psychological clues with which John has provided them. The prongs of a fork indenting a white tablecloth, the stripes on a white bathrobe, the ridges on a white bedspread, the foamy swirl of hairs on a soapy shaving brush: this network of images symbolizes ski tracks on a snowy slope such as the one on which Edwardes met his death at the Gabriel Valley winter resort. Edwardes's demise in turn is subconsciously linked with the death of John's brother in a childhood accident for which John still feels responsible.

In flashback we see John as a youngster sliding down the bannister of a stone porch toward his brother who is sitting at its foot. John unintentionally collides with the lad, causing him to pitch forward and become impaled on a spiked fence (a reminder of the speared railing from which the hero is temporarily suspended in *The Lodger*). Because of his abiding sense of guilt for making his brother die in such a manner, John has convinced himself that he somehow must have precipitated Edwardes's fatal fall into Gabriel Valley's ravine. To ascertain the true facts about the skiing accident, Constance must interpret John's recurring dream about this episode.

Hitchcock brought in the Spanish surrealist Salvador Dali to design this sequence, because he wanted to have the dream photographed in the vivid way Dali painted. Traditionally, he explained, dream scenes in films had always been enveloped in swirling smoke and filmed slightly out of focus to make them look misty and blurred. "But dreams are not

like that; they are very, very vivid."[16] So Hitchcock chose Dali to
conceive this fantasy sequence in his own personal style, which had a
clear-cut, solid, architectural sharpness to it. The fantasy sequence was
then filmed with the (uncredited) help of William Cameron Menzies,
the production designer of *Foreign Correspondent*.

The hallucinatory sequence starts with John and Edwardes playing
cards in a bizarre gambling house. Its walls are hung with black velvet
draperies on which are painted enormous staring eyes, and a man goes
around cutting the eyeballs on the curtains with a gigantic scissors. As a
matter of fact, Dali borrowed the image from *The Andalusian Dog*, an
experimental short film on which he collaborated with Luis Buñuel in
1928 (as film cultists will have recognized.)

The grotesque behavior of the man with the shears implies that he is a
patient in an insane asylum, presumably Green Manors, and that he is
apparently expressing his resentment of the watchful eyes of the institution's staff and guards. A further covert reference to Green Manors is
made when the faceless proprietor of the casino insists with Edwardes
most emphatically that he is the sole owner and operator of the estab-
lishment. This is an implicit allusion to Dr. Murchison (Leo G. Carroll),
the outgoing director of the sanatorium who was known to have been
deeply disturbed by the prospect of being supplanted by Edwardes.

The next time the anonymous proprietor materializes in John's
nightmare, he is holding a wheel in his hand (which suggests a revolver)
and hiding behind a chimney on a slanted roof, as he watches Edwardes
slide off the roof to his death. Constance finally cracks the code of this last
episode of the dream by reasoning that this is a disguised representation
of how the crazed Murchison, in a last desperate attempt to retain his
position at Green Manors, shot Edwardes from behind a tree while the
latter was skiing down a hillside with John, and left John to take the
blame.

When Constance confronts Murchison with this explanation, the
demented psychiatrist pulls out a pistol and threatens to kill her on the
spot. The camera is behind Murchison as it photographs the gun in his
hand slowly turning away from Constance toward himself and then firing
straight at the lens. To keep Constance and the pistol both in focus while
this shot was being photographed, Hitchcock placed a giant artificial
hand holding a revolver, which was itself four times the normal size, in
the foreground while she stood in the background facing the gun. Use of
a magnified prop here recalls the outsized drinking glasses he constructed for a scene in *The Lady Vanishes*, and it was equally effective
here in making the revolver loom threateningly large on the screen.

In the original release prints of *Spellbound*, Murchison's gun went off
in a burst of technicolor scarlet in an otherwise black-and-white movie.

Even without the unexpected flash of color, however, the explosion of the pistol in the filmgoer's face is a startling surprise, as is the discovery that the dapper, staid Dr. Murchison has turned out to be the proverbial lunatic who has taken over an asylum.

By the time Hitchcock made *Spellbound* for Selznick, the producer was willing to concede a greater degree of artistic freedom than he had accorded the director during the shooting of *Rebecca*. This was largely on the strength of Hitchcock's success in working with the other producers to whom he had been farmed out by Selznick in the interim. "Increasingly I learned to have great respect for Hitchcock," Selznick said afterwards. "During *Spellbound* I don't think I was on the set twice" in the course of the shooting period, which lasted from July 10 to October 13, 1944. [17] And when he did come to the set, Ingrid Bergman recalls in Spoto's Hitchcock biography, Hitchcock playfully made believe that the camera was broken and would not operate until the producer left!

After principal photography was completed, Miklos Rozsa composed his Academy Award-winning score. To supply the haunting kind of background music required for a movie dealing with mental illness, Rozsa for the first time in the score for an American movie made extensive use of the theremin, an electronic musical instrument that produces a high-pitched, quavering sound that perfectly augments the weird atmosphere of the picture's scarier scenes, and proves the highlight of a score that is a superb complement to a grand thriller.

The Paradine Case

Hitchcock's last film for Selznick, *The Paradine Case* (1947), also starred Gregory Peck, this time as Anthony Keane, a British barrister who becomes enamored with his client, the haughty, enigmatic Maddalena Paradine (Alida Valli). She is accused of poisoning her elderly and blind but very rich husband. In *Spellbound* Constance Peterson falls in love with her patient, who is also suspected of murder. But he is finally proved innocent of the crime, whereas in the present film the luckless defense attorney is keenly captivated by a femme fatale who is, in fact, guilty as charged.

Keane's infatuation with Mrs. Paradine makes him as blind as her late husband was in physical fact. It impels him to try to exonerate her by shifting suspicion to Mr. Paradine's valet Latour (Louis Jordan), who is also Mrs. Paradine's lover. It is only when Keane's ruthless badgering of Latour in the witness box drives the anguished man to suicide that the attorney recognizes how cruel and inhuman his courtroom tactics have become on behalf of the temptress who holds him in thrall. By the finale,

Mrs. Paradine's widow's weeds have ceased to be a sign of mourning and have come to characterize her as the black widow who has not only literally poisoned her husband, but infected her lawyer with the deadly venom of her spidery charm. Keane is yet another Hitchcock hero who has compromised his position as a guardian of justice, thereby sharing the guilt of the woman of his desires.

Although the film does have some gripping moments, it is on the whole woefully weighted down by a wordy, long-winded screenplay written by none other than Selznick himself. More literary than literate, the script made it difficult even for old pros like Charles Laughton and Ethel Barrymore, as the trial judge and his wife, to infuse a breath of life into some of the moribund scenes Selznick contrived.

Among the ill-advised changes Selznick made in his literary source while writing the screenplay was retooling Latour from the coarse, foul-smelling groom of the novel into the dainty "pretty boy" gentleman's gentleman of the film. Thus Mrs. Paradine's sexual attraction for Latour seems far less the expression of her degrading nymphomania than Hitchcock, following the novelist's lead, thought it should be.

Nevertheless, Hitchcock brought all of his ingenuity to bear on his endeavor to make *The Paradine Case* as imaginative as Selznick's overwritten, patchwork screenplay would allow. The director photographed the sequence in which Mrs. Paradine is brought to police headquarters to be booked for murder in the same lean, documentary style he had used in filming the prologue of *Blackmail* two decades before. Moreover, cinematographer Lee Garmes remembers that to make the trial scenes in *Paradine* come alive as much as possible, Hitchcock opted to cover them with four cameras, two of which were on cranes: one was trained "on the witness box, one on the judge, one on the prosecuting counsel, one on the defending counsel."[18] Yet all of Hitchcock's cinematic invention could not prevent *The Paradine Case* from being trounced on by the critics and avoided by the public—an inglorious end for a creative association that had started so promisingly with *Rebecca*.

Looking back on Hitchcock's first decade in Hollywood, one can see in retrospect how he had sought to test his cinematic craftsmanship by meeting all sorts of self-imposed technical challenges, such as confining himself to one of the smallest sets imaginable in *Lifeboat*; photographing *Rope* in what appeared to be a single, protracted shot; and using muted, natural colors in his two color films, *Under Capricorn* and especially *Rope*. If these experiments did not always work out satisfactorily, they were always worth watching; in the decade ahead he would learn to integrate these technical innovations more smoothly into his work, so that the 1950s became the zenith of his American period.

Meanwhile, those who deigned to speak smugly of the erosion of Hitchcock's talent in the light of films like *The Paradine Case* and *Under Capricorn* were criticized by James Agee, who wrote in the director's defense, "Crocodile tears over the alleged decline of Alfred Hitchcock have for years been a favorite cocktail among those who take moving pictures seriously. That has always seemed to me an impatient and cheap attitude to take toward any kind of change or disturbance in the work of a good artist. It still does."[19]

Some of the crocodile tears were shed by Selznick. He condescendingly chortled that *Under Capricorn* in particular, which, like *Rope*, Hitchcock had made for his own short-lived independent production company, Transatlantic Pictures, demonstrated the difference between Hitchcock under Selznick's supervision and "on his own."[20] This typically self-aggrandizing remark is unfair for several reasons, not the least of which is that *Capricorn* was certainly no more of a debacle than *Paradine*. In any event, after leaving Selznick, Hitchcock acted as his own producer for the rest of his career, regardless of which studio held his contract. Summing up his association with Selznick, Hitchcock made this stoic comment on the producer's misguided attempts to direct a film by remote control: "I think he should have stuck to producing, the thing that he was most proficient at."[21]

As for the mountain of memos which Selznick sent him, Hitchcock noted good-humoredly to a TV interviewer some twenty years after he had left Selznick's employ that he had begun to read Selznick's first missive when he started to work on *Rebecca* in 1939, but had not quite got through it yet, adding that it might be turned into a film entitled *The Longest Story Ever Told*. On the other hand, Hitchcock treasured the congratulatory letter he received from the producer after the opening of *Rear Window* (1954). Nevertheless Selznick remained officious to the last. Characteristically, Selznick left behind him when he died in June 1965 one last memo dictating the details of his own funeral.

6

The Fifties: The Peak Years in Hollywood

Strangers on a Train

JUST WHEN IT SEEMED, in the wake of undistinguished films like *The Paradine Case* and *Under Capricorn*, that the master was losing his touch, Hitchcock snapped back with his film version of Patricia Highsmith's suspense novel *Strangers on a Train* (1951), his first truly masterful movie of the 1950s.

When they meet in the course of a railway journey, Bruno Anthony (Robert Walker), a wealthy young homosexual, shows himself very much attracted to Guy Haines (Farley Granger), a handsome tennis champion. The slightly effeminate, effete Bruno has all the earmarks of a textbook case in abnormal psychology, for he combines a deep-seated, implacable hatred of his tyrannical father with a curious attachment to his eccentric mother. As the two lunch together on the train, it is evident that Guy, who is unhappily married to a conniving, promiscuous spouse, is fascinated by this fey, coyly ingratiating creature. So much so that from the start there is an unacknowledged homosexual undertone to their relationship that immediately recalls the much more overt liaison of Philip (also played by Granger) and Brandon in *Rope*. Screenwriter Arthur Laurents (*Rope*) has said, "Farley Granger told me once that it was Robert Walker's idea to play Bruno Anthony as a homosexual."[1] On the contrary, it should be obvious from foregoing remarks about Bruno's background and behavior that his approach to Guy as a rather blatant homosexual courting a latent one is embedded in the supple screenplay, and not something Walker, as brilliant as he is in the part, superimposed on the characterization on his own.

Before they part company at journey's end, Bruno attempts to manipulate Guy into agreeing to exchange a murder with him, with Guy killing Bruno's father and Bruno doing away with Guy's wife Miriam. Since neither has an ostensible motive for committing the other's crime, they would both, according to Bruno, successfully elude detection. This

James Stewart with two versions of Kim Novak, who, in fact, never appear on the screen together in Vertigo *(1958). (Credit: Larry Edmonds's Cinema Bookshop)*

123

proposal appeals to Guy more than he is prepared to admit even to himself. Consequently, he does not decisively reject it. Taking Guy's hedging for tacit approval, the deranged Bruno soon dispatches Miriam and demands forthwith that Guy keep his part of the bargain, which Guy in a moment of panic agrees to do, just to put Bruno off.

For novelist Patricia Highsmith, the way in which Bruno plays on the baser instincts of the fundamentally good-natured Guy signifies the duality that lies at the heart of human nature. "I'm very much concerned," she has noted, "with the way that good and evil exist in everyone "to a greater or lesser degree."[2] Raymond Chandler, the eminent crime novelist (*The Big Sleep*) and screenwriter, was also very much preoccupied, as was Hitchcock, with bringing to light the dark corners of the human psyche; so he accepted Hitchcock's offer to draft the screenplay for *Strangers*.

A morose, touchy person, Chandler preferred to work alone; so he resented the preliminary script conferences Hitchcock imposed upon him before he was allowed to get to work on his own. He was not even mollified when Hitchcock agreed to come to his home in La Jolla, California, for the sessions. One day, while watching Hitchcock get out of the studio limousine in front of his house, the disgruntled writer mumbled testily to his secretary, "Look at that fat bastard trying to get out of his car," adding that he cared not if the director overheard him. (The director probably did.)

Chandler grumbled that he found these "god-awful jabber sessions" frustrating because Hitchcock was not as troubled as he was by questions of narrative logic and character motivation, paralleling screenwriter Ernest Lehman's later complaints that Hitchcock deleted from *Family Plot* scenes that delineated character. Chandler was particularly worried about the scene in which Guy promises to take the life of Bruno's father. Guy must convince a reasonable percentage of the audience, Chandler recorded in his notes, that "a nice young man might in certain circumstances murder a total stranger just to appease a lunatic." Otherwise the viewers would not be sufficiently involved in the subsequent development of the plot.

To Chandler's chagrin, however, Hitchcock seemed less preoccupied with the fundamental plausibility of the story than with creating a series of strikingly visual scenes. In a letter to a friend, Chandler complained that any writer who worked with Hitchcock found himself trying to work out the story line of a film in such a way that any sort of camera shot "that comes into Hitchcock's mind can be incorporated into it."[3] To Chandler that explained why some of Hitchcock's pictures "lose their grip on logic and turn into wild chases. Well, it's not the worst way to make a picture."[4] As far as Chandler was concerned, it was also not the best way. Referring to Hitchcock in a letter to a studio executive, Chandler remarked dyspeptically that he preferred to deal with a director "who realizes that what is said and how it is said is more important than shooting it upside down through a glass of champagne."[5] (Little did Chandler know that there was a shot something like that in *Champagne!*)

In Hitchcock's defense critic Paul Jensen has written that Chandler's approach to writing a script was in open conflict with Hitchcock's penchant for sidestepping the demands of dramatic logic whenever possible in favor of heading straight for the scenes that were especially fraught with tension. In other words, Chandler, like Graham Greene, was inclined to care more about what Hitchcock termed icebox logic than, all things considered, Hitchcock himself did.

One of the tense scenes to which Jensen refers is that in which Bruno strangles Guy's estranged wife in a secluded corner of the amusement park to which he has followed her. The murder is ironically accompanied by the distant music of the merry-go-round's calliope as it grinds out its cheery rendering of "Strawberry Blonde." Horrified, we watch the murder as it is reflected in Miriam's glasses, which have fallen to the grass during her struggle with Bruno, a shot incidentally, that John Frankenheimer copied in his 1961 film *The Young Savages*. Photographed in this grotesquely distorted fashion, the strangling looks as if it were being viewed in a fun-house mirror, another reminder of the grimly incongruous carnival setting of the crime.

Given the fact that Guy subconsciously wanted to kill Miriam himself, he has in effect done so through the mediation of Bruno as his proxy; to that extent Bruno embodies the underside of Guy's own personality, which underlines Ms. Highsmith's statement that the good and evil forces warring within Guy reflect the duality of human nature itself. In *Strangers on a Train* we have a perfect example of Rohmer and Chabrol's transference of guilt theory, in that a basically decent person is morally stained by capitulating in some degree to a wicked influence on his life, a situation we have noted in films as superficially different but thematically similar as *Shadow of a Doubt* and *The Paradine Case*, to go back no further.

That Guy has become, however inadvertently, allied with the perverse force for evil that Bruno represents is concretized in the scene in which the two men stand on opposite sides of an iron fence as Bruno informs Guy that he has taken Miriam's life. When a squad car appears across the street, Guy instinctively joins Bruno on the same side of the barrier, and thus implicitly acknowledges his share of the guilt for Miriam's demise. Moreover, the image of Guy's troubled face barred by the sinister shadows of the gate grill signals his imprisonment by Bruno

Robert Walker (left) and Farley Granger share an implicit
homosexual relationship in Strangers on a Train *(1951) (Credit:*
Cinemabilia)

in an unholy alliance from which he finds himself for now powerless to escape.

Guy is given the chance to redeem himself by pursuing Bruno back to the scene of Miriam's murder, in one of those "wild chases" that Chandler deplored in Hitchcock's work, and forcing Bruno to confess the truth about her death. As they wrestle each other aboard the carousel, the mechanism suddenly goes berserk, changing what is normally a harmless source of innocent pleasure into a whirling instrument of terror. The carousel thus serves as still another reflection of Hitchcock's dark vision of our chaotic, topsy-turvy planet. As the runaway merry-go-round continues to twirl at top speed, its rendition of "Strawberry Blond" is also accelerated to a dizzying tempo, and mingles with macabre persistence with the screams of the hysterical riders trapped on board. A mechanic at last manages to bring it to a halt, but it stops so suddenly that the riders go sailing off in all directions as the machinery collapses into a heap of smouldering wreckage, bringing this sequence to a spectacular climax.

Bruno dies in the debris, unrepentant to the last. His irredeemably perverse personality distinguishes him, even in death, not so much as the Dr. Jekyll and Mr. Hyde type he has sometimes been called, but solely as Mr. Hyde, since he does not seem to have a good side to his personality.

Besides demonstrating that Hitchcock was back in top form, *Strangers on a Train* marked his first collaboration with cinematographer Robert Burks, who was to photograph no fewer than twelve films, including *To Catch a Thief*, for which he earned an Oscar.

Dial M for Murder

Tony Wendice (Ray Milland), the chief character of *Dial M for Murder* (1954), is another tennis player with murder on his mind; but unlike Guy Haines, Tony takes the initiative to engage someone to strangle his unfaithful wife Margot (Grace Kelly) for him. Because the movie seldom wanders from the Wendice apartment, the sole setting of the play on which it is based, Hitchcock quipped that he could have phoned in his direction of the picture. (*Dial M* is the last Hitchcock movie to be derived from a stage play.) His reason for not opening out the drama for the screen any more than he did was that the needless proliferation of exterior scenes would have dissipated the taut atmosphere generated by confining the action to a limited playing area, an atmosphere that, as in the case of *Rope*, was one of the original play's principal assets.

Furthermore, as Hitchcock said apropos of the circumscribed settings of films like *Lifeboat* and *Rope*, it is the adroit use of the camera, not the

Grace Kelly and Anthony Dawson in the scissors scene in Dial
M for Murder *(1954), Hitchcock's only venture in 3-D filmmak-
ing. (Credit: Bennett's Book Store).*

number of outdoor scenes encompassed by the action, that distinguishes
a motion picture as genuinely cinematic. In this sense, *Dial M* is
authentically cinematic. Take the scene in which Swann, Tony's hired
assassin (Anthony Dawson) is himself stabbed between the shoulder
blades with a scissors while scuffling with Margot, his intended victim.
The camera remorselessly stays on Swann as he lurches around the
room, ineffectually grasping at the shears, an ordinary household article
that has been suddenly transformed into a lethal weapon. As Swann
pitches forward toward the camera, his body pivots, so that he falls face
upward, and in so doing, drives the instrument protruding from his back
deeper into his flesh.

Hitchcock himself believed that this stomach-churning bit of footage
was one of the most frightening murder scenes that he ever devised.
Indeed, after the sequence had been screened during the Lincoln
Center gala in his honor, he remarked to those present, "As you have
seen on the screen, scissors are the best way." He was, of course,
referring not only to the deadly tool responsible for turning Swann's
attempted murder of Margot into his own swan song as a contract killer,
but to the editor's shears that had carefully cut together the sequence.

Like the knifing scenes in *Sabotage* and *Psycho*, the stabbing sequence in *Dial M* proves once and for all the crucial contribution that the editing process, when it is done with the precision that Hitchcock always demanded, can make to the total impact of a strong sequence.

Hitchcock was also conscious of the importance of color coordination in his films, as noted before. In this, his third color feature, he worked out an interesting visual pattern for Margot's costumes, according to which her outfit in a given scene would be dominated by a color that subtly characterized her situation at that point in the story. As Hitchcock explained, Margot wore cheerful hues like bright red to begin with, but "as tragedy overtook her, she went to brick, then to grey," and still more somber shades.[6]

The most prominent technical accomplishment in *Dial M* was the director's use of three-dimensional photography. As Gordon Gow points out in his monograph on Hollywood in the 1950s, most filmmakers chose to exploit 3-D as a gimmick whereby they could create the illusion of objects hurtling outward toward the audience by aiming them right at the camera (a jungle picture in 3-D promised the moviegoer "a lion in your lap"). Hitchcock, on the other hand, saw 3-D as a means of giving certain scenes a greater sense of depth by moving the action on occasion away from the camera rather than toward it. Hence his use of the process in *Dial M* was almost incidental, in contrast to the way in which it was shown off in other films.

Thus he makes the moviegoer watch an intimate love scene taking place in the background, through a row of liquor bottles that stand out in relief as they sit on a cabinet in the foreground. This involves the viewer more deeply in the scene by making him feel as if he were spying on the lovers from his privileged vantage point behind the cabinet.

Having seen *Dial M* in both 3-D and flat versions (the 3-D version was rereleased in the spring of 1982), I can personally testify that all the shots that Hitchcock composed specifically to emphasize the added dimension of depth such as the one just described are nearly as impressive in the ordinary version. That is why Hitchcock was not particularly perturbed when *Dial M* was exhibited in most markets in the conventional format, given the fact that the short-lived fad had just about run its course by the time the film was given large-scale release. Three-D was a nine-day wonder, he said laconically, "and I came in on the ninth day."[7]

Stage Fright

Stage Fright (1950) parallels *Dial M for Murder* in that the male lead in both pictures is a villain rather than a hero. Because the film deals with the milieu of the theater, the opening credits are superimposed on a theater safety curtain, which rises at the conclusion of the credits to show, not a stage setting, but a busy street in downtown London. This reminds us that, as Shakespeare put it, all the world is a stage, and anyone can for his own private purposes get caught up in role playing in daily life as much as an actor in a play.

This overlap of theatrical illusion with reality is most clearly demonstrated by Charlotte Inwood (Marlene Dietrich), a popular musical comedy star who employs the famous feminine wiles that she has displayed so often on the stage to seduce her real-life lover Jonathan Cooper (Richard Todd) into murdering her unwanted husband. Jonathan in turn shows his own propensity for playacting by convincing his sometime girl friend Eve (Jane Wyman) that Charlotte, and not he, actually committed the murder. He does this to talk Eve into shielding him from the police.

Jonathan narrates his fabricated version of the murder in a false flashback that graphically depicts how Charlotte perpetrated the crime and then pinned it on him. Many critics scolded Hitchcock for "cheating" his audience by inserting into the film this spurious flashback, which the viewer initially accepts as a genuine presentation of the facts, because moviegoers usually assume that the camera does not lie. Rohmer and Chabrol try to bail Hitchcock out by saying that the events as portrayed in the course of the flashback are a true depiction of what happened, and that only Jonathan's voice-over commentary on the sound track is a lie. But this hypothesis is simply not supported by close scrutiny of the sequence.

Besides, Hitchcock is in no need of such special pleading to defend the flashback as he filmed it. Motion pictures have been misleading filmgoers in this fashion all the way back to *The Cabinet of Dr. Caligari* (1919), in which the epilogue, by revealing that the whole of the foregoing tale is a madman's hallucination, negates the validity of the entire story. Furthermore, two other important films of the 1950s, Akira Kurosawa's *Roshomon* (1950) and George Cukor's *Les Girls* (1957), not to mention recent film adaptations of Agatha Christie's whodunnits like *Death on the Nile* (1978), dramatize by turns several contradictory accounts of the same past events as remembered by different characters. Only one of these differing versions of the truth, all of which are played out on the screen, can be the accurate rendition of the facts, and the rest, like the false flashback in *Stage Fright*, are not.

Once Jonathan has been smoked out of hiding by the police, they chase him through the theater where Charlotte is appearing and up onto the stage, where the heavy metal safety curtain we saw going up at the beginning of the movie descends like a gigantic guillotine blade and slices him in two. At the moment when Jonathan stands transfixed with terror as he watches the curtain coming down on him, the filmgoers realize that it is he, not the characters in the movie who are professional actors, who winds up with a severe case of stage fright. Unfortunately, the sluggish tempo of many of the movie's earlier passages was not in keeping with the brisk pacing of this climactic sequence, and hence the movie did not find a wide audience.

Dial M and *Stage Fright* are both movies in which the central character tries to dissociate himself from the guilt of a crime in which he is actually involved. Hitchcock matched them with two pictures in which an innocent man narrowly escapes serving a prison sentence for a crime for which he is in no way responsible. These latter two movies are even more closely related by the fact that they are the only ones in which Hitchcock's personal religious convictions, usually presented in a much more muted fashion, are treated rather overtly.

I Confess

In *I Confess* (1953), which is Hitchcock's tribute to the priesthood, Father Michael Logan, a Canadian parish priest (Montgomery Clift), is accused of a murder that in fact was committed by Keller (killer?), the sacristan of his church, who has admitted his crime to the priest as part of the Catholic ritual of Sacramental Confession. As a Roman Catholic trained in a Jesuit prep school, Hitchcock was aware that according to Church doctrine a priest cannot for any reason whatever divulge what has been confided to him in Confession. This is the premise on which the film turns, but it is one that Hitchcock later felt the mass audience as a whole could not fully grasp.

Most non-Catholics assume that the confessional secrecy binding a priest is no stricter than the professional secrecy governing a lawyer or a psychiatrist, both of whom would be permitted to reveal what had been told to them in confidence by a client if it meant extricating themselves from a situation such as that in which Fr. Logan finds himself. Although Hitchcock intended to present the priest in the movie as a heroic individual who is willing to endure severe anguish in order to remain faithful to his priestly commitments, to many moviegoers Fr. Logan's behavior, when compared to that of a lawyer or a psychiatrist in similar circumstances, seemed needlessly self-sacrificing at best and masochistic at worst. Hence the film was not popular.

In working out the screenplay with writer George Tabori, himself a Catholic, Hitchcock stuck closely to the script's literary source, Paul Anthelme's *Our Two Consciences*. In it the priest silently accepts being found guilty at his ignominious trial, signifying his affinity with Christ as innocent victim of the sins of others. When Hitchcock received protests

Brian Aherne cross-examines Montgomery Clift in I Confess
(1953). (Credit: Museum of Modern Art/Film Stills Archive)

from ecclesiastical sources about a Catholic priest being depicted in a
movie as going to prison, even for a crime he did not commit, he recalled
Tabori to Hollywood to revise the screenplay. In the new ending the
killer inadvertently gives himself away at the last moment, and thus
exonerates Fr. Logan. Tabori, however, ultimately refused to have
anything to do with this substantial alteration. "I felt betrayed," he
remembers. "I walked out in the middle of a story conference with the
excuse of taking a leak, went straight to the airport, to New York City,
and never came back."[8] The required revisions were made anyhow by
Hitchcock and another writer, presumably because the director wanted
the cooperation of Catholic diocesan authorities in doing location filming
on Church property around Quebec.

As a matter of fact, Hitchcock committed himself to shooting a substantial part of the movie, interiors as well as exteriors, on location in
Quebec. As cinematographer Robert Burks pointed out at the time, the
extensive location filming not only furnished authentic, ready-made sets
such as churches and courtrooms, which would have cost two million
dollars to build in the studio, it gave the cinematography a spare,
newsreel-like quality that perfectly suited the austere atmosphere of the
story.

One of the exterior sites that seemed made to order for the film was the courtyard of a basilica in which there is an enormous alabaster statue of Christ accompanied by Roman soldiers as He carried His Cross to Calvary. This sculpture dominates the foreground of a shot that shows Fr. Logan passing by on his way to give himself up to the police to be tried for the murder of which he stands accused. The image clearly identifies the priest as a Christ-like martyr who is at this moment journeying toward his own sacrificial Golgotha. As a result of this widespread location filming all over Quebec, Burks concluded, the movie was completely free of that "slick, polished look" that makes many Hollywood films look artificial. In other words, the finished picture turned out to be "exactly what we were striving for."[9]

The Wrong Man

Hitchcock and Burks strove for the same stark, unembellished look for *The Wrong Man* (1956), the equally sobering tale of a man falsely accused of theft. Because the movie was founded on fact, Hitchcock wanted to film the action where it took place. He therefore told Burks while planning the film, "I want it to look like it had been photographed in a style unmistakably documentary."[10] To strengthen this flavor, whenever possible, Hitchcock employed in minor roles persons who had originally participated in the true incidents, including some New York City detectives and several witnesses of the real robberies of which the hero is accused.

Hitchcock's personal appearance in *The Wrong Man* initially was to be a shot of him entering the Stork Club, where the hero of the film works. But he scotched that idea in favor of giving what amounts to a pre-credit curtain speech. He is discovered standing in the shadows of an empty sound stage as he addresses the audience: "In the past I have given you many kinds of suspense pictures. But this time I would like you to see a different one. The difference lies in the fact that this is a true story, every word of it. And yet it contains elements that are stranger than all the fiction that has gone into many of the thrillers that I have made."

With that, we are introduced to Christopher Emmanuel "Manny" Balestrero (Henry Fonda), who is the bass player in the Stork Club band until he is arrested for carrying out a number of armed robberies that are actually the work of a look-alike. Hitchcock documents the routine procedures governing arrest and detention in even more precise detail than he did in *Blackmail* and *The Paradine Case*. He does so not just to give the fullest possible rein to his own personal phobias about policemen and jails. He also underlines the bitter irony that the hapless and helpless individual submitting to the harrowing process has been firmly established in the filmgoer's mind from the outset as an innocent victim of circumstantial evidence.

The director more than once focuses on the handcuffs Manny must wear on the way to his arraignment, because for Hitchcock they signify most powerfully the degradation attendant upon arrest, as highlighted in a newspaper photograph he once saw of a prominent business man being carted off to the station house shackled to a bum. "It's almost a symbol of reduction, as it were, to the lowest form," he explained; "It's like a chain on a dog."[11] That is why handcuff imagery has so often recurred in his films, notably *The Lodger, The Thirty-nine Steps,* and *Saboteur.*

The religious dimension of the movie, already noted, is evident throughout: Manny comes from a devout Italian Catholic background (Christopher means "bearer of Christ" and Emmanuel "God with us"); and he is often shown in the course of the movie praying silently, as when he unobtrusively fingers his rosary beads during the endless hours in court. Manny's deep faith receives its severest test, however, when the ordeal of his trial finally causes his wife Rose (Vera Miles) to be confined to a mental hospital as the result of a complete emotional breakdown.

At this bleakest of moments, Manny's mother encourages him to ask Divine Providence for help once more; and Manny fixes his gaze on a picture of Christ, the most wronged of all men, for inspiration. As he does so, the image of the Savior dissolves into a close shot of Manny murmuring his prayer. This shot in turn slowly melts into a close-up of the real robber, which for a moment is superimposed on Manny's face in double exposure, indicating how close their physical resemblance really is. Manny's face then disappears from the screen, and we now follow the thief into a delicatessen where he plans to commit the robbery that in fact will be his last. This time he is captured and ultimately brought to justice—in a direct, almost miraculous answer to Manny's prayer, Hitchcock clearly implies by his overlapping of the two scenes.

Far from making any apologies for the religious implications of this sequence, Hitchcock told Truffaut that although in retrospect he was not especially fond of the movie as a whole, he retained a predilection for the sequence in which the real culprit was discovered just as Manny was praying for deliverance. "Yes," he said, "I liked that ironic coincidence."[12]

Hitchcock's interlocking Catholic themes of sin, guilt, forgiveness, and redemption are reflected in many of his movies, as when Guy ultimately overcomes the hellish influence of Bruno on his life in *Strangers on a Train.* But usually these themes are integrated into the overall fabric of the film more subtly than they are in *I Confess* and *The Wrong Man,* where the religious dimension draws a trifle too much attention to itself, with the result that the artistic unity of each film suffers somewhat.

The Wrong Man was the last in a series of pictures Hitchcock made for Warner Brothers, which comprises the group of films treated in this chapter so far. Except for *North by Northwest*, which he made under a one-picture contract with MGM, the balance of the movies dealt with in this chapter belong to his Paramount period. All of these thrillers were shot in color and, except for *Rear Window*, in wide-screen as well. They are characterized for the most part by a relatively less serious tone than the Warners films just considered, a mood that is characterized by Hitchcock's impudently funny essay in black comedy, *The Trouble with Harry*.

The Trouble with Harry

The Trouble with Harry (1955) begins when Harry's gaudily attired corpse is discovered lying insolently right out in the open in a golden grove of richly tinted autumn leaves. Hitchcock deliberately brought the corpse out of the pitch-black night associated with melodrama and into the bright sunshine of a New England morning to underscore, as he put it, the ironic contrast between "the sordidness and muddiness of death" and the beauty of the setting.[13] Consequently, film historian Leslie Halliwell, who often misses the point whenever critical acumen rather than historical fact is at issue, is very wide of the mark when he asserts that the gorgeous color photography of the Vermont setting is little more than a distraction in a film whose dark humor would have been better served by bleak black-and-white cinematography.

Critic Robert Haller is closer to appreciating the film when he contends that the universal guilt of fallen humanity symbolically rears its head in the film when nearly everyone who comes across the body, which is as omnipresent throughout the movie as the corpse in *Rope*, assumes for a variety of reasons that he (or she) has been involved in the death of the late, not very lamented gentleman. For example, the wiley Captain Wiles (Edmund Gwenn), himself in the autumn of life, figures that he may have accidentally polished Harry off with a stray bullet while hunting rabbits out of season. Harry's estranged wife Jennifer (Shirley MacLaine, in her first film) thinks she may have precipitated his demise because earlier that morning she had driven him from her door with a blow on the head from a milk bottle. When it transpires that Harry's death was in fact brought about by natural causes, the movie concludes with a closing title that cheerfully assures the audience that "the trouble with Harry is over." To subject this farcical romp to further commentary would be, to use Rohmer and Chabrol's phrase, like trying to analyze a sunbeam.

Hitchcock's television series began around this time, and when James Allardice, the writer of the host's opening and closing monologues, asked Hitchcock what tone he wanted these remarks to have, the latter screened for him a print of this gruesomely amusing movie. Indeed, the director often liked to refer affectionately to *The Trouble with Harry* as a movie that clearly demonstrated his penchant for exploiting what he termed "the fine line between comedy and tragedy"[14]; the film always remained, together with *Shadow of a Doubt*, a personal favorite of his.

The author of the movie's mordantly witty dialogue, the tenor of which Hitchcock had asked Allardice to imitate, was John Michael Hayes, who lent his comic touch to other Hitchcock films of the decade, including *Rear Window* and *The Man Who Knew Too Much* starring James Stewart, and *To Catch a Thief* with Cary Grant. *North by Northwest*, the last and best of Grant's four films with Hitchcock, was scripted by Ernest Lehman, who also had a gift for the understated, tongue-in-cheek, wry repartee that distinguishes the best of Hitchcock's movies all the way back to *The Thirty-nine Steps* and before.

North by Northwest

The seemingly ageless Cary Grant was fifty-four when he made *North by Northwest*, the same age, as a matter of fact, as Jessie Royce Landis, who played his mother in the picture. Yet Grant never looked more handsome and debonair than in the role of Roger O. Thornhill, a Madison Avenue advertising executive. Asked what his middle initial stands for, Roger shrugs, "For nothing at all!" His nonchalant response just could be a private joke on Hitchcock's part aimed at his former producer David O. Selznick, who, like Roger in the film, pretentiously added the same meaningless middle initial to his own name to make it look more prestigious.

In addition, the zero in Roger's name associates him metaphorically with the mythical George Kaplan, an imaginary CIA agent for whom Roger is mistaken by foreign spy Philip Vandamm (James Mason). Kaplan is really a cipher devised as a decoy by a CIA official (played by Leo G. Carroll in the last of his record six appearances in Hitchcock films) just to mislead foreign intriguers such as Vandamm.

The brilliant title sequence was designed by Saul Bass, who also performed the same function for *Vertigo* and *Psycho*. It starts with a shot of a piece of graph paper, whose criss-cross pattern of lines is soon transformed into the grid of a New York City skyscraper, a huge wall of glass in which is reflected midtown Manhattan at rush hour, the frenetic

Cary Grant and the crop-duster in North by Northwest *(1959),*
Hitchcock's "American Thirty-Nine Steps," *as he called it.*
(Credit: Bennett's Book Store)

world in which Roger pursues his hectic career. This telling mirror image implies that Roger's routine pattern of existence is shortly to be shattered by his involvement in the even more frenzied world of spies and counterspies.

In *North by Northwest* Hitchcock once more brings death out of the dark and into daylight as he did in *The Trouble with Harry*, but this time to much more terrifying effect. In the present film the director eschews the shadowy atmosphere of *Strangers on a Train* and his other exercises in film noir in favor of staging several scenes of mayhem in bright sunlight to suggest that in the nasty world of this film, evil is no less likely to strike in broad daylight than under cover of darkness.

In the movie's most renowned sequence, Roger is lured out into the country by enemy spies on the pretext of meeting the fabled Kaplan. As Roger, incongruously attired in a natty business suit, stands on a deserted road sweltering under the relentless rays of the noonday sun, a crop-dusting plane is engaged in dusting a nearby field, which, he suddenly realizes, is devoid of crops. Then without warning, the aircraft swoops down on Roger like some brutal bird of prey and sprays him first with machine-gun fire and then with poison gas. In this single image of Roger frantically running for cover is distilled all the essential elements of the Hitchcock touch, as that term was explained. Here is the Hitchcock hero, isolated and totally vulnerable, being pursued across a parched, desolate prairie by an evil force that at first seemed to him harmless and unthreatening.

The sequence is, of course, especially effective when the film is shown in the wide-screen process in which it was photographed. The more the composition of the image on the screen emphasizes the vast vistas of the setting, the more the viewer is able to grasp the extreme peril of the hero's plight, as he desperately searches the wide open spaces that surround him for a place to hide. Even when the film is shown without benefit of wide screen, as it is on television, the impact of the scene is diminished only slightly. This is because *North by Northwest*, like all of Hitchcock's wide-screen films, was shot in VistaVision, which projected an image whose proportions were closer to the shape of the old rectangular movie screen than that of CinemaScope or any of the other wide-screen systems. Hence relatively little of the wide-screen image is lost when a VistaVision picture is shown in the conventional format, even on TV.

Although Hitchcock was aware that "you don't hold up your story to show a travelog," he believed that a canny director should judiciously use the wide-screen process to exploit to best advantage the eye-filling settings of the story, and thus give moviegoers an experience they cannot get to the same extent on TV.[15] This he did in *North by North-*

west, not only in the sequence just described, but in the cliff-hanging scene on the colossal Mount Rushmore monument. Once again Hitchcock uses a traditional symbol of culture and stability as the background against which the hero undergoes a death-defying confrontation with the hostile forces that have been plaguing him, just as he had done in *Blackmail, Foreign Correspondent,* and *Saboteur.* In this instance Roger and his girl Eve (Eva Marie Saint) are nearly forced by one of Vandamm's henchman to fall down the mountainside, but help arrives in time to save them.

Having firmly established a permanent relationship on the solid rock of Mount Rushmore, Roger and Eve are last seen on their honeymoon as they bed down for the night in their private compartment aboard a train. Hitchcock deftly accomplishes the transition fron one scene to the other by abruptly cutting from a shot of Roger hauling Eve to safety from the mountain ledge on which they had been dangling, to one of him pulling her into an upper berth. As for the film's final shot, that of their train gliding into a tunnel, Hitchcock impishly confessed, "It's a phallic symbol, but don't tell anyone."[16]

The director also volunteered to an interviewer the information that the movie's title represented a bit of sly humor, since, as he noted, "There is no such thing as north by northwest on the compass."[17] The film's original working title was *In a Northwesterly Direction;* but an MGM executive came up with the present title. This was apparently without any conscious reference to Hamlet's remark, "I am but mad north-northwest," that is, his sanity depends on which way the wind is blowing (2.2.396). In any event, as Pauline Kael has observed, the *Hamlet* quotation is appropriate, since Hitchcock really sets the compass spinning by having his hero dash around the country in search of a fictitious secret agent who in fact has no more existence than the spurious point on the compass. It is only when Roger flies north by Northwest (Airlines) to Dakota and Mount Rushmore that he finds the ultimate resolution of his troubles.

To Catch a Thief

To Catch a Thief (1955), an exhilarating action film that also starred Cary Grant, parallels *North by Northwest* by making equally good use of wide-screen photography in filming location scenes, this time on the French Riviera. Since it takes a thief to catch a thief, John Robie (Grant), an ex-cat burglar living on the Riviera, must find the robber for whose crimes he is being blamed and who is imitating Robie's expert methods for stealing jewelry. The French police, doggedly pursuing the wrong man, prove themselves as benighted as the officers of the law in other Hitchcock films.

Meanwhile, Frances Stevens (Grace Kelly), a frivolous heiress who is only slightly more mature than her light-minded counterpart in *Champagne*, falls in love with Robie precisely because she enjoys the excitement of being involved with a man who she prefers to believe is in fact the practicing jewel thief the police say he is. Styling herself as the cat burglar's kitten, Frances coaxes Robie to make love to her in a naughty seduction scene climaxed by a fireworks display that bursts into an incandescent cascade of color in the night sky. The exploding fireworks constitute one of the most playfully discrete, and most often imitated, sexual metaphors in the Hitchcock canon.

Another memorable image occurs in a breakfast scene, when Frances's mother (Jessie Royce Landis) stubs out a lighted cigarette in the yolk of a fried egg (a shot that is repeated in the 1982 film of Agatha Christie's *Evil Under the Sun*). This brings to mind a similar shot from *Rebecca* in which another dowdy dowager extinguishes her cigarette in a jar of cold cream. In both films Hitchcock uses this gesture to define the vulgarity of the woman in question.

One of the movie's most engaging set pieces is the costume ball during which Robie plans to unmask the real cat burglar. In the course of her remarks at the Lincoln Center tribute to Hitchcock, Princess Grace recalled how the shooting of this particular sequence showed the director to be an even-tempered man who possessed "incredible patience and a sense of humor" on the set:

"In the ballroom sequence, which was long and expensive to shoot, I was to wear a very tight gold evening gown with a huge skirt made of yards and yards of material, which was very difficult to get in to. While my dresser and I were struggling with the costume, a frantic assistant director came banging at my dressing room door, reminding me that Mr. Hitchcock was waiting for me. Finally, when I arrived on the set, there were all the extras and technicians who had been getting paid all the time that they were standing about waiting for me to appear. But instead of being cross, Hitch just looked at my very tight gown and said, 'Grace, there are hills in them thar gold.'"

Hitchcock also made a trio of films with James Stewart in the 1950s, one of which costarred Grace Kelly, who of course retired from the screen soon after finishing her three Hitchcock movies to become Princess Grace of Monaco. Sadly, she died in an auto crash on a Riviera road (which had been used for a location scene in *To Catch a Thief*) in the fall of 1982, roughly a week after the death from cancer of another of Hitchcock's favorite actresses, Ingrid Bergman. (Hitchcock was played by Lomax Study in the 1983 television movie *Grace Kelly* starring Cheryl Ladd.)

Rear Window

In *Rear Window* (1954) Hitchcock once more shot an entire film in a confined setting like those of *Lifeboat* and *Rope*, but this time he extended the borders of the single set in a most ingenious way.

Temporarily incapacitated by a broken leg, Jeff Jeffries (James Stewart) indulges his press photographer's inclination to spy on other people's private lives by peeking into the windows of the apartment dwellings across the courtyard from his own Greenwich Village flat. Since the camera remains in Jeff's room throughout the picture, we see the inhabitants of the other apartments largely from his point of view. In fact, the wall of windows that faces Jeff's own rear window become for him a bank of television monitors, by means of which he is able to keep his neighbors under his voyeuristic surveillance without their being aware of it.

Among the assortment of people he observes are a lonely spinster whom he calls Miss Lonelyhearts, a gregarious composer with lots of friends, and Lars Thorwald (Raymond Burr), an adulterous husband whom Jeff comes to suspect of having killed his invalid wife.

Thorwald's ugly deed is eventually brought to light by the efforts of Jeff and his sometimes fiancée Lisa (Grace Kelly), who finds Jeff's morbid curiosity catching. Ultimately, they are not entirely proud of their meddling in other people's lives; as Lisa shamefacedly confesses, she and Jeff were deeply disappointed when it seemed for a time that Thorwald was not actually guilty of homicide after all. "I'm not much on rear-window ethics," she says, "but we're two of the most frightening ghouls I have ever known."

Furthermore, Jeff's increasingly unwholesome interest in the affairs of his neighbors is mirrored in his switching, as his curiosity increases, from a simple pair of binoculars to a high-powered telescope as his means of prying more and more deeply into their private lives. One of his friends (Wendell Corey) suggests that Jeff's fascination with the lives of other people is his way of sidestepping his own pressing need to sort out his unsatisfactory relationship with Lisa, something he has yet to do by the end of the movie. Speaking more broadly, Jeff's nurse (Thelma Ritter) gives all of us something to think about when she comments on Jeff's "window shopping" with his "spy glass": "We have become a race of Peeping Toms. People ought to get outside and look at themselves for a change."

Besides the overall plot dealing with the detection and apprehension of Thorwald, Hitchcock created some interesting little subplots that tell their own stories. In the course of the picture we hear snatches of a romantic ballad being composed by the songwriter who lives in one of the flats across the way. At one point Hitchcock, making his signature appearance in the film, listens to the man work on the composition while fixing his clock. By the end of the film the number is finished, and we at last hear a newly made recording of the entire song being played by its proud composer for the no-longer-lonely Miss Lonelyhearts, as the camera takes one final look into the rear windows of the tenants whose lives Jeff has kept tabs on throughout the film. For his part, Jeff, who has taken a new lease on life and given up spying on others, sits with his back to the window.

Vertigo

In *Vertigo* (1958) Stewart plays Scottie Ferguson, a retired detective who, like Jeff in *Rear Window,* has some unresolved personal conflicts with which he cannot cope. Despondent because an attack of vertigo caused him to allow a policeman to fall from a roof while they were pursuing a criminal, Scottie is temporarily lured out of retirement by Gavin Elster (Tom Helmore), an old school chum. Elster asks Scottie to shadow his wife Madeleine (Kim Novak), who he says may be contemplating suicide. Like the criminal lawyer in *The Paradine Case,* Scottie falls hopelessly in love with a woman in whom he is supposed to have only a professional interest.

He is plunged into a long-lasting fit of guilty depression when he fails to keep Madeleine from apparently hurling herself out of the bell tower of an old California mission church, because acrophobia prohibited him from climbing to the top of the tower in time to save her. Hitchcock simulates Scottie's vertigo for the viewer by an ingenious shot of the tower stairway, taken from Scottie's point of view, as he pauses momentarily and looks downward from the landing on which he is standing, before futilely trying to summon the courage to continue his ascent to the belfry from which he fears Madeleine is about to jump. The director had a miniature bell tower built and laid on its side. Then he photographed the interior of the model with the help of both a dolly and a zoom lens on the camera; that is, he tracked his camera backward from the tower shaft while simultaneously zooming forward, and thus projected for the filmgoer Scottie's dizzying fear of falling.

As we saw in chapter 1, usually Hitchcock opted for suspense over surprise, by giving moviegoers as much advance information as possible. Thus the audience learns long before Scottie does that Elster actually counted on Scottie's vertigo to keep him from interfering with Elster's own plans to do away with his wife under circumstances that falsely imply that she committed suicide. The revelation to the audience occurs in this way:

Scottie meets Judy Barton (Kim Novak again), whom he discovers is both Elster's former mistress and his accomplice in an elaborate hoax to murder his wife. Judy for a time impersonated Mrs. Elster to establish in Scottie's mind the mistaken impression that the real Madeleine harbored suicidal tendencies, so that he would testify at the inquest that Madeleine took her own life. When Scottie forces Judy to reenact for him her part in Madeleine Elster's death at the scene of the crime, she becomes hysterical and herself falls from the belfry just as the real Madeleine had done.

The final shot of Scottie staring glassy-eyed at the dead body of Judy far below summons the image of Barry Kane looking down at the dead Nazi agent who fell from the Statue of Liberty at the end of *Saboteur*. In both cases the viewer is left contemplating the fact that the evil genius who got the hero into trouble in the first place will very likely go scot free. For the record, Hitchcock shot a scene that suggests Gavin Elster's capture by the authorities abroad, but wisely deleted it from the finished film so as not to take the edge off the ending as it stands.

The Man Who Knew too Much: Two Versions

Stewart's other Hitchcock film, *The Man Who Knew too Much* (1956) was actually a remake of a movie with the same title that Hitchcock had originally done in England in 1934. The plot of the first version centered on a kidnapping, which Hitchcock tied in with a group of terrorists who were modeled on a notorious real-life gang known as the Houndsditch anarchists. The metropolitan police, under the personal supervision of Home Secretary Winston Churchill, had run them to ground in London's East End in 1911, when Hitchcock was still a lad growing up in that end of town. Their final shootout with the police became famous in the annals of Scotland Yard as the Sidney Street siege.

The action of the film begins with Bob and Jill Lawrence (Leslie Banks and Edna Best), an English couple, vacationing with their daughter Betty (Nova Pilbeam) at a winter resort in St. Moritz. While Jill is dancing in the ballroom with Louis Bernard (Pierre Fresnay), a Frenchman who is also staying at the lodge, Bob playfully attaches a ball of knitting wool to a button on Bernard's coat. As he and Jill dance, they become hopelessly entangled in the unraveling string of yarn. Bernard smiles good-humoredly when he notices what has happened; but his face is abruptly drained of expression when he is mortally wounded by a gun shot. Hitchcock employed the gimmick of the ball of yarn, not just for comic relief, but as a symbol of the manner in which Bob and Jill have unwittingly become enmeshed in international intrigue by associating with a fellow vacationer who is in reality a French secret agent.

Hitchcock had an overriding interest in the visual dimension of film, a preoccupation which, as we know, Raymond Chandler, for one, thought excessive. This sometimes led the director to conceive compelling images in his imagination that he found so appealing he would then look for ways of integrating them into the screenplay he was working on. In the case of the first version of *The Man Who Knew too Much*, he remembered, "I looked in my mind's eye at snowy Alps and dingy London alleys, and threw my characters into the middle of this contrast."[18]

The bridge that unites these two disparate images is the kidnapping of young Betty Lawrence in the wake of Louis Bernard's death, as the search for her takes Bob and Jill from St. Moritz to the back streets of London. Betty has been abducted by Abbot (Peter Lorre) and his anarchists to silence Bob, who had learned earlier from Bernard about the impending assassination of a foreign diplomat visiting London.

Danger seems to pounce at every turn. Exploiting the viewer's ingrained fear of dentists, Hitchcock has a seedy dentist who is in league with the terrorists try to smother Bob to death with gas. Later, in a scruffy nonconformist chapel, which turns out to be a front for Abbot's mob, a modest-looking, middle-aged woman suddenly produces a revolver from her shopping bag and forces Bob to drop his concealed weapon into the collection plate. With that, the doors of the chapel slam shut with a dreadful echo, and Bob is temporarily shut in with the kidnappers.

Meanwhile Jill has gone to the Royal Albert Hall where the assassination of which Bob had been warned is scheduled to take place in the course of a concert. The featured piece on the program is the "Storm Cloud Cantata," the music for which was written especially for the film by Australian composer Arthur Benjamin, who did the movie's score. The assassin is to fire at his target at the precise moment when a cymbal crash will drown out the sound of the gun fire. Jill calls up the courage to scream out just when the murderer is about to shoot and thus saves the statesman's life. The police then help her to trace Bob and Betty to the anarchists' citadel, where an exciting gun battle brings the film to a close. This scene and the one in the dentist's office were unfortunately not included in the second version.

The Man Who Knew too Much is clearly a film for which Hitchcock retained a great affection, since he had toyed with the idea of remaking it as far back as 1941 as one of his films for Selznick. Finally, more than twenty years after the release of the original version, when he needed to find a vehicle for James Stewart post haste to take advantage of the actor's availability, he decided that the time was right to do this tried and true story a second time.

The remake in 1956 rounds out the quartet of films James Stewart made with Hitchcock, which began with *Rope*. "Stewart is a perfect Hitchcock hero," the director once said, "because he is Everyman in bizarre situations. I mean, let's look at his private life: Princeton, Air

Force colonel—he's not an uneducated oaf. You can believe him as a professor, a doctor, a family man."[19] Having played a professor in *Rope*, Stewart essayed the role of Ben McKenna in *The Man Who Knew too Much*, a fellow who is both a doctor and a family man. In this version of the story, Ben and his wife Jo (Doris Day) have a son Hank, rather than a daughter, and they go on vacation to Morocco rather than to Switzerland. But once Hank is kidnapped in the Casbah, the basic plot line of the first version holds true. The American remake is about forty-five minutes longer than the British version, because Hitchcock concentrates more on character development this time around, and scrupulously tying up the loose plot strands he had left dangling in the 1934 movie.

To cite one example, in the earlier movie the exact nature of Abbot's curious, obviously dependent attachment to the woman of indeterminate age called Nurse Agnes who is his constant companion is never clarified. In the remake, however, they are established as husband and wife, both of whom have clearly defined personalities. Yet the 1956 film, because of this and other refinements in its heavily revised, more substantial screenplay, is not automatically a better or more entertaining film. If the earlier picture left some things unexplained, the filmgoer was kept sufficiently breathless by this fast-moving, seventy-four-minute movie not to notice. As a matter of fact, the London *Observer* judged the 1934 film at the time of its release to be Hitchcock's most promising movie since *Blackmail* five years before simply because of the director's frank refusal to indulge in subtleties that would have got in the way of the forward movement of the exciting plot.

It is only because the director slowed the tempo of the 1956 film to accommodate a thorough delineation of character that he felt a consequent need to develop his screenplay in more elaborate detail than he had in the first version, in effect to make allowances for icebox logic. In any event, the high point of both films is the almost intolerably suspenseful concert sequence, in which the heroine must decide whether or not to stop the assassination that she knows is about to take place, when it might well mean further imperiling the life of her child, still detained as a hostage by the terrorists.

James Stewart remembers delivering a long speech in the course of this sequence in which Ben futilely tries to convince the police that they should interrupt the concert before it is too late. At the end of a take in which the actor had delivered all of this dialogue letter-perfect, Hitchcock advised Stewart that he had decided to cut the entire speech so that the audience could listen to the London Symphony playing the "Storm Cloud Cantata" on the sound track instead. What Hitchcock had realized once he was able to observe the scene taking shape during

The one time Hitchcock repeated himself: (top) Frank Vosper, Leslie Banks, Nova Pil-
beam, and Peter Lorre in the British version of The Man Who Knew Too Much *(1934),*
prior to the assassination at the concert; (bottom) James Stewart in the American remake
of The Man Who Knew Too Much *(1956), at the concert. (Credit: Larry Edmonds's*
Cinema Bookshop)

shooting was that suspense would be heightened if the only thing the audience could hear throughout the sequence's twelve-minute running time was the cantata inexorably galloping toward the cymbal crash (already established in the moviegoer's mind by a recording of the piece played earlier in the film).

For his part, Hitchcock felt that the remake possessed a professional polish lacking in his earlier attempt. Thus in the first version the plot goes into overdrive before the moviegoer gets a chance to become acquainted with the principals, and consequently to sympathize with them to the same degree that one can in the second movie. On the other hand, because the remake is less tightly constructed than its predecessor, it contains a few slow-paced talky stretches that may cause the viewer's interest to flag—something that never happens in the original.

The on-going debate about the relative merits of the British and American periods of Hitchcock's career, which was taken up at the end of chapter 4, can be summed up by comparison of the two versions of *The Man Who Knew too Much*. One can only say that whether one believes that Hitchcock's British thrillers are on a par with his American suspense dramas largely depends on whether one prefers fast-paced action movies with a minimum of plot and character development to longer, somewhat slower, but denser films that reflect deeper probing into the psychology of character. In the last analysis, an individual filmgoer's choice in this matter basically says more about his or her personal cinematic taste than it does about the relative merits of the films themselves.

The remake of *The Man Who Knew too Much* is only one of the six movies that Hitchcock directed in the three-year period between 1954 and 1956. Given this prolific burst of creativity, it is all the more extraordinary that during the very same period he inaugurated a weekly television series that he supervised and hosted for seven seasons. He also personally directed twenty telefilms, mostly for this series. They are the focus of the upcoming chapter, since as a group they are as integral a part of his catalog as any of the theatrical features he directed.

7

"Alfred Hitchcock Presents": The Television Years

"GOOD EVENING, LADIES AND GENTLEMEN, I am Alfred Hitchcock. Tonight I am presenting the first in a series of stories of suspense and mystery called, oddly enough, 'Alfred Hitchcock Presents.' I shall not act in these stories, but I shall only make appearances that will be something in the nature of an accessory before and after the fact, to give the title beforehand to those who can't read, and to tidy up afterwards for those who don't understand the endings."

With these brief remarks Hitchcock introduced on the night of October 2, 1955, the first of some 365 segments of the weekly television series that he supervised from 1955 to 1965, some of which, as noted before, he directed himself. The serio-comic flavor of this introductory speech also set the tenor of the stories to follow, a tone that was further underscored by Gounod's "Funeral March of a Marionette" (not "of the Marionettes," as it is usually called), the theme music. The program always opened with Hitchcock's own celebrated caricature of his profile being transfigured into his silhouette, which in turn gave way to the appearance of the man himself. In hosting the show, Hitchcock was perhaps taking a leaf from fellow-director Cecil B. DeMille's book, since DeMille had once emceed "The Lux Radio Theater," thereby shrewdly making himself, and by extension his films, a household word.

"In selecting the stories for my television shows," Hitchcock explained, "I try to make them as meaty as the sponsor and the network will stand for, and to offset any tendency toward the macabre with humor,"[1] as he had often done in his features, most noticeably in *The Trouble with Harry,* the film that, as mentioned, suggested the flavor of the opening and closing remarks. Hitchcock's impish humor extended even to his references to the sponsor. He playfully introduced one commercial interruption by advising his audience, "Now my sponsor would like to bring you an important message; I needn't tell you to whom it is important."

Two Earlier Short Films

The telefilms that he personally made for the television series were not the first short films Hitchcock had directed. During World War II he felt that he should do something special for the war effort besides making anti-Nazi films like *Lifeboat*. Therefore he agreed to go to London in 1944 to direct two short films sponsored by the British Ministry of Information. These two semidocumentaries were designed to acquaint the French population in newly liberated areas of the country with the work of the Free French resistance movement. They were shot in French, with a French cast and crew. In *Bon Voyage*, Sgt. John Dougall of the RAF escapes to London from occupied France with the aid of the Free French. After recounting in flashback how a Polish officer named Stephan helped him all along the way, the Free French officer to whom he has told his story then relates the same events, also shown in flashback, according to the reports he has received from his agents in France. In filling in details of which John was unaware, the officer reveals that John's "Polish" companion was in fact a member of the Gestapo, and that John unknowingly caused the deaths of several Free Frenchmen by leading Stephan to them.

Hitchcock thus employs the inventive device of showing the audience the same flashback twice, but adding elements the second time round of which John was ignorant at the time the events took place. For example, we see John taking leave of a young girl who has briefly sheltered Stephan and himself just as John is preparing to push on alone. The first presentation of this incident in flashback, because it is seen solely from John's limited point of view, ends here. When the flashback is repeated, however, the episode continues as John leaves, and the girl, who has grown suspicious of Stephan, picks up the telephone to inquire about him of her contacts in the resistance movement. Stephan enters the room at this point and abruptly reaches over and covers the mouthpiece of the phone. He then jabs a revolver into her ribs, and a shot is heard. A puff of gun smoke rises between them, and she drops to the floor.

Because of the static, verbose script of Hitchcock's second short, *Aventure Malgache* (*Madagascar Adventure*), it is of less interest, artistically speaking, than *Bon Voyage*. Set in Madagascar, where at this point in the war emissaries of both the pro-Nazi Vichy government of France and of the anti-Nazi Free French are angling for control of the island, it nonetheless contains some telling images. There is, for example, the scene in which a policeman who wishes to dissociate himself from the Vichy government ceremoniously discards a bottle of Vichy mineral water, just as the police officer played by Claude Rains does in Michael Curtiz's *Casablanca* (1942), and for the same reason. But *Aventure Malgache* has little else to recommend it.

Neither film seems to have received much, if any, distribution in France or anywhere else. The better of the two films, *Bon Voyage*, however, is a neat little melodrama that could have served as a good segment for Hitchcock's television series a decade later.

The Twenty Teleplays

When Hitchcock entered the field of television, he issued a press release in which he said that several people had asked him how he expected to commit a coherent story to film for a half-hour program (really twenty-three minutes of screen time) in three days when he had grown accustomed to working months on filming a theatrical motion picture. "The very idea of Alfred Hitchcock, the calm, complacent Hitchcock, beset by the frantic frenzy commonly associated with television" seems to have caused these people some amusement, he said.[2] He assured them that he could keep up the pace demanded by television production, and the uniform craftsmanship of the teleplays he directed attests to that fact.

Hitchcock staunchly maintained that he did not really make a special effort to choose projects primarily for this series, but simply took over two or three scripts a year whenever his feature schedule allowed. As a result, most critics have felt free to pass over these short films when assessing his work. Yet an examination proves conclusively that Hitchcock consistently elected to direct teleplays, often from stories by his favorite mystery writers such as John Collier and Roald Dahl, that closely paralleled situations and themes associated with his full-length films. In these, he frequently cast actors whom he also used in his features, including Joseph Cotten, Vera Miles, Wendell Corey, John Forsythe, Claude Rains, and John Williams. Hence these films, which amount to around ten hours of total playing time, deserve analysis, especially since the series remains in permanent syndication.

The Half-Hour Teleplays.   The premiere film of the series was entitled *Revenge* (October 2, 1955) and starred Vera Miles as Elsa, a neurotic young woman similar to the character she played in *The Wrong Man*, who sinks into a state of shock after being savagely raped by a man puporting to be a traveling salesman. As her husband Carl (Ralph Meeker) later drives her through the town, she points to a man on the sidewalk and murmurs, "That's the man." Carl, in a fit of rage, immediately follows him into a shabby hotel and bludgeons him to death with a wrench, while the camera remains in the hallways photographing Carl's animated shadow on the wall of the dingy room. Driving away from the scene, Carl tries to reassure his wife that she has been revenged, but she continues to stare out of the car window. Then fixing her eyes on another passerby, she blurts out again, "That's the man." In Elsa's hysterical state, all men have become for her the guilty party.

In choosing rape as the subject of his first telefilm, Hitchcock was already venturing into territory still thought to be fairly taboo for television at the time. But since he carried the film off with the consummate skill and taste that one had learned to expect from his feature pictures, there were no objections from the network. For example, he employed artistic indirection to portray the cruel killing of the salesman. The rape itself is suggested visually by a shot of Elsa's inert hand clutching the crumpled carnation that she had torn from her attacker's lapel, a symbol of how her fragile spirit has been crushed by sexual aggression.

In addition, the transference of guilt theme to be found in Hitchcock's features like *Shadow of a Doubt* is obvious in *Revenge*, since Carl has become infected with the evil he sought to avenge. It is also evident in *Wet Saturday* (September 30, 1956), in which Sir Cedric Hardwicke seeks to foist a murder committed by his emotionally unstable daughter onto an unsuspecting neighbor. In so doing, of course, he becomes implicated in the girl's guilt.

Hitchcock's theme of an ordinary person getting involved in extraordinary events, present in his films even farther back than *The Lodger*, stands out in relief in a quartet of his TV movies that includes "Breakdown," "The Case of Mr. Pelham," "Dip in the Pool," and "Lamb to the Slaughter." *Breakdown* (November 13, 1955) was in actual fact the first teleplay that Hitchcock shot; but it was televised after "Revenge," possibly because he judged it to be a trifle too depressing to inaugurate the whole series. Joseph Cotten, who had already done the story on radio, enacts the role of a calloused, unscrupulous businessman who learns a salutary lesson about one's need for his fellow man when he is completely paralyzed in an auto wreck and has no way of signaling to onlookers that he is still alive.

The story is told entirely from the point of view of the Cotten character, with his thoughts being expressed in voice-over on the sound track. All of the other actors play directly to the camera, thus simulating for the viewer the man's nerve-wracking frustration at being forced to watch a succession of people, including policemen and doctors, peer down at him and assume he is dead because he can neither move nor speak.

He is saved from being enbalmed only when an alert medico perceives a tear trickling down his cheek. This is suggested by a drop of water falling on the camera lens, which causes the image of the doctor observing him to shimmer on the screen. Significantly, this is the first time in living memory that the heretofore insensitive Cotten character has allowed himself to break down and cry.

Joseph Cotten in Breakdown *(1955), the first of Hitchcock's TV films (Cotten had starred in* Shadow of a Doubt, *a decade earlier). (Credit: Movie Star News)*

"The Case of Mr. Pelham" (December 4, 1955) has been correctly called one of the strangest properties on which Hitchcock ever worked in any medium. Pelham (Tom Ewell) is an ordinary businessman whose routine life is gradually taken over by a double who systematically and inexplicably displaces him at home and office. He finally goes completely crazy when his valet accepts the imposter as the genuine article because Pelham's own behavior has lately become increasingly erratic, due to the strain that he has been under while trying to circumvent his look-alike. The result is that the viewer is left wondering whether or not Pelham was demented from the beginning.

Hitchcock's epilogue to this story represents the closest tie-in that any of his appearances as master of ceremonies had with one of the playlets. At the end of the program he is shown being taken away by two asylum attendants in white jackets as he wildly protests that he is the real Alfred Hitchcock. The camera then pans to Hitchcock the host who informs that audience that he, not the other fellow is really Alfred Hitchcock. Then he shakes his head sadly as a pistol shot is heard off-camera.

In "Dip in the Pool" (September 14, 1958), William Rotibol (Keenan Wynn) is a tourist who finds himself short of funds during an ocean cruise (as the Hills did in *Rich and Strange*). He dips into the ship's lottery pool to bet on the time that the liner will reach port. Having foolishly overestimated the duration of the trip, he decides to slow down the ship's's progress by taking a dip in the ocean, thus causing a temporary delay in the voyage while he is fished out.

He assumes that the lady standing nearby on deck will shout "Man overboard!" as soon as she sees him plummet into the sea. But she does no such thing; and William gradually disappears in the distance and finally sinks out of sight, as the steamer continues on its way without him. When she turns away from the rail and stares blankly toward the camera, we realize that she is blind, and not necessarily insane, as Steve Mamber contends in his otherwise excellent essay on Hitchcock's TV films in *Cinema*. Mamber is correct, however, in pointing out that this is the only telefilm in which Hitchcock makes a signature appearance after the manner of the cameos he regularly did in his features. In something of a reprise of his fleeting appearance in *Lifeboat*, Hitchcock is pictured on the cover of a magazine one of the passengers is reading.

"Lamb to the Slaughter" (April 13, 1958), I have found, is the Hitchcock telefilm most well remembered by viewers who have seen the series. Its title, an allusion to the sacrificial lambs of the Old Testament, specifically refers to the frozen leg of lamb with which Mrs. Maloney (Barbara Bel Geddes, Scottie's neglected girlfriend in *Vertigo*) bludgeons her philandering husband. She then proceeds to defrost, bake, and serve the savory joint of meat to the investigating officers, while they speculate about what might have happened to the murder weapon.

Two of Hitchcock's TV segments, "Mr. Blanchard's Secret" and "Back for Christmas," distill elements from *Rear Window*, made two years earlier. "Mr. Blanchard's Secret" (December 23, 1956), the weakest television play Hitchcock ever made, is, in fact, a warmed-over rehash of that basic situation. In this version a mystery writer (Mary Scott) with a hyperactive imagination thinks her next door neighbor Mr. Blanchard has killed his wife because our heroine assumes that Mrs. Blanchard is a hopeless kleptomaniac whose scandalous behavior has ruined her husband's life. In the not-too-surprising finale we learn that Mrs. Blanchard, who is still very much alive, snatched the writer's expensive cigarette lighter, not out of compulsion, but to have her husband, a Mr. Fixit by hobby, repair it for the owner as a surprise.

In "Back for Christmas" (March 4, 1956) Herbert (John Williams) does in fact kill his nagging spouse and bury her body in the cellar, a situation that readily brings to mind Thorwald's attempts to dispose of his wife's corpse in *Rear Window*. Herbert's obsessively efficient wife wins the final round, however. Her vacationing widower receives a letter from a contracter whom she hired before her death, informing him that the firm is excavating his basement while he is away in order to install a wine cellar before he comes back home for Christmas.

The morbid humor, à la *The Trouble with Harry,* that permeates "Back for Christmas" is also present in "Arthur" (September 27, 1959). The title character (Laurence Harvey), a New Zealand chicken farmer, also must get rid of a corpse, this time of his ex-lover Helen. He grinds up her remains in a batch of the chicken feed that he sells to the farmers of the area, and subsequently receives compliments from his customers about the improved quality of his product. Perhaps without realizing it, Hitchcock was anticipating his later feature *The Birds* when he noted at the close of the program that the poultry came to like the new ingredients of blood and bone so much, that one day when Arthur entered the barnyard they turned on him. . . .

In "The Perfect Crime" (October 20, 1957), detective Charles Courtenay (Vincent Price) devises an equally ingenious method of disposing of the remains of a lawyer. He has committed the murder to keep the man from divulging that Courtenay was earlier responsible for sending the wrong man to the electric chair. Courtenay bakes the lawyer's body into clay, which he then molds into a vase that he displays prominently among his curios as a secret souvenir of his perfect crime.

Four other telefilms, like some of Hitchcock's early English feature films, have really nothing to do, strictly speaking, with the world of crime and criminals: "Mrs. Bixby and the Colonel's Coat," "The Horseplayer," "The Crystal Trench," and "Bang! You're Dead." In "Mrs. Bixby" (September 27, 1960) the lady in question (Audrey Meadows) pawns a fur coat given her as a farewell present by the wealthy colonel with whom she has broken off an affair. She subsequently discovers that her cagey husband, much to her chagrin, has redeemed the pawn ticket and made a present of the expensive garment to his secretary.

"The Horseplayer" (March 14, 1961) represents the only other Hitchcock work besides *I Confess* that has a priest as its leading character. Father Amion (Claude Rains) bets on a horse in hopes of raising enough money to make some much-needed repairs on his crumbling church. He then develops scruples about giving in to the temptation to gamble, and penitently prays that God will punish him by making his horse lose. His prayer is not answered, and he wins all the money required to refurbish the church. Surely any effort to ferret out deep religious resonances in this story would be ill advised, since Hitchcock is manifestly having a little good-natured fun at the expense of a naive clergyman, whom he nonetheless treats with affection.

In "The Crystal Trench" (October 4, 1959), my favorite among the teleplays, a young married man is buried in a landslide of snow during a mountain-climbing expedition. His wife Stella (Patricia Owens) waits for four decades to claim the body when the shifting snows at last allow the corpse to surface. The climax of the tale is as finely staged as anything Hitchcock ever did. The well-preserved, handsome young face of the long-deceased husband, fixed permanently in a frozen stare, peers sightlessly out from the crystal trench of ice in which his body is encased and provides a poignant contrast to the withered countenance of his widow, wasted with forty years of waiting. She lovingly takes hold of the locket that is still hanging round her beloved spouse's neck and snaps it open, and is crushed to see the likeness of another woman inside. The raw wind that cuts across her face is nothing compared to the searing revelation of an infidelity that has surfaced so many years too late.

"Bang! You're Dead" (October 17, 1961) is something of a variation on an episode in *Sabotage*, in which a youngster unknowingly carries around a time bomb that finally goes off, destroying a busload of people. Here a lad named Jackie (Billy Mumy) plays cowboys and Indians with a gun that he thinks is a toy, but which is actually a real revolver loaded with live ammunition. Since Hitchcock, as we know, thought that it was a mistake to allow the boy in *Sabotage* to bring about tragedy even inadvertently, he "corrects" himself this time around by having the owner retrieve the pistol before Jackie does any damage with it beyond shattering a mirror with a misfire.

Imminent death is also the theme of "Poison" (October 5, 1958), which takes place in a jungle outpost. Harry (James Donald), a dissolute drunk, believes that a cobra has slithered into bed with him and fallen asleep on his stomach. His companion Woods (Wendell Corey) condescendingly maintains that Harry is only suffering an attack of the DTs, until poetic justice is served when he is himself bitten by the serpent.

The Hour-Long Teleplays.   During this same period Hitchcock directed three hour-long (fifty-two minutes of screen time) television dramas for each of which he had a five-day shooting schedule. The best of the trio is surely "Four O'Clock" (September 30, 1957), the premiere show of the "Suspicion" series. "I had more time to develop character in these films," he pointed out. "For that matter, some stories deserve a longer telling than others," a sentiment he had expressed in contrasting his American thrillers to his shorter British films. "Four O'Clock," as Hitchcock described it, is about Paul, a clock repairman (E. G. Marshall), "who makes a homemade time bomb because he suspects his wife (Nancy Kelly) of having a lover; and he's determined to blow them both up." Right after Paul starts the bomb's timing mechanism, which is set to go off at 4 PM, two burglars break into his house and bind and gag him in the basement (cf. the bondage imagery in *Number Seventeen*, *The Wrong Man*, etc.). They proceed to rob the place. "Then they leave. There he is, helpless, facing his own ticking bomb," and doubting that he has much of a future.[3]

The hands of the bomb's timing device are shown in close-up just as they reach the fatal hour, but inexplicably no explosion occurs. Nevertheless, the strain of waiting helplessly and hopelessly for the bomb to be denotated has driven Paul insane. In the final scene the ropes with which the thieves had tied him are replaced by the straightjacket he is wearing as a couple of asylum attendants take him away. Meanwhile his wife explains to the police that there had been a power failure in the house earlier in the day, which of course kept the bomb from going off. She adds that she had spent the afternoon upstairs talking with her brother, an ex-convict whom Paul had mistakenly assumed was her lover because the two men had never met.

The ironic twists that Hitchcock exploits so marvelously in "Four O'Clock" are less aptly handled in "I Saw the Whole Thing" (October 11, 1962), which he made during the period of his series, when "Alfred Hitchcock Presents" had become "The Alfred Hitchcock Hour." This is a perfunctory courtroom drama that seems to move even more slowly than many of the trial sequences in *The Paradine Case*. The telefilm does have the advantage of an especially effective opening, however: Hitchcock in effect "stretches time" by portraying a hit-and-run traffic accident, which actually took place in an instant, from several points of view. That is, he shows a close-up of the horrified face of each of the five witnesses just as the moment of impact takes place off screen, signified by the sound of the collision being repeated on the sound track with each successive close-up.

Despite the fact that all of the witnesses contend that they "saw the whole thing," in the end it is painfully clear that none of them did, since Barnes (John Forsythe, the boyfriend of Harry's widow in *The Trouble with Harry*), the defendant on trial for the crime, admits that he was not behind the wheel of the car after all. He had gallantly taken the blame for his wife, who was in fact driving, to spare her the ordeal of the trial. It is a pity that the whole telefilm did not live up to its promising opening sequence.

"Incident at a Corner" (April 5, 1960), made for *Ford Star Time*, is drearier still. In fact the spurious plot, which Jack Edmond Nolan mistakenly attaches to this teleplay in his pioneering article on Hitchcock's telefilms, (reprinted in La Valley's *Focus on Hitchcock*) sounds more interesting that the actual scenario. Like "I Saw the Whole Thing," the early passages of this TV drama promise more than it ultimately delivers. A confrontation between a school traffic warden (Paul Hartman) and a woman motorist is repeated from the vantage point of various witnesses. Then the meandering story line takes an unexpected turn and settles down into a turgid tale about the heinousness of poison-pen letters, which seems to have little to do with the deftly designed opening sequence.

Looking Toward Psycho.   If several of Hitchcock's teleplays recall his earlier theatrical features, the two remaining half-hour playlets yet to be discussed look ahead to *Psycho*. In "One More Mile to Go," (April 7, 1957) Sam (David Wayne) has killed his wife and stuffed her body in the trunk of his car. A motorcycle cop stops him because one of his tail lights is flickering on and off. The story ends with the obliging patrolman helping a gas station attendant pry open the trunk of Sam's car to fix the offending light. It finally flutters once more and then goes out, along with Sam's last hope of concealing his crime.

The repeated shots of the policeman reappearing in Sam's rear-view mirror will recur in *Psycho* when Marion Crane, like Sam, keeps hoping that the state highway patrolman who has rightly found her behavior suspicious will give up following her. Moreover, Steve Mamber observes that some shots in an earlier sequence of the telefilm, in which Sam Brings his wife's corpse out to his car and stuffs it in the trunk are virtually re-created in the scene in *Psycho* after the shower slaying, in which a dead body is hidden away in a similar fashion.

The other TV film closely associated with *Psycho* is "Banquo's Chair" (May 3, 1959). John Williams is Inspector Brent, who, like the detective he played in *Dial M for Murder,* is definitely not satisfied that the cause of justice has been served in a case with which he has been associated, and decides to trap the real murderer into a confession. He designs a wily ruse whereby he hires an elderly actress to impersonate the victim and then invites the suspect, the nephew of the murdered woman, to dinner. When a ghostly figure appears accusingly at the dinner table, as Banquo does in *Macbeth*, the murderer goes to pieces and gives himself away. Just as he is being taken into custody, the actress shows up and apologizes for having arrived late.

In both this television film and *Psycho*, made a year later, the killer is haunted for murdering an older woman. Moreover, as James Naremore notes in his fascinating monograph on *Psycho*, each murderer is compared symbolically to a predatory bird that must finally be spied out of its lair and forced into the glaring light of exposure.

In a larger sense *Psycho* is related to all twenty of Hitchcock's television films. Because it was made on a relatively tight budget and schedule, Hitchcock decided to film *Psycho* with the smaller unit of technicians, headed by cinematographer John Russell, and with the same modest technical facilities with which he turned out his telefilms rather than with the more elaborate and expensive crew and facilities that a big movie studio could have provided for him. Given the economy—in every sense of the word—with which *Psycho* was made, the finished film has a stark simplicity that brings the best of his telefilms very much to mind.

Psycho "was an experiment in this sense," Hitchcock said: "Could I make a feature film under the same conditions as a television show?"[4] He not only could but did; for Hitchcock poured into Psycho all of the expertise he had gained from making television as well as theatrical films over the years, and produced as a result what is unquestionably the best and most popular film of his entire career.

8

The Sixties and Seventies:
The Vintage Years

Psycho

THE WIDE PUBLIC ACCEPTANCE of Hitchcock's masterpiece *Psycho* (1960) was no doubt helped by a shrewd publicity gimmick whereby Hitchcock, always the canny showman, insisted that patrons would not be admitted once the picture had started. The ad campaign for the film, which was distributed by Paramount, featured a puckish statement by the director that "*Psycho* is most enjoyable when viewed beginning at the beginning and proceeding to the end. . . . It does not improve when run backwards. This applies even to that portion of the film in which I make a brief but significant appearance." Hitchcock's cameo appearance shows him wearing a ten-gallon hat, visible through the window of an office building in downtown Phoenix, as he stands on the sidewalk outside. He also made what is probably his longest screen appearance in a teasing, ten-minute promotional trailer for the film, in which he conducts a guided tour of the principal sets.

As the film opens, Marion Crane (Janet Leigh) seems to be a typical secretary until, on an impulse, she steals from her boss a large sum of cash with which to finance her marriage to her impecunious fiancé Sam Loomis (John Gavin, who at this writing is U.S. Ambassador to Mexico). Thereupon she immediately sets out to elope with Sam, who lives some distance away. After driving all day and managing to elude the suspicious highway patrolman who had been trailing her, Marion opts to seek shelter from the rainy night in a modest but immaculately kept motel just off the main road.

Norman Bates (Anthony Perkins), the shy, lanky, likeable proprietor of the motel, easily arouses Marion's sympathies when the lonely young man sheepishly admits to her how he is dominated by his elderly mother who lives in the forbidding mansion nearby. Marion has a long conversation with Norman in which he speaks of how human beings become imprisoned in a narrow existence in the course of their lives. "We are all

Anthony Perkins in the shower scene of Psycho *(1960), Hitchcock's finest American film. (Credit: Museum of Modern Art/ Film Stills Archive)*

161

clamped in our private traps, and can never get out," Norman muses out loud. "We scratch and claw, but only at the air, only at each other." Reflecting on Norman's words, Marion elects to redeem herself by going back home the following morning and returning the money she has stolen, and thus extricate herself from the trap in which she herself has been caught. Little does Marion realize that it is by eliciting compassion from an unsuspecting young lady such as herself that the disarming Norman Bates, who stuffs birds as a hobby, baits his traps to ensnare beautiful women. In this case, the bird is one named after the crane, who hails from Phoenix, the name of the fabled bird which, according to legend, possessed the phenomenal ability to be reborn after its death. Truth to tell, Marion Crane will not be as fortunate as the Phoenix.

Before retiring for the night, she takes a cleansing shower, permitting the water to wash away the guilt of the larceny she now repents having committed. At this moment the shower curtain is whipped aside, and Marion is savagely stabbed to death by what appears to be a maniacal woman inexplicably possessed of enormous physical strength. All the while the sound track emits a burst of shrill, high-strung music, with the notes of the slicing string instruments sounding like the piercing shrieks of some carnivorous bird "scratching and clawing" at its prey, to use Norman's dreadfully prophetic phrase.

This is, of course, the film's celebrated shower murder; although it takes less than a minute of screen time, Hitchcock spent about a week filming the stabbing, which is composed of more than sixty individual shots. The very fragmentation of the brutal killing into a rapid succession of close shots makes the act seem even more sudden and violent than if it had been photographed in a single take. The prop department had initially supplied the director with a rubber torso that spurted blood when a knife was plunged into it. But Hitchcock decided that he could suggest the stabbing more vividly by cutting together several separate close-ups of assailant and victim without ever showing the weapon actually penetrating her flesh, and letting the audience's imagination do the rest.

When at last Marion lies bleeding to death on the shower floor, the nozzle continues to spray her body with water. The camera impassively follows the path of her blood as, mixed with water, it trickles down the drain, which appears in extreme close-up to be a black abyss, the very heart of darkness from which her evil attacker seems to have mate-rialized. This sequence of shots, as Rothman notes, is one of the several crucial additions Hitchcock made to the preliminary blueprint for the scene sketched by Saul Bass, who also designed the tiles for the film. One of the reasons that Hitchcock chose to shoot *Psycho* in black and white at a time when feature films were increasingly being done in color was that the slaying photographed in living color would have simply been too gruesome for many moviegoers. As he put it, he wanted to scare his audience, not nauseate them.

Bernard Herrmann, in composing his spare musical score for the film, took his cue from the fact that the movie was in black and white and limited the background music solely to strings as a counterpart to the way in which Hitchcock had limited his color spectrum. As reported in Royal Brown's superlative essay on Hitchcock and Herrmann, the latter said, "In using only strings, I felt that I was able to complement the black-and-white photography of the film with a black-and-white sound."[1]

In killing off his heroine when the movie is less than half over, Hitchcock succeeded in disconcerting his audience into an unsettled state that lasts right up to the finale. Janet Leigh commented at the Lincoln Center gala that she did not mind that her role in *Psycho*, the most important of her whole career, required her to disappear so early from the film; rather, the movie proved that "the length of a part doesn't matter if your associates are real experts like Hitch."

Some moviegoers found the knifing so terrifying that they were afraid to take a shower for some time after seeing *Psycho*, since one is never more vulnerable, after all, than when one stands naked in the shower. One irate father wrote to Hitchcock asking what he should do about his daughter's refusal to bathe after seeing the film, and the director replied that the man should send her to the dry cleaners.

In the end Norman Bates turns out to be the fiendishly deranged villain of the piece. At first, when he dutifully wipes away every trace of the murder in the bathroom and sinks Marion's car, with her corpse in the trunk, in quicksand, one assumes that he is a devoted son, determined to cover up, although misguidedly, his mother's insane behavior. It later develops, however, that Norman, who had an incestuously possessive love for his mother, poisoned both her and her lover after he discovered them in bed together.

To obliterate the intolerable crime of matricide from his conscience, Norman took to nurturing a split personality. In making believe that his mother's personality at times had displaced his own, he was able to maintain the illusion that she was still very much alive. To reinforce this conviction, he employed his otherwise harmless skill as a taxidermist to stuff his mother's corpse with sawdust and preserve it in a state of quasi-permanence. Furthermore, he would invariably don her clothing before he stabbed to death a girl to whom he was attracted, fantasizing all the while that it was his mother who perpetrated these crimes and not he, because in his own diseased imagination he assumed, quite gratuitously, that she was as incestuously jealous of him as he was of her. In addition, because Norman was pathologically shy with women, each of these murders took on the nature of a symbolic rape, giving the dripping knife and the gushing shower nozzle a definite phallic significance.

As Durgnat has written, Norman begins by enjoying his fantasies, and ends up with his fantasies enjoying him. For, by film's end, Norman's frail self-identity has been totally absorbed by the "mother" side of his schizophrenic personality. As he sits staring into space in a jail cell following his arrest, his complete withdrawal from reality is signaled by the blanket in which he has wrapped himself in order to insulate himself completely from any further contact with the outside world. A smile gradually creeps over Norman's face, on which for a moment the grinning skull of his mother's corpse is superimposed. Through Norman's "puckered, mobile features," Peter Cowie comments, "Hitchcock projects an image of humanity clamped in its private trap of frustration and anguish. *Psycho* is not only Hitchcock's greatest film; it is the most intelligent and disturbing horror film ever made."[2] No doubt about it.

Yet after he finished the picture Hitchcock, who financed the film himself, had serious misgivings about its commercial possibilities. (He was even disappointed in the way the shower sequence had turned out, until Herrmann underscored its power with the impressive musical backup already described.) The director feared that it would be dismissed as a low budget potboiler and be dumped on the grind circuit for exhibition in drive-ins and soft-core porn houses. Herrmann once told Brian De Palma, whose own 1980 *Dressed to Kill* was "inspired" by *Psycho*, that he remembered Hitchcock telling him in a moment of panic that *Psycho* "was awful and that he was going to cut it down for his television show."[3] The composer, a volatile, outspoken little man, scoffed at the very idea; but neither he nor Hitchcock could have known at that stage that they had an unqualified masterpiece on their hands, and that with it they had both reached the zenith of their respective careers.

Because *Psycho* is a supreme triumph of the motion picture art, one questions the temerity of the producers who made a sequel to such a classic film more than two decades hence, even when the cast includes Anthony Perkins playing Norman Bates once more. (In Richard Franklin's *Psycho II* Norman has been recently released from the institution to which he was consigned twenty-two years before, at the end of the Hitchcock *Psycho*.) What *Psycho II* (1983) does not have—except when it uses the original shower sequence from Hitchcock's film as a pre-credit sequence—is the genius of the maestro. The closing credits state that "the producers wish to acknowledge their debt to Sir Alfred Hitchcock." That is putting it mildly.

The Birds

Given the references to birds in *Psycho*, it is not surprising that Hitchcock's next movie would be called *The Birds* (1963). It was also, coincidentally, his third Daphne Du Maurier adaptation, after *Jamaica Inn* and *Rebecca*. At this point Hitchcock changed studios for the last time in his career, moving to Universal, where his television series—and *Psycho*—was shot, and on whose back lot the Bates's old dark house still stands.

Hitchcock had once quipped that he envied Walt Disney because working with a herd of trained animals was much less trouble than coaching a single actor. He also thought Disney lucky because the characters in his animated films "are made on paper; when he doesn't like them, he can tear them up."⁴ The closest Hitchcock ever came to making a Disney film was when he collaborated with one of Disney's technicians, Ub Iwerks, on the special effects for *The Birds*.

The film of course involved a great deal of technical trickery to simulate realistically the attacks of man's erstwhile fine feathered friends on the population of a small California coastal town. For the film's final shot, which shows that the birds have occupied the town like an invading army for as far as the eye can see, different groups of birds were photographed at varying distances from the camera, and bits of all of these individual shots were then combined into a single panoramic image. One small section of that final apocalyptic image, Hitchcock recalled, "was shot down a road with five hundred ducks painted grey. . . . It's by far the most complicated single shot I've ever done."⁵

Not all of its special effects worked out as well as the movie's closing image. But Hitchcock firmly believed that audiences would accept an imperfectly contrived special effect so long as their emotions were engaged by the action. That is why, incidentally, moviegoers tend to notice the rather phony process photography that occasionally turns up in *Marnie* (e.g., the fox-hunt scene), while they usually take in stride the special effects in the present film, which is by contrast much more emotionally absorbing than the relatively mediocre, slow-paced *Marnie*.

No explanation is ever offered in *The Birds* for the sudden and unexpected hostility towards humanity that prompts flocks of ordinarily pacific creatures to lay seige to this village, but then one is not really required. Here Hitchcock wishes to examine, as he had already done in such films as *Lifeboat*, how human beings react when thrown together in a crisis, regardless of its cause. If the upheaval that the characters have to contend with in *The Birds* had been an air raid, he said, with planes instead of birds raining havoc from the heavens, the theme of the movie would have remained the same.

Thus, self-centered New York socialite Melanie Daniels (Tippi Hedren), a poor little rich girl who grew up as a bird in a gilded cage, is, like her counterpart Constance Porter in *Lifeboat*, greatly humanized by helping the others with whom she is marooned in a country house during the period of this cataclysm. The most effective use of the movie's birdcage imagery occurs in the scene in which Melanie is trapped in a telephone booth while a flock of birds assault it from all directions in a frenzied attempt to shatter the glass and break in. As Hitchcock himself has commented, Melanie is still in a cage, but it is no longer gilded. Moreover, this scene also sums up the plight of the entire populace, for, as Hitchcock noted, it represents a reversal of the age-old conflict between man and bird, since in this instance human beings are in the cage and the birds are outside.

Perhaps Robin Wood crystallized the movie's theme best when he wrote that the birds "are a concrete embodiment of the arbitrary and unpredictible, of whatever makes human life and human relationships precarious, a reminder of the fragility and instability" of earthly existence that "cannot be ignored or evaded."[6]

Marnie

An unhappy flaw in both *The Birds* and *Marnie* (1964) is the casting of Tippi Hedren as the heroine. Hitchcock had planned to use Grace Kelly in *Marnie* in the title role of a compulsive thief. But Princess Grace's subjects publicly questioned the propriety of her accepting the role of "a lady robber," as Hitchcock called Marnie.[7] Therefore he chose Ms. Hedren, who simply never managed to embody satisfactorily the image of the Hitchcock blonde, a lady whose cool exterior belies the fiery passions burning within—a screen image the director had carefully cultivated in his female stars from Anny Ondra in the 1920s onward, and which Grace Kelly personified to perfection. In the case of Tippi Hedren, the glacial exterior seemed to conceal not an inner fire, but only more ice. Hence she was never able to convey convincingly that the character she was playing was capable of melting into a warm human being, as the script required her to do in both of her Hitchcock films.

In *Marnie* the heroine's rich husband Mark Rutland (Sean Connery) accepts the challenge of attempting to uncover the roots of his wife's neurotic problems by getting her to recall the traumatic childhood experience that she has unconsciously suppressed. At last, with the help of her mother, a wartime prostitute, he is able to make Marnie remember (in flashback) the harrowing night when she clubbed to death with a poker the sailor whom she mistakenly thought was attacking her mother.

The image of the crimson blood running down the sailor's T-shirt, viewed in vivid close-up in the flashback, explains the instances earlier in the film when the sight of any red and white object, such as the scarlet-and-cream outfits worn by the participants in a fox hunt, would trigger a hysterical reaction in Marnie. Her subjective experience at these times is signified by the color red suffusing the screen, pouring downward from the top of the frame to the bottom, in much the same way that the blood of the mortally wounded seaman (Bruce Dern) saturated his shirt. Marnie's compulsive thievery, therefore, was at least partially founded in a subconscious desire to "repay" her mother with a never-ending succession of gifts for taking the rap for the killing that had been virtually wiped from her memory until Mark compelled her to summon it to consciousness.

As Mark and Marnie leave her mother's home, where she has just relived this painful childhood experience, a group of children can be heard chanting a jingle while they skip rope on the sidewalk: "Mother, mother, I am ill; send for the doctor over the hill./Call for the doctor, call for the nurse, call for the lady with the alligator purse." In the context of what has just transpired, the words of this ditty take on added significance: Because the guilt-ridden, mentally ill Marnie felt that she was fundamentally unlovable, she had secretly feared that she would never have any children of her own. Hence she took to cramming her pouchy, womblike purse with stolen loot, not only for the reason already given, but as subconscious compensation for her empty uterus. Indeed, the very first shot in the film is a close-up of Marnie's huge handbag, already bulging with ill-gotten funds. As Mark explains to her, "When a child of any age feels unloved, it takes what it can get, however it can get it."

At film's end Marnie is on the road to recovering her mental health, but she has experienced no miraculous cure. The Hitchcock who as a boy was terrified by father figures such as priests and policemen knew better than to suggest that childhood traumas are easily eradicated; so the film is not mere "cookbook Freud," as one reviewer suggested, giving easy solutions to psychic problems.

For various reasons, *Marnie* was the last film to which some long-time Hitchcock associates contributed, including editor George Tomasini, who had cut every Hitchcock film since *Rear Window,* and cinematographer Robert Burks, whose creative association with the director dated back to *Strangers on a Train.* Both men died after *Marnie* was completed. This was also the last Hitchcock picture for which a Bernard Herrmann score was used, and thereby hangs a tale.

Torn Curtain

Herrmann, whom Hitchcock had sought to employ as early as *Spellbound*, had made a significant contribution to every Hitchcock film from *The Trouble with Harry* to *Marnie*, including helping with the toneless, electronic score of *The Birds* and leading the London Symphony Orchestra on screen in his version of the "Storm Cloud Cantata" in the second *Man Who Knew too Much*. Yet Hitchcock rejected Herrmann's incidental music for *Torn Curtain* (1966), probably because, after the box office failure of *Marnie*, the front office strongly suggested that Herrmann's music was "old-fashioned" and that he should be replaced by a younger composer who could create a snappy, contemporary-sounding score that might yield a hit single that would help promote the film with teenage moviegoers.

Instead of discarding Herrmann's "old-fashioned" score, Hitchcock should have held on to it and simply hired a song-writing team to supply a hummable tune that Julie Andrews, one of the stars of *Torn Curtain*, could have performed in the film and recorded as a single. (Audiences were in fact disappointed that she did not sing a note in the movie.) This, after all, is what Hitchcock had done a decade earlier when he had had Herrmann handle the background music for the remake of *The Man Who Knew too Much*, but brought in Jay Livingston and Ray Evans to write the Oscar-winning "Que Será Será" ("Whatever will be, will be") for Doris Day to sing in the film and to record.

As things happened, however, Hitchcock listened to Herrmann conduct some selections from the *Torn Curtain* score at the studio, decided that the somber, pulsating symphonic music was not the sort of thing that he had commissioned Herrmann to write, and reluctantly told him so on the spot. Then he stalked out of the room and went out and got himself another composer for the film, thus satisfying the studio brass. With that, Hitchcock ended one of the most fruitful associations of composer and director in the history of motion pictures.

It is no reflection on John Addison, who wrote a serviceable substitute score for *Torn Curtain*, that he was no match for Herrmann, who had consistently provided Hitchcock with richly textured orchestral music that was emminently attuned to the director's dramatic requirements. It should come as no surprise that the soundtrack recordings of Herrmann's scores for Hitchcock's films—including the one he did for *Torn Curtain*, which was not used—have deservedly become collectors' items, the only scores for Hitchcock's films that have.

Torn Curtain, together with *Topaz*, are a matching pair of Hitchcock films about the cold war; and ironically, they are both cold films that, like *Secret Agent* and *Sabotage*, present a dim, disenchanted view of the business of being a secret agent.

Torn Curtain begins and ends with Michael Armstrong (Paul Newman) and Sarah Sherman (Julie Andrews) huddled together under a blanket, as if they were trying unsuccessfully to remain insulated from the chilly atmosphere of the cold war. Michael is still another Hitchcock hero whose motives for acting as he does are more mixed than perhaps even he is himself aware. He is an American scientist who agrees to try to make a tear in the Iron Curtain by pretending to defect to East Germany to steal an antimissile formula from a scientist working there. But he does so not so much to help his country as to regain a government subsidy he has forfeited because he could not work out the vital details of the plans himself.

One of the many repulsive things he has to do in carrying out his mission is destroy Gromek (Wolfgang Kieling), a Soviet agent who guesses that Michael is really an American agent and not a defector at all. That Michael's grim odyssey is something of a descent into hell, in which he and others will be purified through the fires of suffering, is suggested in the fantastic credit sequence. It depicts an inferno of leaping orange flames and clouds of smoke from which there materialize the blue-lit, anguished faces of Michael and other key characters. The reference to hell is further underscored late in the film when a ballet based on an episode in Dante's *Inferno* is seen in performance.

The grisly killing of Gromek, referred to above, represents the longest (ten minutes) murder sequence Hitchcock ever shot. Michael, along with a female accomplice no more adept at mayhem than he is, corner their intended victim in a farmhouse kitchen. Because their burly adversary refuses to die, they must transform a variety of household utensils, from soup kettle to butcher knife, into instant weapons in their concerted effort to exterminate him. In this context one readily recalls the scissors in *Dial M for Murder* and the carving knife in *Sabotage* as other examples of domestic items put to deadly use, not to mention the frozen leg of lamb in the teleplay "Lamb to the Slaughter." As a last resort, Michael and his co-conspirator finally force Gromek's head into a gas oven, and in doing so unwittingly summon up the spectre of Auschwitz. In an overhead shot, Gromek's hands are seen gradually relaxing their defensive grip on Michael's neck; they flutter feebly and then fall limply to the floor.

"Even if we win, we ultimately lose," is Richard Schickel's comment on this episode in the script of the TV documentary he did about Hitchcock. For the hero has been dragged down to the ruthless and barbarous level of behavior he had previously decried in the enemy. Hitchcock too has remarked about the sequence that he wanted to show that killing someone involves "a very long and painful process."[8] This was his way of indicating that the work of a secret agent can be dirty and disillusioning, thereby debunking the notion that undercover work is the carefree fun that slick spy films of the James Bond variety make it out to be.

Hitchcock, in consultation with cinematographer John Warren, who had photographed the only two of Hitchcock's half-hour television films ("Dip in the Pool" and "The Crystal Trench") not shot by John Russell, decided that the movie's visual style should reflect the drab, dreary milieu of life behind the Iron Curtain in East Germany. They did so by employing an essentially monochromatic palette of colors that accentuated muted shadows of gray, cream, and beige. Warren also emphasized the film's fundamentally gloomy atmosphere by frequently covering his camera lens with gray gauze and by bouncing the illumination from the battery of huge lamps on the set off white canvas reflectors, which caused soft, indirect illumination to be diffused throughout the shooting area. By this means he created the flat, overcast, pallid look for the film that Hitchcock had asked for.

For the record, the cold, metallic "Iron Curtain" sound that pervaded Herrmann's rejected music for the movie highlighted the brass section of the orchestra. It would have proved a haunting counterpart to the chilly, austere visual design of the movie, had Hitchcock not succumbed to studio pressure and jettisoned it.

Topaz

The script of *Topaz* (1969), like *Torn Curtain*, gives a sardonic slant to its presentation of international espionage. Andre Dévereaux (Frederick Stafford), a French counterspy employed by the United States government at the time of the Cuban missile crisis in 1962, seeks to uncover the identity of Topaz, the code name for a French double agent spying for the Russians in Paris. Topaz is really Jacques Granville (Michel Piccoli), a highly placed French government official.

An interesting sidelight on the film is that Hitchcock experimented with no fewer than three different resolutions before finally settling on the one eventually approved for the release prints, calling to mind the multiple endings of *Suspicion*. In the first denouement that Hitchcock concocted, Dévereaux and Granville have what amounts to an old-fashioned pistol duel on a deserted Paris football field. Granville is brought down by a bullet fired not by Dévereaux, but by a sharpshooter hidden in the arena stands, on orders from Granville's Russian employers who have no further use for him.

This scene was scrapped after the picture was previewed, however, perhaps because the narrative exposition necessary to lead up to it needlessly protracted the running time of a movie that was already too long and whose story line was already too complicated.

Hence Hitchcock recalled cast and crew to shoot an alternate scene, one that I happened to see at a private screening of the film. This time Granville, who is boarding a plane that will carry him into exile behind the Iron Curtain, turns to wave flippantly at Dévereaux as the latter prepares to get on a plane bound for Washington. The French government allows Granville to get away and thus avoids admitting publicly that he has hoodwinked them for so long. Nevertheless, Hitchcock scuttled this perfectly plausible resolution, too, perhaps because he feared that audiences would feel frustrated and dissatisfied that a disreputable traitor has been allowed to get away, despite the fact that it is unlikely that this bungling double agent will receive a very warm reception from the Russians. (Hitchcock had no qualms about allowing the villains of both *Saboteur* and *Vertigo* to elude capture successfully.)

In any event, the director hastily manufactured still another wrap-up just before the film was released. In this instance he employed the simple expedient of repeating a shot of Granville's house used earlier in the movie and freezing it on the screen while a gun shot is heard off screen, signaling that Granville blew his brains out after Dévereaux blew his cover. In this way the treasonous Granville's retribution is brought about in the most swift and straightforward manner possible, since he is disposed of with a single shot, in both senses of the word.

The scene just discussed is followed by a codalike epilogue that presents a series of shots picturing all the people who risked or lost their lives in the course of the film helping Dévereaux to fulfill his mission. This montage is superimposed on a shot of a man on a park bench pouring over a newspaper account of the Cuban missile crisis just ended. Then the man tosses the newspaper into a trash can and nonchalantly goes on his way. This tableau, which depicts the kind of anonymous casualties who are behind the big news stories that are headlined in the press, is, like the credit sequence in *Torn Curtain*, a thought-provoking reminder of the terrible toll of suffering and death that the game of secret agentry exacts of the players.

Hitchcock's last-minute tampering with the film reflects his own dissatisfaction with it; critics and public alike agreed that, in spite of the fact that the movie was his most expensive film ever, *Topaz* was not the finely cut gem they had hoped it would be. One critic compared the overpopulated plot to a relay race in which a fresh set of characters seems to take over the telling of the complex story every time Dévereaux's work brings him to another country. Hence, this reviewer complained with good reason that the beleaguered spectator has difficulty trying to keep track of all of the players without a score card.

Conversely, the director's next film fulfilled just about everyone's expectations of what a vintage Hitchcock thriller could be.

Frenzy

The story line of *Frenzy* (1972), which was derived from Arthur La Bern's novel *Goodbye, Piccadilly, Farewell Leicester Square*, in essence recapitulates the Jack the Ripper plot of Hitchcock's first major motion picture, *The Lodger*, made almost a half-century before. Also, it was shot in London where the director's career began. Thus with *Frenzy*, Hitchcock's professional life in a real sense had come full circle. Here once again is the archetypal Hitchcock hero intrepidly chasing down the criminal of whose crimes he is himself falsely accused. Meanwhile the police pursue him because, as one character acridly comments, the cops have, "as usual, got everything ass-about-face."

Richard Blaney (Jon Finch) is thought to be the "necktie murderer," a sexual psychopath terrorizing London, because both his estranged wife Brenda Blaney (Barbara Leigh-Hunt) and his girl friend Babs Milligan (Anna Massey) have fallen victim to the killer. The real maniac, however, is none other than Richard's old mate Bob Rusk (Barry Foster), whose amiability marks him as one of Hitchcock's superficially attractive psychotics, a long line of lunatics that reaches back to Levet, the villain of his very first film, *The Pleasure Garden*.

Hitchcock wisely depicts only one of Rusk's hideous rape-murders in detail, that of Brenda, since, once the filmgoer has witnessed one of these atrocities, the director need only suggest thereafter that another is taking place off screen. Thus when Rusk leads the unsuspecting Babs into his flat, the camera stops at the doorway and does not venture to follow them inside. Instead it slowly retreats down the shadowy staircase and out into the sunshine of the busy street, as if recoiling from the unspeakable act that is taking place behind curtained windows. Once outside, the camera pauses for a moment to survey the pedestrians going about their business unaware of what is transpiring inside the building. By means of this brilliantly executed shot, Hitchcock once more reminds his audience, perhaps more effectively than he ever had before, of his disturbing conviction that catastrophe surrounds us all, and can strike when we least expect it.

Frenzy also yields several rich examples of Hitchcock's characteristically ghoulish humor, as when Inspector Oxford (Alec McCowen), the police inspector in charge of the case, who happens to be the most downright likeable cop in all of Hitchcock's films, explains over dinner to his wife (Vivien Merchant) how the culprit had to pry open the stiffened fingers of Babs's corpse with a pocket knife to recover the initialed stickpin Babs had torn from his coat lapel while she struggled with him. As Oxford describes how the murderer sytematically snapped open each

Barry Foster overpowering Barbara Leigh-Hunt in Frenzy
*(1972), which marked Hitchcock's return to form. (Credit: The
Cinema Bookshop, London)*

of his victim's fingers to retrieve the incriminating object, his wife
appropriately accompanies him by absentmindedly breaking bread
sticks as she listens.

At another point, when a repulsively fat barmaid remarks to a customer that the necktie murderer always rapes his victims before killing
them, the chap gives the sex-starved creature the once-over and quips,
"Every cloud has a silver lining."

I was fortunate enough to be on hand one day in the summer of 1971
when Hitchcock was shooting a location scene for *Frenzy* in the minipark
in the center of London's Leicester Square. He tended to stay unobtrusively on the sidelines out of the way of the crew while they set up each
shot according to his detailed advance instructions. Then, when all was
in readiness, he would come forward and watch the filming. When the
day's shooting was completed, the director climbed into his limousine
and disappeared from sight, having conducted himself in the same
formal, detached fashion while shooting in the open air in downtown
London that customarily characterized his manner when filming in the
controlled atmosphere of a sound stage.

Family Plot

In January 1975, following a mild heart attack, Hitchcock had a pacemaker installed in his chest shortly before starting work in earnest on what would be his last completed film, *Family Plot* (1976). Although his health was not what it had been, he assured everyone that his batteries were fully charged, and applied himself with his usual verve to collaborating on the screenplay with Ernest Lehman (*North by Northwest*). He clearly had no intention of retiring. When a tactless journalist inquired what the mandatory retirement age for directors in Hollywood was, he responded courteously that he thought it was somewhere around reel twelve.

The movie, which was based on Victor Canning's suspense novel, *The Rainbird Pattern*, turned out to be a good film, though not in a class with *Frenzy*. Mrs. Julia Rainbird (Cathleen Nesbitt), a wealthy dowager, enlists the aid of a fake medium, Blanche Tyler (Barbara Harris) and the medium's boyfriend George Lumley (Bruce Dern) in finding her last surviving relative, so that she can bequeath her entire estate to him. The two amateur sleuths do track down the long-lost heir, who turns out to be a master kidnapper going by the name of Adamson (William Devane). Adamson fears that Blanche and George will discover the secret scheme he and Fran, his accomplice (Karen Black) have hatched to abduct an archbishop. Adamson is more interested in the ransom the church dignitary will bring than in acquiring the Rainbird fortune legally.

Principal photography for the film commenced at Universal on May 12, 1975, and included location work in Los Angeles and San Francisco. Some time after shooting was completed on August 18 (about thirteen days over schedule), I asked Devane how he found working with Hitchcock. "Acting in a Hitchcock film is just the way it has always been described," the actor told me. "He really does have the entire film worked out in his own mind, right down to the last detail, before he steps onto the studio floor. As a result, the shooting moves along very smoothly, but it's not very challenging to shoot a film that is so carefully worked out in advance." Other actors have said that they at times have found themselves stretching to be inventive within the tight framework Hitchcock set up for them. Therefore in the end they perhaps did a better job than they would have had they been allowed more freedom of interpretation and movement. Nonetheless, Devane said he still preferred directors who allowed him more leeway.

Significantly, Hitchcock's cameo appearance in *Family Plot* consists in his silhouette being viewed through the frosted glass of an office door. This vision of his portly profile, seen "through a glass darkly" (which recalls the way he appeared at the beginning of his TV show each week)

Modish Karen Black in Hitchcock's last film, Family Plot *(1976). (Credit: Cannes Film Festival)*

was hardly meant to imply that the director was but a shadow of his former self. On the contrary, in the context of the remarks that William Devane and other actors have made about Hitchcock's total control over a production, the director's signature appearance in the film brings into relief how his shadow fell across every aspect of the film-making process, from script to scoring.

Ernest Lehman told me when he appeared with *Family Plot* at the Cannes Film Festival in 1976 that, although he spent several months working on the script on his own after some preliminary conferences with the director, "somehow the picture turned out the way *he* wanted it to. He always gets his own way, and I have never figured out how he does it." Neither, as we have seen, could Raymond Chandler, who grudgingly admitted that in the end *Strangers on a Train* was clearly a Hitchcock picture, not a Chandler picture. As Samuel Taylor, who worked on the screenplays of *Vertigo* and *Topaz*, put it at the Lincoln Center gala, Hitchcock was a genuine auteur, the true author of every film he made.

One only has to read Canning's novel to see how Hitchcock changed much more than the title to bring it into line with his own creative impulses. The key kidnapping episode is not directly depicted in the book at all, but it is a major sequence in the film, elaborately staged in San Francisco's Grace Cathedral. John Russell Taylor has noted that "clearly the idea of snatching a bishop in the midst of High Mass, before the eyes of a crowded congregation, has a special devilish appeal for Hitchcock, the one-time sufferer from strict Jesuit schooling."[9] The director's motive for opting to depict the abduction graphically probably had less to do with the discipline he associated with his days in a Jesuit prep school than with a canny movie maker's wish to capture a colorful and exciting sequence on film. (It is true, however, that Hitchcock's religious training made him adept at portraying Catholic ritual on the screen in authentic detail, as he does here, and in *I Confess* and his telefilm "The Horseplayer.")

"These so-called 'Catholic touches' in Hitchcock's films are often as much the work of Jewish screenwriters like myself as they are of Hitchcock himself," Lehman explained. "In the present instance, we realized that having the bishop kidnapped while vacationing in the country, which is what happens in the novel, would not be as interesting as showing the kidnapping taking place right in the middle of a Sunday service." Hitchcock agreed, adding on another occasion that the abduction of a bishop should take place at the moment when he is functioning most evidently as a bishop; kidnap him alone in a wood, the director said, and he might as well be a stockbroker.

Hitchcock accomplished the abduction scene in a quick succession of short, separate shots. While the prelate is making his way to the pulpit,

Adamson, dressed in clerical garb, unobtrusively sinks a hypodermic needle into his arm, and then spirits the unconscious man out of the church into a waiting car before anyone in the packed congregation gets an inkling of what has transpired.

Commenting on this sequence, Taylor observed that it is hard to believe that the man who directed it made his first feature a half century before that; "and yet there is a dogged line of consistency through everything he has done." For a sequence such as the one in the cathedral, "with its rapid montage, its emphasis on visual story-telling, could be transplanted complete to the silent cinema."[10] Because Hitchcock joined the film industry long before the movies learned to talk, he clearly developed at the outset of his career a respect for the primacy of the visual over the verbal that served him well the rest of his days.

9

Epilogue: The Touch of Class

FRANCOIS TRUFFAUT WAS NOT EXAGGERATING when he said that during Hitchcock's career the director created "a staggering body of work—the richest, longest, and most complete filmography of the directors who began in silent film."[1] Nor is it an overstatement to suggest that Hitchcock was a creative artist who impressed the entire corpus of his work with the unmistakable stamp of his own style and vision, as I have tried to demonstrate.

There is consequently a discernible line of consistency in his work, as Taylor noted at the end of the previous chapter. Nevertheless, as one who shares Hitchcock's Catholic, Jesuit background, I feel compelled to say that any attempt to ransack his films with a view to uncovering a coherent religious philosophy in them, would be imprudent. Asked if there was a search for God in his films, the director responded thoughtfully, "A search for good? Oh, yes. . . . A search for God? Maybe."[2] Elsewhere he added that it was useless to attribute profound metaphysical intentions to him. As a matter of fact, all the "philosophical" theories about his work, as far as he was concerned, "hold no water at all."[3]

This is not to suggest that Hitchcock's films do not dish up much food for thought for the reflective moviegoer to digest. But he does this by implicit suggestion, not by explicit statement. Indeed, many moviegoers have come away from his movies with more than just the satisfaction of being entertained, as *Newsweek* once noted. They also carry with them some sobering thoughts about human nature: that people are not always what they seem, neither as good nor as bad as they perhaps might at first appear; or that good and evil can bundle together, like sly lovers, in the same personality. In addition, the more perceptive filmgoers might just realize that these same truths also apply in some degree to themselves, and not just to others. In Hitchcock's own words, if one has been brought up by the Jesuits, "as I was, these elements are bound to intrude."[4]

Hitchcock with Tippi Hedren pre-planning a scene for The Birds *(1963), carrying on an essential part of his work from the earliest days. (Credit: Larry Edmonds's Cinema Bookshop)*

Throughout his last years Hitchcock was moved by the recognition that he received from various quarters. These acknowledgments included the Lincoln Center tribute, and the coveted Irving Thalberg Award he received at the 1967 Academy Award ceremonies, perhaps in belated acknowledgment of the fact that, although he had been nominated for an Oscar as the best director for *Rebecca, Lifeboat, Spellbound, Rear Window,* and *Psycho,* it had never been conferred upon him. Never at a loss for wit, he always expressed his appreciation for these accolades with humor: after accepting the Thalberg Award, he said he had not minded never getting an Oscar for being best director because he already had a doorstop. He was also knighted by Queen Elizabeth II a few months before his death.

Sir Alfred Hitchcock died at the age of eighty on April 20, 1980, primarily of arthritis and kidney ailments, in his home in the Bel Air section of Los Angeles. Hitchcock's old friend, Jesuit Father Thomas Sullivan of Loyola-Marymount University, who had years before served as religious advisor on *I Confess,* presided at the funeral rites held in Good Shepherd Church in Beverly Hills, after which the body was cremated.

It has been said that artists like Hitchcock helped to popularize the thriller by taking murder out of the rose garden and dropping it into the alley. He put it quite differently in the remarks he addressed to the audience at the close of the Lincoln Center gala; and it seems altogether appropriate as this study draws to a close to let him have his last whimsical word by quoting from that "curtain speech," which he recorded on film in advance of the occasion. One can almost hear his TV theme, "Funeral March of a Marionette," playing in the background as he says:

As I do not approve of the current wave of violence that we see on our screens, I have always felt that murder should be treated delicately; and, in addition, that with the help of television, murder should be brought into the home where it rightly belongs. Some of our most exquisite murders have been domestic, [probably referring to *Sabotage* and *Psycho*] performed with tenderness in simple, homey places like the kitchen table or the bathtub. Nothing is more revolting to my sense of decency than the underworld thug who is able to murder anyone—even people to whom he has not been properly introduced. After all, I'm sure you will agree that murder can be so much more charming and enjoyable, even for the victim, if the surroundings are pleasant.

Then he concluded, "They tell me that a murder is committed every minute, so I don't want to waste any more of your time. I know you want to get to work."

In eulogizing Hitchcock after his death, Ernest Lehman said that while writing a screenplay for a Hitchcock movie one was always aware "that the fact that it was a *Hitchcock* made it ultimately memorable. And there *are* no Hitchcocks any more, God rest his soul."[5]

Amen to that.

Notes and References

Chapter One

1.   Alfred Hitchcock, "Production Methods Compared," in Richard Koszarski, ed., *Hollywood Directors: 1941–76* (New York, 1977), pp. 156, 160. N.B.: Any direct quotations from Hitchcock that are unfootnoted are derived from television interviews given by the director during the last few years of his life.
2.   Pete Martin, "Hitchcock," in Harry M. Geduld, ed., *Film Makers on Film Making* (Bloomington: Indiana University Press, 1969), pp. 127–28.
3.   Ibid., p. 128.
4.   Charles Higham and Joel Greenberg, "Alfred Hitchcock," in *The Celluloid Muse* (New York: New American Library, 1972), pp. 103, 98.
5.   Roger Manvell, *New Cinema in the USA* (New York: Dutton, 1968), p. 43.
6.   Gorham Anders Kindem, *Toward a Semiotic Theory of Visual Communication: The Color Films of Alfred Hitchcock* (New York: Arno, 1980), p. 75.
7.   Maurice Yacowar, *Hitchcock's British Films* (Hamden, Conn., 1977), p. 14.
8.   "Hitchcock's Three Nightmares," *Newsweek*, January 24, 1966, p. 89.
9.   George Sadoul, *Dictionary of Film Makers*, trans. and ed. Peter Morris (Berkeley: University of California Press, 1972), pp. 116–17.
10.   Richard Schickel, "Alfred Hitchcock," in *The Men Who Made the Movies* (New York: Atheneum, 1975), p. 273.

Chapter Two

1.   Oriana Fallaci, "Alfred Hitchcock," in *The Egotists* (Chicago: Regnery, 1963), p. 249.
2.   Francois Truffaut, *Hitchcock* (New York: Simon and Schuster, 1967), p. 18.
3.   Fallaci, "Alfred Hitchcock," p. 244.
4.   Bob Thomas, "Alfred Hitchcock," in Bob Thomas, ed., *Directors in Action* (New York: Bobbs-Merrill, 1973), p. 28.
5.   Yocawar, *Hitchcock's British Films*, p. 20.
6.   Truffaut, *Hitchcock*, p. 31.

7.   Lindsay Anderson, "Alfred Hitchcock," in Albert J. La Valley, ed., *Focus on Hitchcock* (Englewood Cliffs, N.J., 1972), p. 50.
8.   Herb A. Lightman, "Hitchcock Talks about Lights, Camera, Action," *American Cinematographer,* May 1967, p. 333.
9.   John K. Newnham, "My Screen Memories," *Film Weekly* (London), May 9, 1936, p. 7.
10.   Alfred Hitchcock, "Film Production," in *Encyclopedia Britannica,* vol. 15 (1972), 908.

Chapter Three

1.   John Russell Taylor, *Hitch: The Life and Times of Alfred Hitchcock* (New York, 1978), p. 104.
2.   John Grierson, "Directors of the Thirties," in Daniel Talbot, ed., *Film: An Anthology* (Berkeley: University of California Press, 1966), p. 122.
3.   George Perry, *The Films of Alfred Hitchcock* (New York: Dutton, 1965), p. 45.
4.   *Graham Greene on Film,* ed. John Russell Taylor (New York: Simon and Schuster, 1972), p. 222.
5.   Donal Henahan, "He Served as 'Pilot' for Frederick Delius," *New York Times,* June 28, 1981, p. 2.

Chapter Four

1.   Robert Harris and Michael Lasky, *The Films of Alfred Hitchcock* (Seacaucus, N.J.: Citadel, 1976), p. 64.
2.   Yacowar, *Hitchcock's British Films,* p. 300.
3.   Taylor, ed., *Greene on Film,* p. 123.
4.   Alfred Hitchcock, "Direction," in *Focus on Hitchcock,* pp. 34–35.
5.   Charles Thomas Samuels, "Sir Carol Reed," in *Encountering Directors* (New York: Putnam, 1972), p. 167.
6.   Andre Bazin, "Hitchcock Versus Hitchcock," in *Focus on Hitchcock,* p. 64.
7.   Pauline Kael. *I Lost it at the Movies* (New York: Bantam Books, 1966), p. 8.
8.   *Focus on Hitchcock,* pp. 52, 53.

Chapter Five

1.   *Memo from: David O. Selznick,* ed. Rudy Behlmer (New York: Avon Books, 1973), p. 313.
2.   Truffaut, *Hitchcock,* p. 144.
3.   Ronald Haver, *David O. Selznick's Hollywood* (New York: Knopf, 1980), p. 321.
4.   Alfred Hitchcock, "Murder—With English on It," *New York Times Magazine,* March 3, 1957, p. 42.
5.   Martin, "Hitchcock," p. 131.

6. Cf. Fallaci, "Alfred Hitchcock," p. 245.
7. David Freeman, "The Last Days of Alfred Hitchcock," *Esquire*, April 1982, p. 94.
8. Harris and Lasky, *Films*, p. 119.
9. Charles Higham and Joel Greenberg, "The Forties," in Peter Cowie, ed., *Hollywood: 1920–70* (New York: Barnes, 1977), p. 120.
10. Vito Russo, *The Celluloid Closet: Homosexuality in the Movies* (New York: Harper and Row, 1981), p. 62.
11. Ingrid Bergman with Alan Burgess, *My Story* (New York: Dell Books, 1981), pp. 234–35.
12. Ibid., p. 200.
13. Gavin Lambert, "Hitchcock and the Art of Suspense: Part I," *American Film*, January–February 1976, p. 23.
14. Truffaut, *Hitchcock*, p. 118.
15. Tony Thomas, *Gregory Peck* (New York: Pyramid Books, 1977), p. 52.
16. Higham and Greenberg, *The Celluloid Muse*, p. 103.
17. Behlmer, ed., *Memo from: Selznick*, p. 345.
18. Charles Higham, *Hollywood Cameramen* (Bloomington: Indiana University Press, 1970), p. 50.
19. James Agee, *Agee on Film* (New York: Grosset and Dunlap, 1969), p. 71.
20. Behlmer, ed., *Memo from: Selznick*, p. 453.
21. Higham and Greenberg, *The Celluloid Muse*, p. 105.

Chapter Six

1. Russo, *Celluloid Closet*, p. 94.
2. Gordon Gow, "The Fifties," in *Hollywood: 1920–70*, p. 184.
3. Frank MacShane, "Stranger in a Studio: Raymond Chandler and Hollywood: Part II," *American Film*, May 1976, pp. 57–59.
4. Raymond Chandler, "Notebooks on *Strangers on a Train*," in *Focus on Hitchcock*, p. 102.
5. Larry McMurtry, "Selected Letters of Raymond Chandler," *New York Times Book Review*, November 15, 1981, p. 46.
6. Alfred Hitchcock, "*Rear Window*," in *Focus on Hitchcock*, p. 42.
7. Gow, "The Fifties," p. 174.
8. Robert LaGuardia, *Monty* (New York: Avon Books, 1977), p. 98.
9. Hilda Black, "The Photography Is Important to Hitchcock: *I Confess*," *American Cinematographer*, December 1952, p. 547.
10. Frederick Foster, "Hitch Didn't Want it Arty," *American Cinematographer*, February 1957, p. 85.
11. Schickel, "Alfred Hitchcock," p. 276.
12. Truffaut, *Hitchcock*, p. 183.
13. Raymond Durgnat, *The Strange Case of Alfred Hitchcock*, Cambridge: MIT Press, 1974), p. 268.
14. Peter Bogdanovich, *Pieces of Time* (New York: Arbor House, 1973), p. 26.

15.   Gow, "The Fifties," p. 176.
16.   Robin Wood, *Hitchcock's Films* (New York, 1970), p. 106.
17.   Durgnat, *The Strange Case of Alfred Hitchcock*, p. 320.
18.   Hitchcock, "Direction," pp. 33–34.
19.   Bogdanovich, *Pieces of Time*, p. 137.

Chapter Seven

1.   Martin, "Hitchcock," p. 125.
2.   John Crosby, "Macabre Merriment," in *Focus on Hitchcock*, p. 139.
3.   Martin, "Hitchcock," pp. 129–30.
4.   Truffaut, *Hitchcock*, p. 211.

Chapter Eight

1.   Royal D. Brown, "Herrmann, Hitchcock, and the Music of the Irrational," *Cinema Journal*, Spring 1982, p. 35.
2.   Peter Cowie, *Seventy Years of Cinema* (New York: Barnes, 1969), p. 235.
3.   Brian De Palma, "Remembering Herrmann," *Take One* (Special Hitchcock Issue), May 1976, p. 41.
4.   Fallaci, "Alfred Hitchcock," p. 254.
5.   Higham and Greenberg, *The Celluloid Muse*, p. 112.
6.   Wood, *Hitchcock's Films*, p. 137.
7.   Fallaci, "Alfred Hitchcock," p. 255.
8.   "Hitchcock's Three Nightmares," p. 89.
9.   John Russell Taylor, "Hitchcock's Fifty Years in Films," *Times* (London), July 19, 1975, p. 7.
10.   Ibid.

Chapter Nine

1.   Francois Truffaut, "Hitchcock: His True Power is Emotion," *New York Times*, March 4, 1979, sec. 2, p. 1.
2.   Robert Haller, "Alfred Hitchcock: Beyond Suspense," in *American Motion Picture Directors* (Notre Dame, Ind.: Ave Maria Press, 1965), p. 22.
3.   Higham and Greenberg, *The Celluloid Muse*, p. 114.
4.   Charles Champlin, "Paying Homage to 'King Alfred,'" *Los Angeles Times*, March 7, 1979, sec. 4, p. 18.
5.   John Brady, "Ernest Lehman," in *The Craft of the Screenwriter* (New York: Simon and Schuster, 1981), p. 205.

Selected Bibliography

(Note: Some of the more significant research materials are highlighted here. Critical works which are subject to specific comment in the text, where they also receive a full note reference, are not mentioned again below.)

Books

La Valley, Albert J., ed. *Focus on Hitchcock.* Englewood Cliffs, N.J.: Prentice-Hall, 1972. A random sampling of reprints, including two essays in which Hitchcock discusses the art of direction.

Rohmer, Eric, and Claude Chabrol. *Hitchcock: The First Forty-Four Films.* Translated by Stanley Hochman. New York: Ungar, 1979. A sophisticated analysis of Hitchcock's work up to *The Wrong Man* (1956), emphasizing how he reshaped his literary sources according to his own personal vision.

Rothman, William. *Hitchcock: The Murderous Gaze.* Cambridge, Mass.: Harvard University Press, 1982. An analysis of five Hitchcock features that is so detailed that it at times drifts into overinterpretation.

Spoto, Donald. *The Art of Alfred Hitchcock.* New York: Hopkinson and Blake, 1976 (republished by Doubleday, 1979). A long-winded account of the films which, like just about every other critical study of the director, gives short shrift to his early English films and omits any consideration whatever of his wartime semi-documentaries and his TV films. Equally long-winded is Spoto's gossipy follow-up, *The Dark Side of Genius: The Life of Alfred Hitchcock.* Boston: Little, Brown, 1983. The author cheapens the substantial scholarly worth of the latter book by salting it with tawdry tidbits about the director's personal life.

Taylor, John Russell. *Hitch: The Life and Times of Alfred Hitchcock.* New York: Pantheon, 1978. Although this authorized biography contains material not available elsewhere, it paraphrases too many anecdotes already recorded elsewhere. Still, Spoto's unauthorized biography, for all its plethora of detail about Hitchcock's personal and public life, has not superseded it.

Truffaut, Francois. *Hitchcock.* With the collaboration of Helen Scott. New York: Simon and Schuster, 1967. An incisive book-length interview with the director, ending with *Torn Curtain.* It is by nature anecdotal, and treats in detail only those points the interviewee wished to pursue.

Weis, Elizabeth. *The Silent Screen: Alfred Hitchcock's Sound Track.* East Brunswick, N.J.: Fairleigh Dickinson University Press, 1982. The author concedes Hitchcock's desire to integrate musical and visual concepts in his films, then slights the director's close collaboration with composers like Bernard Herrmann for uncompelling reasons.

Wood, Robin. *Hitchcock's Films.* New York: Paperback Library, 1970. This study of some of the later films is certainly not the complete guide to Hitchcock's movies that the cover proclaims it to be, even in the 1977 version published by Barnes, which adds only a new introduction. Some of the author's more mercurial judgments in the book are rightly criticized in his essay, "Hitchcock: Lost in the Wood," which he wrote under the pretentious pseudonym of George Kaplan (the mythical spy in *North by Northwest*), which appears in Don Whittmore and Philip Alan Cecchettini, eds., *Passport to Hollywood* (New York: McGraw-Hill, 1976), pp. 370–84.

Yacowar, Maurice. *Hitchcock's British Films.* Hamden, Conn.: Archon Books, 1977. This study of Hitchcock's first twenty-three films is very good as far as it goes.

Parts of Books

Hitchcock, Alfred. "Film Production." In *The Encyclopedia Britannica*, vol. 15, 1972, pp. 907–10. This thorough analysis of the various phases of motion picture production appears in all editions of the encyclopedia issued between 1958 and 1972.

————. "Production Methods Compared." In Richard Koszarski, ed., *Hollywood Directors: 1941–76.* New York: Oxford University Press, 1977, pp. 156–61. Like the pieces by the director in *Focus on Hitchcock*, this 1949 essay is a revealing account of how Hitchcock viewed his craft.

Periodicals

Freeman, David. "The Last Days of Alfred Hitchcock." *Esquire*, April 1982, pp. 81–105. Although there is some interesting exclusive interview material with the director included here, this indiscreet article by the last screenwriter to work with him is a basically one-sided presentation of Hitchcock's final year or so of life, dwelling excessively on his drinking habits and his depression at being forced by ill health to abandon his last film project at the script stage. The Spoto biography covers Hitchcock's declining years in its later pages in a similar fashion.

Hitchcock, Alfred. "Murder—with English on it." *New York Times Magazine*, March 3, 1957, pp. 17, 42. A chatty discussion by the director of how the traditional English taste for mystery and crime yarns influenced his work.

Filmography

NUMBER THIRTEEN (unfinished) (Wardour and F., 1922)
Producer: Alfred Hitchcock
Director of Photography: Rosenthal
Cast: Clare Greet and Ernest Thesiger

THE PLEASURE GARDEN (Gainsborough/Emelka, 1926)
Producer: Michael Balcon
Script: Eliot Stannard, from the novel by Oliver Sandys
Director of Photography: Baron Giovanni Ventigmilia
Sets: C. Wilfred Arnold and Ludwig Reiber
Assistant Director: Alma Reville
Cast: Virginia Valli (Patsy Brand), Carmelita Geraghty (Jill Cheyne), Nita Naldi
(native girl), Miles Mander (Levet), and John Stuart (Hugh Fielding)
Running time: 7,058 feet (about 92 minutes)
Premiere: March 1926, London
16mm rental: Raymond Rohauer and Twyman

THE MOUNTAIN EAGLE (USA: *Fear O'God*) (Gainsborough/Emelka, 1926)
Producer: Michael Balcon
Script: Eliot Stannard and Charles Lapworth
Assistant Director: Alma Reville
Director of Photography: Baron Giovanni Ventigmilia
Sets: Willy and Ludwig Reiber
Cast: Bernard Goetzke (Judge Pettigrew), Nita Naldi (Beatrice), Malcolm Keen
(Fear O'God), and John Hamilton (Edward Pettigrew)
Running time: 7,503 feet (about 98 minutes)
Premiere: October 1926, London
16mm rental: The film is lost.

THE LODGER: A STORY OF THE LONDON FOG (Gainsborough, 1926)
Producer: Michael Balcon
Script: Alfred Hitchcock and Eliot Stannard, from the novel by Marie Belloc-
Lowndes
Director of Photography: Baron Giovanni Ventigmilia

Sets: C. Wilfred Arnold and Bertram Evans
Editor: Ivor Montagu
Assistant Director: Alma Reville
Cast: Ivor Novello (the lodger), June (Daisy Bunting), Marie Ault (Mrs. Bunting), Arthur Chesney (Mr. Bunting), and Malcolm Keen (Joe Betts)
Running time: 7,685 feet (about 100 minutes)
Premiere: September 1926, London (shot after *The Mountain Eagle* but released a month before it)
16mm rental: Films Inc., and Images Film Archive

DOWNHILL (USA: *When Boys Leave Home*) (Gainsborough, 1927)
Producer: Michael Balcon
Script: Eliot Stannard, from the play by David LeStrange (Ivor Novello and Constance Collier)
Director of Photography: Claude McDonnell
Editors: Ivor Montagu and Lionel Rich
Sets: Bertram Evans
Cast: Ivor Novello (Roddy Berwick), Ben Webster (Dr. Dowson), Robin Irvine (Tim Wakely), Sybil Rhoda (Sybil Wakely), and Lillian Braithwaite (Lady Berwick)
Running time: 8,635 feet (about 112 minutes)
Premiere: May 1927, London
16mm rental: Unavailable

EASY VIRTUE (Gainsborough, 1927)
Producer: Michael Balcon
Script: Eliot Stannard, from the play by Noel Coward
Director of Photography: Claude McDonnell
Sets: Clifford Pember
Editor: Ivor Montagu
Cast: Isabel Jeans (Larita Filton), Robin Irvine (John Whitaker), Franklin Dyall (M. Filton), Eric Bransby Williams (Claude Robson), and Ian Hunter (Filton's counsel)
Running time: 7,592 feet (about 99 minutes)
Premiere: August 1927, London
16mm rental: Films Inc., and Images Film Archive

THE RING (British International Pictures, 1927)
Producer: John Maxwell
Script: Alfred Hitchcock, Alma Reville, and Eliot Stannard
Director of Photography: Jack Cox
Sets: C. Wilfred Arnold
Cast: Carl Brisson (One-Round Jack Sander), Lilian Hall Davis (Nelly), and Ian Hunter (Bob Corby)
Running time: 8,454 feet (about 116 minutes)
Premiere: October 1927, London
16mm rental: Janus; Em Gee (condensed)

THE FARMER'S WIFE (British International Pictures, 1928)
Producer: John Maxwell
Script: Eliot Stannard and Alfred Hitchcock, from the play by Eden Philpotts
Director of Photography: Jack Cox
Editor: Alfred Booth
Sets: C. Wilfred Arnold
Cast: Lilian Hall Davis (Minta Dench), Jameson Thomas (Samuel Sweetland), Maud Gill (Thirza Tapper), Gordon Harker (Churdles Ash), and Gibb McLaughlin (Henry Coaker)
Running time: 67 minutes
Premiere: March 1928, London
16mm rental: Janus

CHAMPAGNE (British International Pictures, 1928)
Producer: John Maxwell
Editor: Alfred Hitchcock
Script: Eliot Stannard and Alfred Hitchcock, from a story by Walter C. Mycroft
Director of Photography: Jack Cox
Sets: C. Wilfred Arnold
Cast: Betty Balfour (Betty), Gordon Harker (her father), Ferdinand Von Alten (the mysterious passenger), and Jean Bradin (Betty's fiancé)
Running time: 8,038 feet (about 104 minutes)
Premiere: August 1928, London
16mm rental: Janus; and Em Gee (condensed)

THE MANXMAN (British International Pictures, 1929)
Producer: John Maxwell
Script: Eliot Stannard, from the novel by Sir Hall Caine
Editor: Emile de Ruelle
Director of Photography: Jack Cox
Sets: C. Wilfred Arnold
Cast: Carl Brisson (Peter Quilliam), Malcolm Keen (Philip Christian), and Anny Ondra (Kate)
Running time: 8,163 feet (about 106 minutes)
Premiere: January 1929, London
16mm rental: Janus; and Em Gee (condensed)

BLACKMAIL (British International Pictures, 1929)
Producer: John Maxwell
Script: Alfred Hitchcock, Benn W. Levy, and Charles Bennett, from the play by Charles Bennett
Director of Photography: Jack Cox (Ronald Neame was one of his assistants)
Sets: Wilfred C. Arnold and Norman Arnold
Music: Campbell and Connely, arranged by Hubert Bath and Henry Stafford
Editor: Emile de Ruelle
Cast: Anny Ondra (Alice White [Joan Barry spoke Ms. Ondra's lines]), Sara Allgood (Mrs. White), John Longden (Frank Webber), Charles Paton (Mr.

White), Cyril Ritchard (Crewe, the artist), and Donald Calthrop (Tracy, the blackmailer)
Running time: 86 minutes
Premiere: June 1929, London
16mm rental: Films Inc., and Images Film Archive

ELSTREE CALLING (British International Pictures, 1930)
Directors: Adrian Brunel, with Alfred Hitchcock, Andre Charlot, Jack Hulbert, and Paul Murray
Script: Val Valentine
Director of Photography: Claude Freise Greene
Music: Reg Casson, Vivian Ellis, and Chic Endor
Lyrics: Ivor Novello and Jack Strachey Parsons
Cast: Anna May Wong, Donald Calthrop, and Gordon Harker
Running time: 7,770 feet (about 101 minutes)
Premiere: September 29, 1930, London
16mm rental: Unavailable

JUNO AND THE PAYCOCK (British International Pictures, 1930)
Producer: John Maxwell
Script: Alfred Hitchcock and Alma Reville, from the play by Sean O'Casey
Director of Photography: Jack Cox
Sets: Norman Arnold
Editor: Emile de Ruelle
Cast: Sara Allgood (Juno), Edward Chapman (Captain Boyle), Sidney Morgan (Joxer), Marie O'Neill (Mrs. Madigan), and John Longden (Charles Bentham)
Running time: 85 minutes
Premiere: September 22, 1930
16mm rental: Unavailable

MURDER! (British International Pictures, 1930)
Producer: John Maxwell
Script: Alma Reville, Alfred Hitchcock, and Walter Mycroft, from the novel and play by Clemence Dane [Winifred Ashton] and Helen Simpson, *Enter Sir John*
Director of Photography: Jack Cox
Sets: John Mead
Editors: René Harrison and Emile de Ruelle
Cast: Herbert Marshall (Sir John Menier), Nora Baring (Diana Baring), Phyllis Konstam (Dulcie Markham), Edward Chapman (Ted Markham), and Esmé Percy (Handell Fane)
Running time: 102 minutes
Premiere: November 1930, London
16mm rental: Films Inc., and Images Film Archive

MARY (German version of *Murder!* shot simultaneously) (Sud Film A.G., 1930)
Cast: Alfred Abel and Olga Tchekowa

THE SKIN GAME (British International Pictures, 1931)
Producer: John Maxwell
Script: Alfred Hitchcock and Alma Reville, from the play by John Galsworthy
Directors of Photography: Jack Cox and Charles Martin
Editors: René Harrison and A. Gobett
Cast: Edmund Gwenn (Mr. Hornblower), Jill Esmond (Jill), John Longden (Charles), C. V. France (Mr. Hillcrist), Helen Haye (Mrs. Hillcrist), and Phyllis Konstam (Chloe)
Running time: 85 minutes
Premiere: October 1931, London
16mm rental: Janus

NUMBER SEVENTEEN (British International Pictures, 1932)
Producer: John Maxwell
Script: Alfred Hitchcock and Rodney Ackland, from the play and the novel by Jefferson Farjeon
Director of Photography: Jack Cox
Cast: Léon M. Lion (Ben), Anne Grey (Miss Ackroyd), and John Stuart (Detective Barton)
Running time: 63 minutes
Premiere: No date traced, but it was shot before *Rich and Strange*, though released after it.
16mm rental: Em Gee and Images Film Archive

RICH AND STRANGE (USA: *East of Shanghai*) (British International Pictures, 1932)
Producer: John Maxwell
Script: Alma Reville, Val Valentine, and Alfred Hitchcock from an idea by Dale Collins
Directors of Photography: Jack Cox and Charles Martin
Sets: C. Wilfred Arnold
Music: Hal Dolphe
Editors: Winifred Cooper and René Harrison
Cast: Henry Kendall (Fred Hill), Joan Barry (Emily Hill), Percy Marmont (Commander Gordon), Betty Amann (the princess), and Elsie Randolph (Elsie)
Running time: 83 minutes
Premiere: June 1932, London
16mm rental: Janus

WALTZES FROM VIENNA (USA: *Strauss's Great Waltz*) (Gaumont-British, 1933)
Producer: Tom Arnold
Script: Alma Reville and Guy Bolton, from his play
Sets: Alfred June and Peter Proud
Music: Johann Strauss the elder and Johann Strauss the younger
Cast: Jessie Matthews (Rasi), Edmund Gwenn (Strauss Senior), Fay Compton (the countess), Frank Vosper (the prince), and Esmond Knight (Strauss Junior)

Running time: 80 minutes
Premiere: October 1933, London
16mm rental: Unavailable

THE MAN WHO KNEW TOO MUCH (Gaumont-British, 1934)
Producers: Michael Balcon and Ivor Montagu
Script: A. R. Rawlinson, Charles Bennett, D. B. Wyndham-Lewis, Edwin
Greenwood, and Emlyn Williams
Director of Photography: Curt Courant
Sets: Alfred June and Peter Proud
Music: Arthur Benjamin; "Storm Cloud Cantata" by Arthur Benjamin, with text
by D. B. Wyndham-Lewis
Editor: H. St.C. Stewart
Cast: Leslie Banks (Bob Lawrence), Edna Best (Jill Lawrence), Peter Lorre
(Abbot), Nova Pilbeam (Betty Lawrence), Pierre Fresnay (Louis Bernard), and
Frank Vosper (the assassin)
Running time: 74 minutes
Premiere: December 1934, London
16mm rental: Films Inc. and Images Film Archive

THE THIRTY-NINE STEPS (Gaumont-British, 1935)
Producers: Michael Balcon and Ivor Montagu
Script: Charles Bennett, Alma Reville, and Ian Hay, from the novel by John
Buchan
Director of Photography: Bernard Knowles
Sets: Otto Werndorff and Albert Jullion
Costumes: J. Strassner
Music: Louis Levy
Editor: Derek N. Twist
Cast: Madeleine Carroll (Pamela), Robert Donat (Richard Hannay), Lucie
Mannheim (Annabella Smith), Godfrey Tearle (Professor Jordan), Peggy
Ashcroft (the farmer's wife), and Wylie Watson (Mr. Memory)
Running time: 87 minutes
Premiere: June 6, 1935, London
16mm rental: Images Film Archive and Em Gee

SECRET AGENT (Gaumont-British, 1936)
Producers: Michael Balcon and Ivor Montagu
Script: Charles Bennett, Alma Reville, Ian Hay, and Jesse Lasky, Jr., from the
play by Campbell Dixon adapted from the Ashenden stories of Somerset
Maugham
Director of Photography: Bernard Knowles
Sets: Otto Werndorff and Albert Jullion
Costumes: J. Strasser
Music: Louis Levy
Editor: Charles Frend
Cast: Madeleine Carroll (Elsa Carrington), John Gielgud (Edgar Brodie/Richard

Ashenden), Peter Lorre (the general), Robert Young (Robert Marvin), Percy
Marmont (Caypor), and Lilli Palmer (the maid)
Running time: 86 minutes
Premiere: May 1936, London
16mm rental: Films Inc. and Images Film Archive

SABOTAGE (USA: *A Woman Alone*) (Gaumont-British, 1936)
Producers: Michael Balcon and Ivor Montagu
Script: Charles Bennett, Alma Reville, Ian Hay, Helen Simpson, and E. V. H.
Emmett, from the novel by Joseph Conrad, *The Secret Agent*
Director of Photography: Bernard Knowles
Sets: Otto Werndorff and Albert Jullion
Music: Louis Levy
Costumes: J. Strassner
Editor: Charles Frend
Cast: Sylvia Sidney (Mrs. Verloc), Oscar Homolka (Verloc), John Loder (Ted),
Desmond Tester (Stevie), William Dewhurst (Mr. Chatman), and Martita Hunt
(his daughter)
Running time: 76 minutes
Premiere: December 1936, London
16mm rental: Films Inc. and Images Film Archive

YOUNG AND INNOCENT (USA: *The Girl Was Young*) (Gainsborough, 1937)
Producer: Edward Black
Script: Charles Bennett and Alma Reville, from the novel by Josephine Tey, *A
Shilling for Candles*
Director of Photography: Bernard Knowles
Sets: Alfred Junge
Music: Louis Levy
Editor: Charles Frend
Cast: Derrick de Marney (Robert Tisdall), Nova Pilbeam (Erica Burgoyne),
Percy Marmont (Colonel Burgoyne), Edward Rigby (Will), John Longden
(Kent), Basil Radford (Uncle Basil), and George Curzon (Guy)
Running time: 84 minutes
Premiere: November 1937, London
16mm rental: Films Inc. and Images Film Archive

THE LADY VANISHES (Gainsborough, 1938)
Producer: Edward Black
Script: Sydney Gilliatt, Frank Launder, and Alma Reville, from the novel by
Ethel Lina White, *The Wheel Spins*
Director of Photography: Jack Cox
Sets: Alec Vetchinsky, Maurice Cater, and Albert Jullion
Music: Louis Levy
Editors: Alfred Roome and R. E. Dearing
Cast: Margaret Lockwood (Iris Henderson), Michael Redgrave (Gilbert), Dame

May Whitty (Miss Froy), Paul Lukas (Dr. Hartz), Cecil Parker (Mr. Todhunter), Naugton Wayne (Caldicott), and Basil Radford (Charters)
Running time: 97 minutes
Premiere: October 1938, London
16mm rental: Images Film Archive and Em Gee

JAMAICA INN (Mayflower Pictures, 1939)
Producers: Erich Pommer and Charles Laughton
Script: Sydney Gilliat, Joan Harrison, Alma Reville, and J. B. Priestley, from the novel by Daphne Du Maurier
Directors of Photography: Harry Stradling and Bernard Knowles
Special Effects: Harry Watt
Sets: Tom N. Moraham
Costumes: Molly McArthur
Music: Eric Fenby
Editor: Robert Hamer
Cast: Charles Laughton (Sir Humphrey Pengallan), Leslie Banks (Joss Merlyn), Maureen O'Hara (Mary, the Merlyns' niece), Wylie Watson (Salvation), and Robert Newton (Jem Traherne)
Running time: 98 minutes
Premiere: May 20, 1939, London
16mm rental: Em Gee and Kit Parker

REBECCA (Selznick International, United Artists, 1940)
Producer: David O. Selznick
Script: Robert E. Sherwood, Joan Harrison, Philip MacDonald, and Michael Hogan, from the novel by Daphne Du Maurier
Director of Photography: George Barnes, ASC
Sets: Lyle Wheeler
Music: Franz Waxman
Editor: Hal C. Kern
Cast: Joan Fontaine (the second Mrs. de Winter), Laurence Olivier (Max de Winter), Judith Anderson (Mrs. Danvers), George Sanders (Jack Favell), Nigel Bruce (Major Giles Lacey), Florence Bates (Mrs. van Hopper), and Leo G. Carroll (the doctor)
Running time: 130 minutes
Premiere: March 21, 1940, New York
16mm rental: Twyman and Images Film Archive

FOREIGN CORRESPONDENT (United Artists, 1940)
Producer: Walter Wanger
Script: Charles Bennett, Joan Harrison, James Hilton, and Robert Benchley
Director of Photography: Rudolph Maté
Sets: William Cameron Menzies and Alexander Golitzen
Music: Alfred Newman
Editors: Otto Lovering and Dorothy Spencer
Cast: Joel McCrea (Johnny Jones/Huntley Haverstock), Laraine Day (Carol Fisher), Herbert Marshall (Stephen Fisher), George Sanders (Herbert Folliott),

Albert Basserman (Van Meer), Robert Benchley (Stebbins), and Edmund Gwenn (Rowley)
Running time: 120 minutes
Premiere: August 16, 1940, New York
16mm rental: Films Inc. and Images Film Archive

MR. AND MRS. SMITH (RKO, 1941)
Producer: Harry E. Edington
Script: Norman Krasna
Director of Photography: Harry Stradling, ASC
Sets: Van Nest Polglase and L. P. Williams
Music: Roy Webb
Editor: William Hamilton
Cast: Carole Lombard (Ann Krausheimer Smith), Robert Montgomery (David Smith), Gene Raymond (Jeff Custer), and Jack Carson (Chuck Benson)
Running time: 95 minutes
Premiere: February 1941, New York
16mm rental: Films Inc.

SUSPICION (RKO, 1941)
Producer: Harry E. Edington
Script: Samson Raphaelson, Joan Harrison, and Alma Reville, from the novel by Francis Iles [Anthony Berkeley Cox], *Before the Fact*
Director of Photography: Harry Stradling, ASC
Sets: Van Nest Polglase and Carroll Clark
Music: Franz Waxman
Editor: William Hamilton
Cast: Joan Fontaine (Lina MacKinlaw), Cary Grant (Johnny Aysgarth), Cedric Hardwicke (General MacKinlaw), Nigel Bruce (Beaky), Dame May Whitty (Mrs. MacKinlaw), Isabel Jeans (Mrs. Newsham), and Leo G. Carroll (Capt. Mahlbeck)
Running time: 99 minutes
Premiere: November 1941, New York
16mm rental: Films Inc.

SABOTEUR (Universal, 1942)
Producers: Frank Lloyd and Jack H. Skirball
Script: Peter Viertel, Joan Harrison, and Dorothy Parker, from an idea by Alfred Hitchcock
Director of Photography: Joseph Valentine, ASC
Sets: Jack Otterson
Music: Charles Previn and Frank Skinner
Editor: Otto Ludwig
Cast: Robert Cummings (Barry Kane), Priscilla Lane (Patricia Martin), Otto Kruger (Charles Tobin), Alma Kruger (Mrs. Van Sutton), and Norman Lloyd (Fry, the saboteur)
Running time: 108 minutes
Premiere: May 1942, New York
16mm rental: Twyman and Clem Williams

SHADOW OF A DOUBT (Universal, 1943)
Producer: Jack H. Skirball
Script: Thornton Wilder, Alma Reville, and Sally Benson, from a story by
Gordon McDonell
Director of Photography: Joseph Valentine, ASC
Sets: John B. Goodman, Robert Boyle, A. Gausman, and L. R. Robinson
Costumes: Adrian, and Vera West
Music: Dimitri Tiomkin
Editor: Milton Carruth
Cast: Joseph Cotten (Charles Oakley), Teresa Wright (Charlie Newton), Patricia
Collinge (Emma Newton), MacDonald Carey (Jack Graham), Henry Travers
(Joe Newton), and Hume Cronyn (Herb Hawkins)
Running time: 108 minutes
Premiere: January 1943, New York
16mm rental: Twyman and Clem Williams

LIFEBOAT (20th Century-Fox, 1944)
Producer: Kenneth MacGowan
Script: Jo Swerling, from a screen story by John Steinbeck
Director of Photography: Glen MacWilliams
Sets; James Basevi and Maurice Ransford
Music: Hugo Friedhofer
Costumes: René Hubert
Editor: Dorothy Spencer
Cast: Tallulah Bankhead (Constance Porter), William Bendix (Gus), Walter
Slezak (Willy), John Hodiak (Kovac), Henry Hull (Charles Rittenhouse), and
Hume Cronyn (Stanley Garrett)
Running time: 96 minutes
Premiere: January 1944, New York
16mm rental: Films Inc.

BON VOYAGE (MOI 1944) (documentary short for the British Ministry of
Information)
Script: J. O. C. Orton and Angus McPhail, from an original subject by Arthur
Calder-Marshall
Director of Photography: Gunther Krampf
Sets: Charles Gilbert
Cast: John Blythe and the Moliere Players
Running time: 25 minutes

AVENTURE MALGACHE (*Madagascar Adventure*) (MOI, 1944) (docu-
mentary short for the British Ministry of Information)
Director of Photography: Gunther Krampf
Sets: Charles Gilbert
Cast: The Moliere Players
Running time: 31 minutes

SPELLBOUND (Selznick, United Artists, 1945)
Producer: David O. Selznick
Script: Ben Hecht and Angus McPhail, from the novel by Francis Beeding
[Hilary St. George Saunders and John Palmer], *The House of Dr. Edwardes*
Director of Photography: George Barnes, ASC
Sets: James Basevi and John Edwing
Music: Miklos Rozsa
Costumes: Howard Greer
Editors: William Ziegler and Hal C. Kern
Dream Sequence: Salvador Dali
Cast: Ingrid Bergman (Dr. Constance Petersen), Gregory Peck (John
Ballantine), Leo G. Carroll (Dr. Murchison), Norman Lloyd (Garmes), and
Michael Chekhov (Dr. Brulov)
Running time: 111 minutes
Premiere: October 1945, New York
16mm rental: Films Inc. and Images Film Archive

NOTORIOUS (RKO, 1946)
Producers: Alfred Hitchcock and Barbara Keon
Script: Ben Hecht, from an idea by Alfred Hitchcock
Director of Photography: Ted Tetzlaff, ASC
Sets: Albert S. D'Agnostino, Carrol Clark, Darrell Silvera, and Claude Carpenter
Costumes: Edith Head
Music: Roy Webb
Editor: Theron Warth
Cast: Ingrid Bergman (Alicia Huberman), Cary Grant (Devlin), Claude Rains
(Alexander Sebastian), Leopoldine Konstantin (Mrs. Sebastian), and Louis
Calhern (Paul Prescott)
Running time: 101 minutes
Premiere: August 1946, New York
16mm rental: Films Inc. and Images Film Archive

THE PARADINE CASE (Selznick Releasing Organization, 1947)
Producer: David O. Selznick
Script: David O. Selznick with Alma Reville, from the novel by Robert Hichens
Director of Photography: Lee Garmes, ASC
Sets: J. MacMillian Johnson and Thomas Morahan
Costumes: Travis Banton
Music: Franz Waxman
Editors: Hal C. Kern and John Faure
Cast: Gregory Peck (Anthony Keane), Ann Todd (Gay Keane), Charles Laughton
(Judge Horfield), Alida Valli (Maddalena Paradine), Ethel Barrymore (Sophie
Horfield), Charles Coburn (Simon Flaquer), Louis Jordan (Andre Latour), and
Leo G. Carroll (Sir Joseph Farrell)
Running time: 115 minutes
Premiere: December 31, 1947, Los Angeles
16mm rental: Films Inc. and Twyman

ROPE (Transatlantic Pictures, Warner Bros., 1948)
Producers: Sidney Bernstein and Alfred Hitchcock
Script: Arthur Laurents and Hume Cronyn, from the play by Patrick Hamilton
Directors of Photography: Joseph Valentine, ASC, and William V. Skall, ASC
(Technicolor)
Sets: Perry Ferguson
Music: Leo F. Forbstein, based on the theme "Perpetual Movement No. 1," by
Francis Poulenc
Costumes: Adrian
Editor: William H. Ziegler
Cast: James Stewart (Rupert Cadell), John Dall (Shaw Brandon), Farley Granger
(Philip), Cedric Hardwicke (Mr. Kentley), Constance Collier (Mrs. Atwater),
and Dick Hogan (David Kentley)
Running time: 80 minutes
Premiere: August 1948, New York
16mm rental: Swank

UNDER CAPRICORN (Transatlantic Pictures, Warner Bros., 1949)
Producers: Sidney Bernstein and Alfred Hitchcock
Script: James Bridie (O.H. Mavor) and Hume Cronyn, from the novel by Helen
Simpson
Director of Photography: Jack Cardiff, ASC, Paul Beeson, Ian Craig, David
McNeilly, and Jack Haste (Technicolor)
Sets: Tom Morahan
Music: Richard Addinsell
Editor: A. S. Bates
Costumes: Roger Furse
Cast: Ingrid Bergman (Henrietta Flusky), Joseph Cotten (Sam Flusky), Michael
Wilding (Charles Adare), and Margaret Leighton (Milly)
Running time: 117 minutes
Premiere: September 1949, New York
16mm rental: Kit Parker

STAGE FRIGHT (Warner Bros., 1950)
Producer: Alfred Hitchcock
Script: Whitfield Cook, Alma Reville, and James Bridie (O.H. Mavor), from two
stories by Selwyn Jepson, "Man Running" and "Outrun the Constable"
Director of Photography: Wilkie Cooper
Sets: Terence Verity
Music: Leighton Lucas
Editor: Edward Jarvis
Cast: Marlene Dietrich (Charlotte Inwood), Jane Wyman (Eve Gill), Michael
Wilding (Inspector Wilfred Smith), Richard Todd (Jonathan Cooper), Alastair
Sim (Commodore Gill), and Dame Sybil Thorndike (Mrs. Gill)
Running time: 110 minutes
Premiere: February 1950, New York
16mm rental: Films Inc. and Twyman

STRANGERS ON A TRAIN (Warner Bros., 1951)
Producer: Alfred Hitchcock
Script: Raymond Chandler, Czenzi Ormonde, and Whitfield Cook, from the
novel by Patricia Highsmith
Director of Photography: Robert Burks, ASC
Sets: Ted Hawortt and George James Hopkins
Music: Dimitri Tiomkin
Costumes: Leah Rhodes
Editor: William H. Ziegler
Cast: Robert Walker (Bruno Anthony), Farley Granger (Guy Haines), Ruth
Roman (Ann Morton), Leo G. Carroll (Senator Morton), Patricia Hitchcock
(Barbara Morton), Laura Elliot (Miriam Haines), and Marion Lorne (Mrs.
Anthony)
Running time: 101 minutes
Premiere: July 1951, New York
16mm rental: Swank

I CONFESS (Warner Bros., 1953)
Producers: Alfred Hitchcock, Barbara Keon, and Sherry Shourdes
Script: George Tabori and William Archibald, from the play by Paul Anthelme,
Our Two Consciences
Director of Photography: Robert Burks, ASC
Sets: Edward S. Haworth and George James Hopkins
Music: Dimitri Tiomkin
Editor: Rudi Fehr, ACE
Costumes: Orry-Kelly
Technical Consultants: Father Paul la Couline and Inspector Oscar Tangvay
Cast: Montgomery Clift (Father Michael Logan), Anne Baxter (Ruth Grandfort),
Karl Malden (Inspector Larrue), Brian Aherne (Willy Robertson), and O. E.
Hasse (Otto Keller)
Running time: 95 minutes
Premiere: March 1953, New York
16mm rental: Films Inc. and Twyman

DIAL M FOR MURDER (Warner Bros., 1954)
Producer: Alfred Hitchcock
Script: Alfred Hitchcock, from the play by Frederick Knott
Director of Photography: Robert Burks, ASC (3-D, Warnercolor)
Sets: Edward Carrère and George James Hopkins
Music: Dimitri Tiomkin
Costumes: Moss Mabry
Editor: Rudi Fehr
Cast: Ray Milland (Tony Wendice), Grace Kelly (Margot Wendice), Robert
Cummings (Mark Halliday), Anthony Dawson (Swan/Lesgate), and John
Williams (Inspector Hubbard)
Running time: 88 minutes
Premiere: May 1954, New York
16mm rental: Films Inc. and Clem Williams

REAR WINDOW (Paramount, 1954)
Producer: Alfred Hitchcock
Script: John Michael Hayes, from a novelette by William Irish (Cornell Woolrich)
Director of Photography: Robert Burks, ASC (Technicolor)
Sets: Hal Pereira, Joseph McMillan Johnson, Sam Comer, and Ray Mayer
Music: Franz Waxman
Editor: George Tomasini, ACE
Costumes: Edith Head
Cast: James Stewart (L. B. Jeffries), Grace Kelly (Lisa Fremont), Wendell Corey (Tom Doyle), Thelma Ritter (Stella), Raymond Burr (Lars Thorwald), and Judith Evelyn (Miss Lonelyhearts)
Running time: 112 minutes
Premiere: August 1954, New York
16mm rental: Swank

TO CATCH A THIEF (Paramount, 1955)
Producer: Alfred Hitchcock
Script: John Michael Hayes, from the novel by David Dodge
Director of Photography: Robert Burks, ASC (VistaVision, Technicolor)
Sets: Hal Pereira, Joseph MacMillan Johnson, Sam Comer, and Arthur Krams
Music: Lynn Murray
Editor: George Tomasini, ACE
Costumes: Edith Head
Cast: Cary Grant (John Robie), Grace Kelly (Frances Stevens), Jessie Royce Landis (Jessie Stevens), and John Williams (the insurance inspector)
Running time: 97 minutes
Premiere: August 1955, New York
16mm rental: Films Inc.

THE TROUBLE WITH HARRY (Paramount, 1955)
Producer: Alfred Hitchcock
Script: John Michael Hayes, from the novel by John Trevor Story
Director of Photography: Robert Burks, ASC (VistaVision, Technicolor)
Sets: Hal Pereira, John Goodman, Sam Comer, and Emile Kuri
Music: Bernard Herrmann
Editor: Alma Macrorie
Costumes: Edith Head
Cast: Edmund Gwenn (Captain Wiles), John Forsythe (Sam Marlowe), Shirley MacLaine (Jennifer), Mildred Natwick (Miss Gravely), and Mildred Dunnock (Mrs. Wiggs)
Running time: 99 minutes
Premiere: October 1955, New York
16mm rental: Swank

THE MAN WHO KNEW TOO MUCH (Paramount, Filwite Prod., 1956)
Producers: Alfred Hitchcock and Herbert Coleman
Script: John Michael Hayes and Angus McPhail, from a story by Charles Bennett and D. B. Wyndham-Lewis

Director of Photography: Robert Burks, ASC (VistaVision, Technicolor)
Sets: Hal Pereira, Henry Bumstead, Sam Comer, and Arthur Krams
Music: Bernard Herrmann; songs by Jay Livingston and Ray Evans; "Storm Cloud Cantata" by Arthur Benjamin with text by D. B. Wyndham-Lewis
Editor: George Tomasini, ACE
Costumes: Edith Head
Cast: James Stewart (Dr. Ben McKenna), Doris Day (Jo McKenna), Daniel Gélin (Louis Bernard), Brenda de Banzie (Mrs. Drayton), Bernard Miles (Mr. Drayton), and Reggie Malder (the assassin)
Running time: 120 minutes
Premiere: May 1956, New York
16mm rental: Swank

THE WRONG MAN (Warner Bros., 1956)
Producers: Alfred Hitchcock and Herbert Coleman
Script: Maxwell Anderson and Angus McPhail, from "The True Story of Christopher Emmanuel Balestrero," by Maxwell Anderson
Director of Photography: Robert Burks, ASC
Sets: Paul Sylbert and William L. Kuehl
Music: Bernard Herrmann
Editor: George Tomasini, ACE
Technical Consultant: Frank O'Connor (Police Magistrate to the District Attorney, Queens County, New York)
Cast: Henry Fonda (Christopher Emmanuel Balestrero), Vera Miles (Rose Balestrero), Anthony Quayle (Frank O'Connor), and Esther Minciotti (Mrs. Balestrero)
Running time: 105 minutes
Premiere: December 1956, New York
16mm rental: Films Inc.

VERTIGO (Paramount, 1958)
Producers: Alfred Hitchcock and Herbert Coleman
Script: Alec Coppel and Samuel Taylor, from the novel by Pierre Boileau and Thomas Narcejac, *D'entre les morts*
Director of Photography: Robert Burks, ASC (VistaVision, Technicolor)
Sets: Hal Pereira, Henry Bumstead, Sam Comer, and Frank McKelvey
Music: Bernard Herrmann
Editor: George Tomasini, ACE
Costumes: Edith Head
Titles: Saul Bass
Nightmare Sequence: John Ferren
Cast: James Stewart (Scottie Ferguson), Kim Novak (Madeleine Elster/Judy Barton), Barbara Bel Geddes (Midge Wood), Tom Helmore (Gavin Elster), and Ellen Corby (manager of the McKittrick Hotel)
Running time: 120 minutes
Premiere: May 1958, New York
16mm rental: Swank

NORTH BY NORTHWEST (Metro-Goldwyn-Mayer, 1959)
Producers: Alfred Hitchcock and Herbert Coleman
Script: Ernest Lehman
Director of Photography: Robert Burks, ASC (VistaVision, Technicolor)
Sets: Robert Boyle, William A. Horning, Merrill Pyle, Henry Grace, and Frank McKelvey
Music: Bernard Herrmann
Editor: George Tomasini, ACE
Titles: Saul Bass
Cast: Cary Grant (Roger O. Thornhill), Eva Marie Saint (Eve Kendall), James Mason (Philip Vandamm), Jessie Royce Landis (Clara Thornhill), Leo G. Carroll (the Professor), and Martin Landau (Leonard)
Running time: 136 minutes
Premiere: August 1959, New York
16mm rental: Films Inc.

PSYCHO (Paramount, 1960)
Producer: Alfred Hitchcock
Script: Joseph Stafano, from the novel by Robert Bloch
Director of Photography: John L. Russell, ASC
Sets: Joseph Hurley, Robert Claworthy, and George Milo
Music: Bernard Herrmann
Titles: Saul Bass
Editor: George Tomasini, ACE
Costumes: Helen Colvig
Cast: Anthony Perkins (Norman Bates), Janet Leigh (Marion Crane), Vera Miles (Lila Crane), John Gavin (Sam Loomis), Martin Balsam (Milton Arbogast), John McIntire (Sheriff Chambers), Lurene Tuttle (Mrs. Chambers), and Patricia Hitchcock (Caroline)
Running time: 109 minutes
Premiere: June 1960, New York
16mm rental: Twyman and Swank

THE BIRDS (Universal, 1963)
Producer: Alfred Hitchcock
Script: Evan Hunter, from the novella by Daphne Du Maurier
Director of Photography: Robert Burks, ASC (Technicolor)
Special Photographic Effects: Lawrence A. Hampton and Ub Iwerks
Sets: Robert Boyle and George Milo
Sound Consultant: Bernard Herrmann
Bird Trainer: Ray Berwick
Editor: George Tomasini, ACE
Cast: Tippi Hedren (Melanie Daniels), Rod Taylor (Mitch Brenner), Jessica Tandy (Mrs. Brenner), Suzanne Pleshette (Annie Hayworth), Ethel Griffies (Mrs. Bundy), and Charles McGraw (Sebastian Sholes)
Running time: 120 minutes
Premiere: April 1963, New York
16mm rental: Swank and Twyman

MARNIE (Universal, 1964)
Producer: Alfred Hitchcock
Script: Jay Presson Allen, from the novel by Winston Graham
Director of Photography: Robert Burks, ASC (Technicolor)
Sets: Robert Boyle and George Milo
Music: Bernard Herrmann
Editor: George Tomasini, ACE
Cast: Tippi Hedren (Marnie Edgar), Sean Connery (Mark Rutland), Diane
Baker (Lil Mainwaring), Louise Latham (Bernice Edgar), Martin Gabel (Strutt)
and Bruce Dern (the sailor)
Running time: 130 minutes
Premiere: June 1964, New York
16mm rental: Clem Williams and Twyman

TORN CURTAIN (Universal, 1966)
Producer: Alfred Hitchcock
Script: Brian Moore and (uncredited) Keith Waterhouse and Willis Hall
Director of Photography: John F. Warren, ASC
Sets: Frank Arrigo
Music: John Addison
Editor: Bud Hoffman
Cast: Paul Newman (Michael Armstrong), Julie Andrews (Sarah Sherman), Lila
Kedrova (Countess Kuchinska), Wolfgang Kieling (Gromek), and Ludwig
Donath (Professor Lindt)
Running time: 128 minutes
Premiere: July 1966
16mm rental: Clem Williams and Twyman

TOPAZ (Universal, 1969)
Producer: Alfred Hitchcock
Script: Samuel Taylor, from the novel by Leon Uris
Director of Photography: Jack Hildyard
Art Directors: Alexander Golitzen and Henry Bumstead
Music: Maurice Jarre
Editor: William H. Ziegler
Costumes: Edith Head
Cast: Frederick Stafford (Andre Dévereaux), Dany Robin (Nicole Dévereaux),
Michael Piccoli (Jacques Granville), Philippe Noiret (Henri Jarré), John For-
sythe (Michael Nordstrom), John Vernon (Rico Parra), Roscoe Lee Browne
(Philippe), and Karin Dor (Juanita)
Running time: 126 minutes
Premiere: December 1969, New York
16mm rental: Clem Williams

FRENZY (Universal, 1972)
Producers: Alfred Hitchcock and William Hill
Script: Anthony Shaffer, from the novel *Goodbye Piccadilly, Farewell Leicester
Square* by Arthur La Bern

Director of Photography: Gil Taylor
Music: Ron Goodwin
Editor: John Jympson
Sets: Sydney Cain, Robert Laing, and Simon Wakefield
Cast: Jon Finch (Richard Blaney), Barry Foster (Bob Rusk), Barbara Leigh-Hunt (Brenda Blaney), Anna Massey (Babs Milligan), Alec McCowen (Inspector Oxford), and Vivien Merchant (Mrs. Oxford)
Running time: 116 minutes
Premiere: June 1972, New York
16mm rental: Clem Williams and Twyman

FAMILY PLOT (Universal, 1976)
Producer: Alfred Hitchcock
Script: Ernest Lehman, from the novel *The Rainbird Pattern* by Victor Canning
Director of Photography: Leonard J. South
Music: John Williams
Editor: J. Terry Williams
Sets: Henry Bumstead and James W. Payne
Costumes: Edith Head
Cast: Karen Black (Fran), Bruce Dern (George Lumley), Barbara Harris (Blanche Tyler), William Devane (Adamson), Ed Lauter (Maloney), and Cathleen Nesbitt (Julia Rainbird)
Running time: 120 minutes
Premiere: April 1976, New York
16mm rental: Swank and Twyman

Index

There Is No Balm
in Birmingham

ANN DEAGON

There Is No Balm
in Birmingham

DAVID R. GODINE · BOSTON

David R. Godine, Publisher
Boston, Massachusetts

★

Copyright © 1972, 1974, 1975, 1976, 1978
by Ann Deagon
LCC 75–41623
ISBN 0–87923–177–7
Printed in the United States of America

Acknowledgments: Some of these poems first appeared in
Aura, Cold Mountain Review, Crucible, Guilford Review, International Poetry Review, New Collage, Review '74, Southern Poetry Review, and *St. Andrews Review.*

A Godine Poetry Chapbook
Third Series

For Andrea

Contents

A GYNECOLOGY

I   There Is No Balm in Birmingham

Among the agents used by counterfeiters
to age their stock are: glycerine,
whale oil, rose water. I know this art.
To make their tender legal, to pass current,
my petaled, my limpid aunts
distilled in the coiled copper of their afternoons
animal, vegetable, mineral
into a balmy essence that preserved
their beauty moist.
                  Leathered as I am,
Aunties, sisters, I smear my page
with crafty balsam, beauteous conceit,
hide to the last, last line the truth that's not
beauty but bone. bone. bone. bone.

II   Customs of the Esquimaux Women

They do not stalk the caribou
tall-boned over hard white.
Kneeling fur-trousered low to
the bleak of ice they cut one
pure hole, prise up its flat moon.
In under sea the muscled seal
like dark pigs root for air.
One woman loosens furs, dips one
bare breast into the breathing hole:
its nipple spurts a thread of scent.
Seal veer and rise, their snouts
nudge, nuzzle, strike. The woman
screams, they grapple, tug the black
clenched beast on ice, hack off
its head, the woman's cry still coming hoarse,
rhythmic.

        Nights in the igloo she crouches,
softens stiff skin between her teeth.
Beside her in a shallow stone
seal blubber flickers the whole night.

III Jugglers All

Let the balls be round as oranges, rounder
than eggs, than babies. Let them cluster
the air like grapes before they fall.
Let the Indian Clubs glide and hover
svelte as the legs of sorority sisters
turning cartwheels in the leaf of spring.
Let the glasses brim with order
tinkling in pyramids and not a drop
suggest time shatters even pyramids.

And when the juggler climbs stair upon stair
lofting to miracle glass water chair,
let her then spin around her in great arcs
eggs oranges babies grapes and human parts,
like God by compass rounding out the skies.
Like any woman juggling for her life.

Moving North

The Brown Recluse, also known as the Hermit Fiddler, a
spider whose bite produces a gangrenous sore, is apparently spreading northward. From its original home in
the Southwest it has now migrated as far as North
Carolina.

Not it. She. The one with eggs.
Demographer with the future in her belly,
moving up in the world. Texas rots
dry, Louisiana wet. Twenty
years in Alabama: closets, drawers,
silver chests, the backs of portraits
cottoned with eggs and everywhere the sweet
festering scent. In Tennessee
she homed into the woodpile, roughed it,
budded the boards with eggs. Now here
holed up in my ornamental block
she babysits a quiet contagion.

                                        Lady,
I know your bite. I am myself
something of a recluse and given
to wearing brown. My Odyssey—
no, my Penelopeid up the dry
shins of girlhood to the wetter parts
was not unlike your own. We are heading
both of us north. The cold, I hear,
is shriveling, the cold bites back.
Even in this lush midway state I feel
a touch of gangrene on my hither leg,
some deadlier hermit fiddling in my brain.

Certified Copy

I have xeroxed my navel
bare-bellied in the public library
borne on the hymeneal cries
of hysteric librarians, inserted a coin
prone on the glass slab steeled myself against
the green light's insolent stroke
and viewed emerging
instantaneously, parthenogenously from the slit
this reproduction of my reproduction
this evidence of my most human birth.

Archives forget, Bibles prevaricate
aged witnesses from age grow witless—
only the skin remembers, swirling to clench
the archetypal wound: the center holds.

Games for the Root-House Children

1. First find something dead.
   Bury it. Wait a month.
   Dig it up. You will learn
   How the dead come alive.

2. Watch spider wrap cricket
   In a cocoon. She will have
   Music in the gut all winter.
   Learn how the small survive.

3. Learn the bee-dance. Follow the bee.
   Glut your eye on wild blooms.
   Follow the bee back home.
   Honey is sweeter than art.

4. Take a stone. Draw a circle.
   Whatever comes inside the circle
   Smash it. You are learning
   What stones are for.

5. Cut off a finger: trout strike.
   Lie still in the field: a buzzard
   Centers down. Wring its neck.
   The body is the only bait.

6. Tie a mouse to a thistle.
   Lean your hoe to a tree.
   When the snake comes, teach him
   A new way to shed skin.

7. When you are big, wrestle the bear.
   Win, and you feast in a fur coat.
   Lose, and you sleep underground
   All winter long next his heart.

8. When you have learned all the games
   Lay your axe to the tree's root.
   Knowledge, quoth Lilith, is firewood.
   The winters here are hard.

The Tree House

I

At Chimney Place (the chimney long gone
to lizards) grape vines swallowed
boxwood rows. The tumbled
pony shed buried a half-
glimpsed still saddled cadaver.
(Nights we heard faint whinnies.)
We built the tree house there.

We nailed our childhood to
the great maple—each cleat
a splintered year. Skates made pulleys
to hoist our booty: duckboards ripe
with fungus, tin signs from rotted
fruit stands, boards that said KEEP OUT.
The sled my uncle split against a tree
framed the entrance. Gripping its runners
we swung into our own high keep.

II

Was there a dead pony? you question.
I had no uncle, either. And who
would have had a sled in Birmingham?
Why did I say *we* when I was always
alone? Is there no truth? you ask—
only this shape-shifting, this growth
of lies like kudzu altering the trees
into a stand of monsters? No.
I never built a tree house.
Until now.

III

Why does a grown woman build
a tree house of words (a word house
of trees)? The metaphor at best
is inexact. True, we scrounge
anything to cage us from the wind.
True, from there we see
further than the yard. True,
what once streaked on snow
falters in the melting, hangs
at rust. Call it allegory.

But if it wasn't true, why these
flakes of rust along my palm? Why
these dreams of falling?

The House of Three Pianos

I

Every high corner of the porch
is fluted with dirt-daubers' tunnels.
I ream them out with my broom handle.
Each one houses at its upper end
some insect's shrouded body. Cliff dwellers,
was it from you I learned to hide
a succulent corpse in every fluted
corridor of my brain? Where poems
hatch and feed, grow wings, issue
into air.

II

It is the body of a girl.
The room is called *la grande salle*
or perhaps *the conservatory.*
The door opens. Inside
are three pianos. At dusk they are like
misshapen coffins. Some thing
with hump or wing, some Quasimodo
lies here or stalks abroad. Dreamed by day
they hum like great transformers:
throw back the cover—the sun
short-circuits, you burn white.
At night by chandelier they play
like machines the infinite repertoire
of what has never been written, of what
I will never write.

III

This room was real once. I came in
out of a wood. There were three:
the Father too hard, the Mother too soft,
the Young One right. Somewhere between
bed and chair and table I learned
hate. pity. desire. But not which
of these is the greatest. That shell game
I still play.

IV

I know those people
are nothing to me. What they were
I could not have known. They rest
now in low houses. Only
the mind that sly mortician replays
continually the past's imposture.

On this white pad by slow curettage
poem by poem I ream the tunnels out,
scrape clean the high hollow of my skull.
Abort the myth. Let in the air.

Of Mice

Post holes sunk by plumb line in this
muddy April deep cored
well with dank cider, float mouse
cadavers. O you pink-footed furriers,
not all holes are home. At best you'll
strand in May's draining, mush under
concrete-bedded fence posts that stripe
the neighbor view like print against page.

Well mouse, your betters fare no better. All
stark words deep set in lines
bed against some battering of flesh
some draggled fur of lovers.
                    Scurry, Eduardo:
I have dug this poem for you.

Dreams of Affluence

I am a housewife vacuuming
her swimming pool. Under my toes
under the blue vinyl, moles
hump their tunnels. The cat
lays them pale and dripping at
our doorstep. She has learned
how to dive. The chlorine
has bleached her white.
You cannot tell her from a mole.

I am diving through my life.

The Weather Balloon

In June at seven from the pool
the clearest-eyed child
cries out, has sighted
the weather balloon, tiny as
a bead of quicksilver, a bubble
caught under fathoms of blue.
It will not surface here
where our yard beaches the sky.
At sea in air it drifts, its whole
purpose that drifting. Meteorologists
plot its azimuth. We train
binoculars and our binocular gaze
on its uncaring passage. Our round
pool blinks back the sky. We think
we are tethered. We are all of us
at sea.

Deadwoman's Float

This way of drowning, this element
buoys me above you: I breast your waves,
ride at your anchor, plunge and crest,
shudder, break against your coral, drown.
Drowning upward, stars turn fish,
fish dart like stars. You smile, reach up
to part my hair like water, my face
surfaces watery as nymphs. You beach me
on your chest, stranded, gasping
your briny sweat, clenched in my hand
that pearl your nipple, clenched in my mind
this way of drowning, this element.

Basic Rescue

1. OPEN THE AIRWAY

Green cement has flooded the firehall.
We unfold chairs. The instructor
lays flat a white sheet.
He inflates Resusci-Anne,
pumps till her bent legs kick straight.
LOOK LISTEN AND FEEL FOR BREATHING.
She does not breathe. GIVE FOUR
QUICK BREATHS. We kneel and breathe
turn by turn in a discreet pavane
each of us with her own death in tow.

2. FEEL FOR A PULSE

Each of us with her own death in tow:
the baby turned blue in the highchair
the boy at the bottom of the pool
like a mosaic, the daughter OD'd
the man in the bed not waking up.

We crouch, fingertips to carotid
feeling for pulse we know's not there.
All the world has a single throat.

3. BEGIN COMPRESSION

All the world has a single throat.
See how she lolls, lips parted, knowing
she is born to this, hers to invite
the mouths of strangers. She inhales us
not tasting our garlic or our mouthwash
tasting only our pale clear lives.

The heel of our hand is between her breasts.
We are pumping up the world, see how
its vasty chambers fill. We will breathe
life into the mouths of corpses:
their lungs redden like a forge.

Man and Wife Is One Flesh

I

Barely acceptable in grammar,
it is not mathematically sound.
An equation incapable of proof,
we assert it merely.

II

Because he was dying, they let me stay.
In the corridor speakers called over and over.
Something is happening in the corridor,
he said. (But nothing was.) They gave him
more morphine. Check the altitude,
he said, do we have enough? I told him,
Yes. The dog's collar is a quarter-
inch too small. I'll exchange it, I said.
(But we had no dog.) The monitor
faltered and beat on, faltered and beat.

On the third night he had not yet died.
I leaned back in the reclining chair.
It is hard to put in words: he lay
propped into living; I lay back
level with death. A great plane
sliced through the tissue of the world.
We lay against it, smears on a slide.
Falling asleep I fell continually
into his body, feeling the tubes
dry my nostrils, feeling the slow
swell of fluid up my wrist,
my hair thinning to his fine golden
my eyes blurring blue, blue.

III

He lived, for the time. We all
live for the time only, the time
a great shearing between dead
flesh and the quick. No way
but by its sting to know
we live and live together.

Gestalting the Dream

Yes, yes, you explained all that—
how every figure of whatever nightmare
is me, all things acts beings places
all myself, myself the delicate
sinister whisper on the phone: my child
unharmed, she says, or soon will heal;
myself the boy sent for help who never . . .
myself the three workmen rough with beer
fondling me toward the shack, crumpling
the scrap of paper with the license number
of the kidnappers' van; myself the squad-car
passing one street over out of hearing
unable (as I am unable) to prevent
anything; myself the final woman
preacher: Let's see what miracle the Lord
hath wrought this day—lugging out of the trunk-
altar the clothes bag with something in it,
unzipping the child's body miraculously dead.

Yes, Doctor, I admit everything, everyone,
every malice and forethought. Yet, Doctor:
I am the mother who did not kill the child
who did not lock her in the trunk. I am
in fact the child, wanted dead or alive,
the missing savior-cop as well as the missing
killer, the missing aunts uncles lovers
the father most of all who never appears.
(I am him so entirely he never appears
he is my dreaming eye my dreams turn blue
at their edges from his iris.) Calm yourself,
Doctor, I am you with your extravagant

expectations of healing what the dream
knows dies. Doctor, I am the poet
of every one of my dreams and of this poem.
And you, Reader, looking away—
when did you first suspect that I am you?

Variations in an Unknown Key

I

The improvisations of the tone-deaf
imply a slant aesthetic.

II

Ellen's octave's seven keys
(her limit metacarpal,
not metaphysical. She's
stretched past fifths and sixths to fall
some half inch short of resolve).
Her rounds come back to nowhere
we've been, her scherzos reprove
our tonal set. Child, I fear
those black harmonics, austere,
unearthly, whose heavy bruit
hangs on the air like iron fruit.

III

Dreaming I halt
through sparse stubble
on the ashen hill.
Below, the stadium
teems with natives. They stalk
between the goal posts. One
lofts a bat, perpendicular to god.
Another dances, masked
catcher of souls. A dozen
blackened balls arc from a juggler.
The ones with gloves

have no right hands.
                    When it is over
I hobble down. They show
reverence to the stranger, no
hostility. I am led inside
the ruined conservatory. The hall
miraculously still enshrines
a Steinway, closed. We do obeisance.

Here is the hard part
to tell: the walls streaked
with murals—hierophonics, one
might call them. Staffs dark inked
(with gall or ash), notes somber,
rich earth and ore tones. An art become
holy in just that forgetting
its name and note.
                    I break the lock,
uncover keyboard, raise top, play.
What music comes
where space not pitch configures,
I cannot wake to say. Its resonance
subsumes me. I fade from
my view.

IV

The house has become
her instrument.
In the chambers of the house
her flawed heart scribes
its syncopated beat, its cardio-
grammatic scale. We play
cautious quartets.
In the chambers of the house
her breath becomes
music.

V

We are the tone.
Listen, friend:
we forked creatures—
strike us against stone,
we ring. Touch us
against your cheek,
feel us
ring to the bone.

MEASURES

I Pythagoras at the Piano

Your fingers depress the keys, your foot
depresses the pedal: from out that mechanism
comes a vibrance (having to do, you explain,
with the lengths of strings). We have been told
God is a number. These geometries
oppress me. (But when I answer
how the poem makes in the mind,
in the marrow, there a dark girl
ripe as olives kindles in the dingy
studio a crescendo of light.)

In the absence of numbers
where line and space no longer alternate
where only space is given, these lines
are drawn like blood.

II *The Antiquarians*

We are agreed the earth is round;
the quadrangle square; the lawns
rectangular; the museum oblong;
the galleries cubicular; the cases
visible intersections of planes. Look:
sudden beyond glass, the dead potter's
incalculable fingers from the wheel
stroked a bowl round as breasts.

Observe among the Egyptiaca
that fulsome figurine, her naked
symmetry: only the feet missing—
broken off, so the card informs,
to forestall escape from the dead
man's embraces. But don't we all
take off our feet before we go to bed?
(His hand in my hair, at my back the wall:
between the rock and the hard place I have
savored necessities.) The card omits
whether the sculptor modeled from life,
whether he broke her feet
to keep her still.

III *Epicycles*

Above the Sunset Inn
some hours past sunset
the moon pulls in
to the earth's shadow. Observatories
congratulate the punctual
universe. (If we find another
planet, you said, it will be round
and roll.)
        In room 11 my
terrestrial mechanic and I
map out the body's paths,
turning past each other
in the night.

IV Leonardo's Wheel

On the coffee table between us
the drawn man (da Vinci, figure 1)
squares with theory: head to toe
fingertip to fingertip aligns
a perfect square—bisects at groin,
is quartered at knee and nipple—the square
root of Man. A compass fixed
at navel circumscribes his limbs' orbit.
(Projected on my bed, the spread-
eagled figure struggles, strains,
steadies to my stroke, shudders—the voice
breaking upward, the blond cry.)

Leonardo, your figures do not
lie. Ringed in we wheel toward
earth's shadow cone. We eclipse.

V Fugue

I have observed
measure, though never moderation.
Say Man's the measure: all the same,
Man is not always the same.
The man in every stanza is not
always the same. (The woman is.
Always the same.)
                    Musician,
I have not made this poem to say
Woman is the measure. But that
what signifies is measureless.
(Your touch on ivory or woman's breast
defying calibration—the note
we strike together resonating
out of key and out of time.) Man
woman figure figurine, our modes
diverge, our sameness draws us in:
mon semblable, mon frère,
all ways my same.

Untitled

There are names for everything we do.
(The classicist recalls them from Catullus.)
You can find them in the manuals.
They are illustrated by photographs
of a young man who does not much
notice the girl he fondles. He remembers
how his older brother tied his hands
and pushed the end of a toy gun inside him,
whipping him with the gun-belt over and over.
He is hard and straight like the barrel of a gun.
Under the lights the girl's skin warms.
She concentrates on the blond photographer,
angling her breasts toward the camera.
The manuals have so little to teach.

Those words, those pictures do not define our acts.
Yes, we committed that one, this one
we tried and failed, in the motel room
where ice melted with a sound like footsteps
as our separate lives came loose and fell away.
Our own exposures blurred in the half-dark
defy our captioning. I have no name
to give them, or give you.

Getting Out the Thorns

Tjens Jensen, known as "the Human Hedgehog," has
had a total of 32,131 inch-long thorns removed from his
body since falling into a barberry hedge in April 1971.
His doctors are puzzled.

One needn't tell the doctors everything.
Does it matter to them what story you fell from,
or that the woman had long hair
and a name like a vegetable?
It's the count that counts.
I tell you, Tjens, we hedgehogs know
a thing the M.D.'s don't: the real thornbush's
inside. A sort of acupuncture
in reverse. When I was twelve
a little south of McBurney's Point
I felt the first pricking. It spread
along the Meridians, through the Four Seas,
to the Great Connecting Point of the Spleen.

They tell me Chinese women in old times
from modesty would point to where they hurt
on the practitioner's doll. And then he'd ease
their fevers with la grande piqûre.
Times change. We needle our doctors.
We become the instruments of our own need.
(Sleeping with us you sleep on pins and needles:
like porcupines we must do it carefully.)
We become the instruments of our own need.
We are opening out: each spine pushes
open another Window of the Sky,
another Gilded Temple, another
Gushing Well. Soon we will be translucent,
our lacy flesh at bloom on the sharp tree.

39

Early November

"Lay on more weight."
    —Giles Cory, at Salem

I

The turtle in Friends Homes parking lot
has had it, has spilled like soup
from her cracked tureen. What we fear,
panic in the crawl space (the furnace moans
wanting its filters changed, the house on top
encrusted, thickening). My grandmother's dog
under the springs humped up when my grandfather
humped down: one night the slats fell.
Let a joist break, we crack like coconuts,
our milk runs out. What it is to live
in houses made by hands.

II

Gestalt the dream: I am the helmsman's wheel,
he turns me point by point. I am the mariner.
(I will not qualify him, call his eyes blue
with absence. Let that be as it may.)
We have gone below. The boat unhelmed
wallows. He bears me down.
Under the keel swooning seas
shift. Yes, I am the boat
uncaptained, stunned, directionless.
I am the stunning sea: the boat staggers
between my thighs.

III

With a dark man in a night dark
as the one that killed him, I kneel
at Randall Jarrell's grave. We brush away
rained leaves. Broken sky
comes down in drops. The slab has gathered
light from nowhere, we see it float.
It bears us like a raft. I am half adrift
in the nighted world, half weighted here
under the grinding stone my bones to dust.

IV

You would not think books like these heavy,
my yearly output each in its paper back.
They ruffle on the lectern. Where's the weight,
you ask. Over my head
the iron glossary not yet set down,
that unabridgement of the great unspoken,
there's the infinity that breaks the pencil's point
in early November.

V

To my twelve readers and you in your gown
I make no plea guilty or not guilty,
will testify only to the weight of the stones
the men houses books my weighted body
under which I run like cider
under which I am running like a tide.

The String Lady

The string lady is in her room.
She has unraveled the city.
Great hanks snarls ravelings
of twine net her. She is a salty
catch, an octopus untangling
America. She rolls it up. Balls
orbit her like moons. They snowball.

This is no yarn I spin: the lady
is real. Her room is on 46th Street,
the 9th floor. She has lived there
for years. This is what she does.
Why did she begin? Did she
watch a beachcomber shoulder
a great rope, its frayed end
down his back like a mane
raveled to ringlets? Or
on Sunday morning opening
the broom closet found the roomer
with an extension cord close
around his throat? She does not say.

It gets harder to find string.
Soon the world will come unstrung.
Then she will unravel the drapes
the bedspread her socks sweater
underwear her white hair her skin
coarse threads slubbed with moles
then her stringy flesh veins tendons
wound round. Last the ganglia
the spinal cord—oh Ariadne's clue

out of the labyrinth and all it takes
is winding! She winds down
the last spidery ball. The room
is in order. The room waits.

After a thousand years or so, listen:
Do the balls stir? Is something
beating like a heart?

Tod und das Weib

No flowers. I will not lie
in state or under the astroturf
of cemeteries. (Earth has been
often enough my bed, but with
livelier bedfellows than these
morticians.) I have other plans.

I am engaged to Johns Hopkins.
Packed in that cool drawer
I hold my breath. My new lovers
scrub up. They clip their nails.
They put rubbers on their fingers.
They make jokes. They will uncover
all my secrets. They will know me
inside out.

I do not say all love is like this.
But if it is I choose it still:
as I came naked from my mother
as I went naked to my man
to feel at dying as at borning
against my flesh in their sweet fumble
the brash tentative hands of men.

The Old Mine

I

Crouch at
the tunnel's mouth:
cold pours your lap full.
If cold's only
heat's absence
here absence
floods, here nil
rides to the knee.

II

A monk once slept seven days:
from his mouth a green mouse crept,
found out a hole in the hill,
came back at week's end. The monk
woke up with intimations
of great wealth, mined the mousehole's
emerald droppings, died rich
and damned.

III

Something is coming out of this hole
squared with square beams. Not
something square, something not
dug with hands.
It keeps coming. There is no
half-life to cold.

IV

Two hundred years back
took the sapphires, that jelled blue
like flowers hacked from ice—
the flower melts
the ice blooms, at its core
a rift of blossoming light.

Next century garnered corundum:
its wily grit ground down
the mountain, left this
spill of cold rock. Now we.

V

Now we mine
pure absence
pure sense
of hole
that has already outlived
the mountain.
Inside our mind the mine
wells cold. Air eats
the mountain down.
Out and In
approach each other like
two jaws. We eat the air.
The air eats us.

VI

Only
in such cold
your eyes splinter
blue as
what once
was worth
the perilous descent.

PRINTED AT THE STINEHOUR PRESS, LUNENBURG, VERMONT